P9-DXH-716

The Limits of
Influence

The Limits of Influence

Psychokinesis and the Philosophy of Science

Stephen E. Braude

London and New York

First published in 1986
by Routledge & Kegan Paul Inc.

First published in paperback in 1991
by Routledge
11 New Fetter Lane, London EC4P 4EE

Simultaneously published in the USA and Canada
by Routledge
a division of Routledge, Chapman and Hall, Inc.
29 West 35th Street, New York NY 10001

Phototypeset in Times, 10 on 12 pt
by Input Typesetting Ltd, London
and printed in Great Britain
by T. J. Press (Padstow) Ltd,
Padstow, Cornwall

British Library Cataloguing in Publication Data
Braude, Stephen E.
    The limits of influence: psychokinesis and the philosophy
    of science.
    1. Psychokinesis
    I. Title
    133.8

Library of Congress Cataloging-in-Publication Data
Braude, Stephen E.
    The limits of influence.
    Bibliography: p.
    Includes index.
    1. Psychokinesis.   2. Psychical research.
3. Apparitions.   I. Title.
BF1371.B73   1986   133.8'8   85–25756

ISBN 0–415–06203–9

For my parents

CONTENTS

Contents

PREFACE

This book documents, among other things, my growing disenchantment with the intellectual community. Not too long ago, before I began to investigate the evidence of parapsychology, I still believed that intelligence was a weapon in the war against evil, that my colleagues in academia (especially in philosophy and science) were committed to discovering the truth, and that intellectuals would be pleased to learn they had been mistaken, provided the revelation brought them closer to this goal. I now realize how thoroughly naive I was.

Since dipping into the data of parapsychology, I have encountered more examples of intellectual cowardice and dishonesty than I had previously thought possible. I have seen how prominent scholars marshal their considerable intellectual gifts and skills to avoid honest inquiry. I have seen how intelligence can be as much a liability as a virtue – in particular, how it sometimes affords little more than complicated ways of making mistakes, entrenching people in views or opinions they are afraid to scrutinize or abandon. I have seen, in effect, how intelligence often expands, rather than limits, a person's repertoire of possible errors.

I have also come to realize that members of academic and other professions tend to be strikingly deficient in the virtue that, ideally, characterizes their field. I have seen how scientists are not objective, how philosophers are not wise, how psychologists are not perceptive, how historians lack perspective – not to mention how physicians are not healers, and how attorneys are not committed to justice.

Some of my revelations (however long overdue they may be) spring from personal experiences. I have observed with amazement – and, I suppose, ill-concealed disdain – how academics are able to proclaim confidently that the evidence of parapsychology is insubstantial, and then display that they don't even know what the evidence is – a lacuna about which they could hardly have been unaware. I have seen college professors, and also a well-known, ambitious, and (I believe) thoroughly unscrupulous magician move from relative obscurity to considerable notoriety, by cultivating reputations as debunkers and defenders of clear-headedness – in large part through their sedulous avoidance of evidence they *know* they cannot explain. More disappointing still, I have discovered from my investigations of nineteenth-century mediumship that none of this is new, and that prominent intellectuals have been behaving in these dishonest ways all along.

I must add, however, that there is a further and somewhat embarrassing personal reason for the present clarity of my perceptions. Frankly, I cannot pretend always to have achieved the sublimity of thought whose absence I criticize in my colleagues. Some of what I now understand about the varieties of intellectual dishonesty and cowardice I owe to having observed them in myself; they are demons with whom I am intimately acquainted. For many years I was content to dismiss reports of ostensibly paranormal phenomena as, at best, the result of confusions or delusions of various sorts. Of course, I hadn't bothered actually to *read* any of the evidence and assess it for myself. My opinions were fashioned after those of my mentors, who (I later learned) were equally ignorant of the evidence, but with regard to whom I was too insecure and intimidated to display much independence of thought (especially on a matter that so easily provoked their derision). Even after I became tenured and finally began to study the experimental evidence of parapsychology, I continued to accept uncritically the received view that laboratory evidence was inherently cleaner, and more respectable and reliable, than the non-experimental evidence.

Admittedly, I had no idea at the time how few of those who promulgated this wisdom had bothered to examine the latter body of evidence with any care. In fact, only recently have I come to appreciate how few *parapsychologists* are familiar with the material. But at no point along the way was my ignorance benign; it was, in fact, a lazy and craven expedient. For one thing, it facilitated the disgracefully scornful attitude I occasionally adopted, initially toward parapsychology in general, and then later toward those who defended the non-experimental evidence. For another, it simply reinforced the complacency with which I held my beliefs. Even after I began to study the evidence of parapsychology and develop a respect for the field and its data, it allowed me to remain smugly comfortable with my moderate radicalism. I made no effort to examine the non-experimental evidence for myself; I was content not to have to admit into my universe phenomena that seemed to me bizarre and frightening (both personally and professionally). Of course in my heart I knew what I was doing. But at that stage in my career I lacked the courage to challenge, not only an increasing number of orthodox academicians, but also the majority of active parapsychologists. Because of my sympathetic interest in parapsychology, my alliance with the former was in a state of flux – collapsing in some places and solidifying in others; and I was insecure about its future. And my alliance with the latter was new, and presumably fragile.

I have now spent more than five years carefully studying the non-experimental evidence of parapsychology – in fact, just that portion of it which is most contemptuously and adamantly dismissed by those academics who all along have been blithely ignorant of the facts. I started with the expectation that the received wisdom would be supported, and that my belief in the relative worthlessness of the material would merely be better-informed. But the evidence bowled me over. The more I learned about it, the weaker the traditional skeptical counter-hypotheses seemed, and the more clearly I realized to what extent skepticism may be fueled by ignorance. I was forced to confront the fact that I could find no decent reasons for doubting a great deal of strange testimony. It became clear to me that the primary source of my reluctance to embrace the evidence was my discomfort with it. I knew that I had to accept the evidence, or else admit that my avowed philosophical commitment to the truth was a sham.

I am hardly comfortable about announcing to my academic colleagues that I believe, for example, that accordions can float in mid-air playing melodies, or that hands may materialize, move objects, and then dissolve or disappear. I have taken abuse and ridicule for the far more modest opinions expressed in my previous book. But I have reached my recent conclusions only after satisfying myself that no reasonable options remain. Actually, I find that my discomfort tends to diminish as I discern more clearly how little the most derisive and condescending skeptics really know about the evidence, and how their apparent confidence in their opinions is little more than posturing and dishonest bluffing. In fact, I am less comfortable about stating my present views on parapsychology than I am about confessing how my intellectual independence was won, in part, through learning not to respect my colleagues.

It is no accident, then, that the tone of this book is occasionally polemical and antagonistic. In the past, those who defended the evidence for large-scale psychokinesis have too easily allowed themselves to be put on the defensive. In my opinion they have responded too timidly – or graciously – to their most vocal opponents, especially to those motivated more by the love of publicity than by the love of knowledge. I believe, however, that the skeptic must be put on the defensive. The more evangelical of the lot inveigh against the forces of irrationalism. But I believe that their greatest enemies might be full information and an open mind. It is a simple (and often profitable) matter to be a professional skeptic about parapsychology, especially when one suppresses the best cases and perpetuates misconceptions among those who know even less about the field. I hope, therefore, to inject some relevant data and clear reasoning into a debate where those commodities have been in short supply. I believe that the evidence I present will seem respectable – if not coercive – to anyone without a scientific or metaphysical axe to grind. And I hope that my discussion will make it more difficult for the self-styled debunker to dismiss the evidence with feigned confidence, bogus or irrelevant facts, and facile arguments.

The empirical part of this book deals primarily with a rather restricted portion of the total evidence for psychic (now called 'psi' or 'paranormal') phenomena – namely, the evidence from physical mediumship. A *medium* is an ostensible psi agent, who purports to be an intermediary between the spirit world and this world. A *mental* medium is a medium who apparently transmits and receives communications from the world of spirits. A *physical* medium is a medium in whose presence psychokinesis (PK) is observed.

I shall take no stand here on whether mediums really are what they purport to be. Although I shall make some comments on the topic of survival in Chapter 3, I shall postpone an in-depth treatment to a later occasion. This book is concerned primarily with psychokinesis – particularly, *large-scale* PK – and its significance for the world of souls incarnate. I want to challenge certain widespread beliefs about the nature and quality of the data, and consider the implications of a sensible appraisal of the evidence for familiar views about the world. Many commentators (parapsychologists included) have been ignorant of the full evidence for large-scale PK, although that has not deterred them from expressing firm opinions on the subject and promulgating various standard misconceptions. And many others have simply been confused. Their assessments have been colored by unwarranted assumptions about the possible range or efficacy of PK (and psi phenomena generally), as well as the utility of laboratory experimentation. And they have misunderstood the importance of psi phenomena for our received body of scientific knowledge.

My first task, then, will be to compare the evidence for large-scale PK to the allegedly superior laboratory evidence. In the process, I shall expose the defects in the principal skeptical arguments against the former body of data, and argue that psi phenomena do not pose a clear or serious threat to the fabric of science. Then, in Chapter 2, I shall examine in detail some of the best evidence for PK, paying particular attention to the cases of D. D. Home and Eusapia Palladino. In Chapter 3 I survey the leading theories of apparitions, and consider the extent to which the evidence – especially the evidence for *collective* apparitions – can be explained by an appeal to PK. Chapter 4 examines the central issues in PK theory, and contains a sustained critique of mechanistic theories of action and cognitive phenomena. Finally, in Chapter 5, I consider the viability of explaining the evidence for precognition in terms of real-time large-scale psi, and present reasons for rejecting the possibility of retrocausation.

Although I am writing primarily for philosophers and parapsychologists, this book (like my last) is intended for a diverse audience. I would like it to be useful to the broad range of academics, students, and educated laypersons who are unfamiliar with the evidence, and who have innocently (or not so innocently) accepted the many received misconceptions about it. But certain sections of the book presuppose familiarity with background philosophical issues, while others will be most fully appreciated by those acquainted with the problems and data of parapsychology. Since the topics I address should interest readers in many disciplines, I have tried to make the book as generally accessible as possible without making it trite. Nevertheless, it is inevitable that some will find parts of it too advanced, elementary, or cursory. Unfortunately, I know of no way to maximize the book's utility and avoid this problem. I can only hope that readers will be tolerant of passages tailored for those at some other level of philosophical or parapsychological sophistication.

One of my major tasks in preparing this book was to locate and digest the mountains of obscure and out-of-print documents on physical mediumship. I would like to express my gratitude to those who helped me to acquire the relevant materials, and who guided me through the imposing maze of cases. In particular, I wish to thank Carlos S. Alvarado, Rhea A. White, George Zorab, Eleanor O'Keeffe, and Patrice Keane. For their valuable comments on portions of the manuscript, I wish to thank John Beloff, G. Lee Bowie, Alan Gauld, and Michael Martin. And I am especially grateful to Jule Eisenbud and Bruce Goldberg for their stimulation, encouragement, and conceptual guidance. Finally, I must express my debt to the late Laura A. Dale, whose research assistance and criticism fueled my early enthusiasm for this project, and whose ideals of clarity and accuracy I found both intimidating and inspiring. Laura would probably have disagreed with some of my views; but I hope my scholarship would have received her blessing.

1

THE IMPORTANCE OF NON-EXPERIMENTAL EVIDENCE

1.1 INTRODUCTION

The evidence for psi phenomena generally, and for psychokinesis in particular, may provisionally be divided into three broad categories: experimental, semi-experimental, and anecdotal. Into the first category fall twentieth-century laboratory studies, as well as the more tightly designed investigations of the nineteenth century – for example, some French studies of mesmerism and ESP. The second category consists of investigations of what are sometimes called *recurrent spontaneous psi phenomena* – i.e., psi phenomena that (a) occur outside a laboratory setting, and (b) occur repeatedly in connection with either a certain person or a certain place. Mediumistic phenomena and most poltergeist phenomena are person-centered members of this class, while some poltergeist phenomena and most haunting phenomena are place-centered members.[1] I call the evidence for these phenomena *semi*-experimental because, although the phenomena are recurrent and therefore lend themselves to investigation (and not merely after-the-fact inquiries), the investigations are typically not controlled or designed in a way generally regarded as characteristic of scientific experimentation. This is not to say that they are therefore more careless or more vulnerable to trickery or fraud than laboratory experiments. In fact, certain of the semi-experimental studies – for example, some investigations of the great superstar mediums of yesteryear (see Chapter 2) – seem to be at least as well-guarded against fraud as most contemporary laboratory experiments (even in orthodox science). But the general consensus about the study of mediums, poltergeists, etc., is that these investigations are not full-blown experiments, either because they are exploratory and post-hoc in nature and are not intended to test specific hypotheses, or because they don't allow for the proper isolation and manipulation of experimental variables, or else because they are not conducted in a laboratory and accordingly more closely resemble a field investigation than an experiment. Whether or not such judgments are justified (especially with regard to the study of physical mediums) is a matter I prefer to postpone for now; and so I am willing to regard such investigations as semi-experimental.[2] Into the final category of evidence for psi fall what have been termed *sporadic spontaneous psi phenomena* – i.e., psi phenomena that (a) occur outside a laboratory setting, and (b) are unique or almost unique occurrences in the life of the person(s) involved (either as agent or as subject). Most reports of apparitions belong in this category.

The reader might wonder why the term 'spontaneous' should ever have been applied to mediumistic phenomena – particularly those intentionally provoked or encouraged for the scrutiny of prepared observers. As far as I can determine, there are two reasons for that use of the term. First, the phenomena studied in the lab tend to be more or less contrived events; often they are of a kind that would occur only or primarily in a laboratory setting. Before electronic tests for PK became the rage, laboratory psychokinetic phenomena were principally nonrandom falls of carefully controlled tosses of dice, coins, or other objects. Now they tend to be nonrandom outputs of electronic random event generators (see Braude, 1979). By contrast, the phenomena apparently produced by mediums occurred originally in real-life situations. Levitations, materializations, and apports, for example, had been reported centuries before laypersons and scientists made organized attempts to evoke and study them. Second, the arguments leveled against the semi-experimental and anecdotal evidence are quite similar, and differ from those typically advanced against the experimental evidence. Here, perhaps, we find the main reason for including mediumistic phenomena with the rest of the so-called spontaneous phenomena, recurrent and sporadic. The received wisdom, even among parapsychologists, seems to be that only the experimental evidence is (or *can* be) reputable, and that the other two classes of evidence share serious common weaknesses. Supposedly, the two types of non-experimental evidence are inherently defective, and for more or less the same general reason – namely, that they are not as 'clean' (i.e., reliable or trustworthy) as the experimental evidence with its associated contrived phenomena.

In any case, we need not detain ourselves over the use of the term 'spontaneous.' That seems really to be a side issue. Of more central concern is the piece of received wisdom that simultaneously condemns the semi-experimental and anecdotal evidence for psi. I want to examine carefully whether the customary opposition to non-experimental evidence is justified. And here I must part company, not only with most academics, but also with many (perhaps the majority of) parapsychologists. I cannot support the prevailing view that the non-experimental evidence of parapsychology is either inherently weak or at least inferior to the laboratory evidence. Interestingly, this common attitude toward non-experimental evidence is a somewhat new development. Only in recent years has the data of parapsychology been heavily weighted in favor of the experimental. Most of the evidence preceding the work of Rhine around 1930 is semi-experimental and anecdotal. It is only relatively recently, then, that parapsychologists have been able to luxuriate in the apparently clean evidence drawn from laboratory studies. Of course, Rhine and many others felt that this was all for the good. But for reasons I shall mention below, I must challenge this judgment. The belief in the superiority of experimental evidence seems to me to be based on several major confusions.

My current favorable assessment of the non-experimental evidence for psi is by no means unprecedented. But no doubt many will consider it to be either reactionary or radical (depending on their point of view). Certainly, my present views are more extreme than those I took in my previous book on philosophy and parapsychology (Braude, 1979). At that time, I was (at best) only mildly attracted to some of the views I now hold. I now believe that the non-experimental evidence of parapsychology has been unjustly maligned. I now consider it to be an extremely valuable source of information concerning the nature and limits, and even the reality, of psi functioning. Even more important, I now believe that such material is at least as valuable and reliable as the evidence gathered from laboratory experiments, and probably more so.

3

No doubt many will be surprised by this evolution of my position. After all, they might say, experimental evidence is gathered under controlled conditions, and offers the promise of replication of results. Non-experimental evidence, on the other hand, tends to be collected under non-controlled conditions, and suffers from the inevitable unreliability of human testimony and perception. Moreover, the phenomena reported in these cases are often so bizarre as to be antecedently incredible, and probably the result of ingenious chicanery and conjuring. This is precisely the received opinion regarding non-experimental material, and there is enough truth in it to render the response initially plausible. But I have come to believe that the received view is ultimately superficial, and that it withers under close scrutiny. In what follows I shall explain why I believe this to be the case.

1.2 THE LIMITATIONS OF EXPERIMENTAL RESULTS

In some ways, experimental parapsychology has been very disappointing. Most laboratory evidence appears to suffer from two major – and as far as I can see, ineliminable – weaknesses: (a) its inability to convince skeptics of the reality of psi functioning, and (b) its inability to reveal vital facts or data concerning the nature of psi.

As far as (a) is concerned, the problem is not that there have been no good or impressive experiments. In my opinion, there have been quite a few (some discussed in Braude, 1979). Often the designs have been ingenious and clean, and sometimes the results have been quite striking. Nor is the problem the alleged paucity of repeatable experiments. For reasons I have explored elsewhere (Braude, 1979), I think both skeptics and believers are deeply confused about this issue, and have made far too much of it. To see what is really wrong with experimental evidence, we must begin by placing recent psi experimentation into historical perspective.

Most parapsychologists today work in the shadow of J. B. Rhine, and either knowingly or implicitly adopt certain of his assumptions about the nature of science and the value of experimentation (in the behavioral sciences generally, and in parapsychology in particular). And although it is certainly false (contrary

4

to what some believe) that Rhine almost singlehandedly made parapsychology scientific, many nevertheless believe that his experimental, quantitative procedures afforded the best possible opportunities for obtaining clean evidence for psi, and hence for silencing the skeptic.

My own view, on the other hand, is that Rhine's so-called revolution has failed, and in just those respects in which it was expected to succeed. Skeptics have rarely (if ever) been converted, or even deeply impressed by laboratory experiments. Nor have they been more effectively swayed than they were in the past by séances or anecdotal reports. The reasons all concern the fact that the laboratory evidence is quantitative. Most successful experiments boast odds against chance, *at best*, of 100 or 1,000 to 1. And although some reach staggering levels of significance, they are rare enough for the skeptic or parapsychological fence-sitter to wonder whether they represent nothing more than a statistical anomaly, rather than occasional spasms of outstanding – or conspicuous – psi. Certainly, laboratory results in PK are never as viscerally compelling or mind-boggling as experiences – or even mere reports – of large-scale physical phenomena (e.g., object levitations or materializations). Not even Schmidt's experiments with pre-recorded targets (see, e.g., Schmidt, 1976, and the discussion in Braude, 1979) carry the same impact as tangible object movement under good conditions. As important as Schmidt's tests may be, the items of data themselves – signals recorded on tape – are colorless. The experiments are arresting only in the light of statistical arguments and abstract considerations about the nature of causality.

The problem, in my opinion, is that applying the laws of chance to real-life situations is a complex and subtle business. Under non-existent ideal conditions the laws are relatively straightforward. But when it comes to actual cases it is often extremely difficult to pinpoint nonrandom occurrences with any confidence. (That is why parapsychologists abandoned PK tests with dice and coins and turned to comparatively simple experiments with random number generators.) But even in the more straightforward cases, one can still wonder whether enough trials have been conducted to iron out present anomalies. By contrast, however, an object flying slowly and gracefully through the air in good light poses a clear-cut problem, and therefore tends to be more impactful right from the start. Similarly, quantitative evidence will invariably be less interesting and arresting than a vivid ostensible precognitive dream or a lifelike apparition.

Quantitative evidence, then, is by its nature less compelling than evidence impressive independently of statistical analysis. Moreover, the statistical evidence has simply not been compelling enough, and perhaps it can never be. To be sure, some skeptics might be swayed if odds against chance were regularly billions to 1. But others – perhaps many others – would still wonder whether our figures were right, whether the number of trials was great enough, or whether some non-paranormal factor in the experimental situation had been overlooked. Intransigent skeptics, of course, can always generate a reason for dismissing the evidence of parapsychology, quantitative or otherwise. But even if some never yield in the face of data (no matter how strong), it still seems as if statistical arguments are highly unlikely to produce substantial belief changes in more flexible minds. Many will be unable to shake the suspicion that the arguments are either intentional or inadvertent bits of mere number-fiddling.

Some parapsychologists, of course, would say that it is in the nature of psi not to be more dramatic than it is (see, e.g., Eisenbud, 1963b, 1970, 1982a, 1983). They would argue that psi functioning occurs in response to real human needs, not those contrived for the purposes of scientific examination. Hence, they would argue, psi is unlikely to be testable in any way satisfying the canons of behavioral research. But this takes us to the second major weakness of experimental evidence in parapsychology.

Even if the entire skeptical community became firmly convinced of the mere existence of psi phenomena – in fact, even if quantitative evidence caused the conversion – it is doubtful that further laboratory experimentation would yield much enlightenment. Naturally, partisans of experimental parapsychology disagree. They would urge that quantitative formal tests fulfill certain vital scientific requirements in the attempt to understand psi functioning, and that only through rigorous experimental procedures can we isolate, control, and manipulate crucial variables, and thereby learn subtle facts about psi.

But that position strikes me as completely wrong. Ironically, it also suggests that parapsychologists have not been paying attention to their own arguments. For example, in debates over repeat-

6

ability, parapsychologists often claim that skeptics don't take seriously enough the type of phenomena they are trying to investigate. They protest when skeptics object to their claim that some experimental situations may inhibit psi (due, say, to experimenter effects, poor subject/experimenter rapport, shifts in the subject's mood, etc.). They protest when skeptics are suspicious of claims that *experimenters* may be paranormally producing results (rather than the official subjects who get chance results with other experimenters or when tested by the skeptic). In response to the skeptic, they point out – *correctly* – that psi may well (for all we know) be highly situation-sensitive, and that it may also work in mysterious ways, under the surface. Experimental controls, for example, can never prevent unwanted psi effects of various kinds from interfering with the proceedings. The quest for standard hard-scientific experimental repeatability, then, may be ill-conceived. Too many critical variables are unknown and uncontrollable. Not only may the state of the participants and the experimental environment vary critically from one occasion to the next; we cannot even determine conclusively who the real agent is, and whether participants are exerting a positive or negative influence on the final results.

It is rather curious, then, that many parapsychologists – for similar reasons – appear not to take psi seriously enough when they defend the utility of conventional experimentation. Their perfectly legitimate objection to the skeptic is relevant to far more than the limited issue of repeatability. Obviously, if success may depend on psychological or dynamical factors which one can never conclusively discern or isolate, then already the experimenter can't tell for certain why an experiment has succeeded or failed. But to make matters worse, if success or failure may be due to *psi* effects other than those officially under investigation (including unconsciously motivated psi influences), then it is a kind of conceit to think that one can *ever* be sure who did what to whom or to what, when it was done, or the extent to which a given experimental environment is psi-conducive or psi-repressive.

Nevertheless, many parapsychologists cling obdurately to their faith in the utility of conventional experimental designs. They seem tacitly and naively to assume that subjects will use only the psi abilities being investigated, that they will use them only after the experiment has begun and then only according to their

7

appointed role in the experimental design, and that others (experimenters, judges, onlookers) will use no psi at all in order to influence the outcomes. But this supposed 'gentleman's agreement' as Eisenbud (1963a) called it, is quite preposterous. There is no reason to think that people will be so well-behaved in exercising their psi abilities. Many of those concerned with an experiment will have a psychological investment in its outcome; and their personal goals may well be more genuinely motivating than – and perhaps at variance with – those contrived for the experiment. But since no conventional experimental controls can prevent people from using whatever psi abilities they can muster to achieve whatever result they desire, experimenters can only pretend to have matters really well in hand. For example, if ESP is possible, then there can be no way to insure that experiments are really double-blind (blind, that is, from paranormal information-acquisition). Hence, once we take seriously the possibility of sneaky or naughty psi and the importance of elusive contextual factors in the experimental situation, we can only be rather pessimistic about the prospects for studying psi by conventional means.

Therefore, despite the impressive extrachance scores of many psi experiments, Eisenbud was justified in claiming that

> parapsychological experiments . . . amount to little more than formalized arrangements for one or more investigators to be on hand with a notebook or two to observe whatever occurrence may happen to take place under conditions that remain for the most part obscure. (Eisenbud, 1963a, p. 255)

Furthermore (for reasons I discuss in more detail in the next section), we must be open to the possibility that psi phenomena can be of *any* magnitude. Once we allow psi (even if only for the sake of argument) to violate familiar spatial and temporal constraints on organic interactions, we cannot determine in advance of further inquiry how extensive those violations may be – i.e., where we may draw the line. If only small-scale psi effects are possible, we will know that only after extensive empirical investigation and on the basis of a carefully and thoroughly developed and well-supported psi theory. But at present, no decent theory forbids large-scale or super psi, and no evidence weighs against it (see also Chapter 4). At our current level of understanding, super psi is as viable as puny psi.

For all we know, then, small-scale laboratory results might not be produced by small-scale psi. For example, in our current state of ignorance, we must be open to the possibility that Schmidt's evidence for apparent small-scale retro-PK may in fact be due to super PK running in the temporally conventional direction (see, e.g., Schmidt, 1976, and the discussion in Braude, 1979; also Chapters 4 and 5 for a discussion of super PK). For reasons I shall explore later, it might be psychologically comforting to set up experiments that appear to test for small-scale psi effects. But if (as far as we know) psi may be unlimited in scope or power, then experimenters cannot even be sure what magnitude of effect they are testing for. Granted, most parapsychologists are loathe to countenance the possibility of grand psi. (Some even resist mundane psi.) But that position, I shall argue, is indefensible; and it only fosters the illusion that it is possible to isolate and control experimental variables.

And to make matters still worse, there are good reasons for thinking that parapsychological experiments will never elicit important or revealing facts about psi. For example, many have suggested (plausibly) that psi functioning is need-determined – i.e., that the occurrence of psi typically depends on an organism's real or perceived physical or psychological needs. It would be absurd to think that psi is something that occurs only or primarily in the lab. After all, psi-experimentation is merely a response to apparent occurrences of psi in life. And it is reasonable to think that when we attempt to produce psi in the lab, we are simply trying to harness or manipulate for our limited purposes a kind of organic functioning developed, used, or adapted to serve real or perceived needs. But in that case, the situations that elicit psi functioning are unlikely to be those found in formal experiments, which at best create only artificial or contrived needs. No matter how interesting or attractive the experimental tasks may be (e.g., embedded in video games or other visually arresting displays), it is inexcusably naive (especially for a trained psychologist) to suppose that subjects will find the tasks deeply motivating, or more motivating than the experimenter's real investment in success (*or* failure). Hence, test situations might fail to motivate all but the very rare psychic virtuoso (or freak) from producing dramatic phenomena, and the rest from producing even modest phenomena reliably. Certainly one would not expect formal experiments to yield results representative of psi in its full development, or to simulate conditions that would provoke psi occurrences in real life.

Moreover, laboratory experiments may have yet another drawback, related to their artificiality. Even in relatively congenial experimental settings, the demands of laboratory research and the nature of the tasks required of the subject may be cripplingly inappropriate to the phenomena under investigation. For all we know, it might be as unnatural and difficult to function psychically in an experiment as it would be for most people to relax in a tank of sharks, or reveal their most intimate secrets to stern and judgmental authority figures. Or perhaps more relevantly, it might be as difficult to exhibit psi as it would be for most people to commit a crime knowing that the police are watching.

Undoubtedly, some will dismiss these suggestions as evasive – i.e., as attempts to rescue parapsychology from the proper demands of scientific research. But one needn't even believe in psi to agree that formal experimentation in parapsychology may be useless or counter-productive. *If* psi exists, then it takes only an open mind to see that it may not be the sort of thing that can be elicited, or at least elicited in a dramatic and skeptic-shriveling way, in the tightly-controlled, often sterile, and at best artificial and contrived environment required for a test. In all honesty, I think we must admit that we know too little about psi (assuming it exists) to rule out such a possibility. For all we know, perhaps only the greatest psychic superstars could transcend typical laboratory or test conditions. And for those whose psychic endowments are more ordinary and apparently less versatile or controllable, experimental situations may simply be too inhibiting, repressive, or perhaps just not stimulating in the appropriate way. Analogously, while some people can arouse themselves sexually under almost any conditions, few can do so under laboratory conditions. For most people, sexual arousal can occur only in more congenial, and often *characteristically special* environments. And since there are, presumably, more such ordinary people than there are great psychic virtuosi, or people totally lacking fears or inhibitions, non-experimental evidence may be our single best source of information about psi, at very least in its most customary form. Certainly, it seems more likely than experimental evidence to help us determine the range or limits of psi. (This viewpoint, I submit, will seem increasingly plausible as one becomes acquainted with the material surveyed in Chapter 2.)

My pessimism concerning experimental evidence, then, is due in part to the possibility that psi may simply be a slippery phenomenon, one that by its very nature is not likely to be caught in the parapsychologist's net (even if it leaves occasional traces as it passes through). But in part it results from a broader methodological problem, imported from experimental psychology. My views, here, run contrary to what I perceive as a widespread and completely unwarranted confidence in the utility of experimentation in the behavioral sciences. I believe there is very little of interest to be learned experimentally about cognitive or intentional organic abilities or capacities. And we clearly do not need to look to parapsychology to substantiate this claim. Experimental procedures are impotent to reveal fundamental facts about most behavioral or intentional regularities – for example, the ability to be charismatic, whimsical, manipulative, self-deceptive, dogmatic, playful, poetic, obsequious, or courageous. But then for all we know, psi functioning may likewise not be the sort of organic capacity that can profitably be investigated experimentally.

In fact, psi might be analogous in crucial respects to athletic abilities that can be studied *only* during the pressure of actual contests. If we want to assess a tennis player's ability to hit accurate serves, we must see how well he performs during a game. Some players, of course, practice better than they play, and others play better than they practice. A tennis player's serving ability, therefore, is partly a function of how the player deals mentally with the pressures of an actual match. But even if we ignore the ways in which psychological pressures of a game affect athletic performance, many athletic abilities still can be studied only in the context of a game. Only in actual playing situations, in which opponents are trying their hardest to win, will we be able to evaluate a quarterback's ability to read defenses, or a base-runner's ability to steal second. And we simply are in no position to assert that psi abilities can more easily be studied out of context.

Now while the above considerations do not in any way demonstrate that the experimental evidence for psi is totally useless or insubstantial, I think that parapsychology would be in a sorry state indeed if the experimental evidence were the only evidence available. It is regrettable, then, that many parapsychologists today fail to acknowledge the enormous reservoir of non-experimental evidence, especially the material prior to 1930. In fact, many of those who entered the field in the wake of enthusiasm for Rhine's approach – as well as many of their students or protégés – have never even studied the non-experimental evidence. And since the majority of active parapsychologists fall into this class, it is no wonder that most current theoreticians have nothing to say about non-experimental evidence, especially the older cases. No doubt it also explains why most research is confined to the lab, without attempting to relate the work to the rich vein of material that drove scientists to the lab in the first place.

And there are other reasons as well for the narrow compass of recent work. To some extent it results from the views about psi, science, and scientific method discussed above. But connected with those views is a widespread reluctance to examine seriously the quality and nature of the testimony, and to question the currently orthodox position on the limits of the empirically possible. And of course the reasons for that reluctance may be very deep. Eisenbud (1982a), for instance, traces the resistance to psi generally and PK in particular to the fear of admitting into the universe phenomena overtly accepted only in 'primitive' societies, and more specifically to the fear of responsibility for distant events (including the deaths of friends and relatives, and also large-scale disasters). (See Chapters 2 and 4 for more on this topic.) Others, I believe, are simply embarrassed by the extreme nature of many of the reported phenomena, and fear that their interest in them will be judged to be uncritical, weak-minded, or unscientific. And that fear is not without foundation. Historically, as a matter of fact, serious investigators of large-scale PK have been treated very badly by fellow scientists (see, e.g., section 1.4 below, Chapter 2, and also Inglis, 1977, 1984); and the tradition continues to this day. Not only do both skeptics and parapsychologists have a longstanding bias against PK (more so than for the 'higher' mental phenomena), but in addition they have often harbored a general prejudice against phenomena produced by members of the non-professional or working classes.[3] Therefore, researchers have little incentive for investigating the apparent spontaneous PK of 'just plain folk'. One cannot blame them for preferring to avoid the almost inevitable barrage of attacks on their competence or integrity. On the whole, then, the psychological atmosphere surrounding the study of large-scale phenomena is even less inviting than that surrounding more conventional forms of psi research. The study of large-scale PK, in particular, receives little encouragement or support (moral or financial).

Nevertheless, some parapsychologists continue to defend the quality of non-experimental evidence; but they constitute a small minority. And only certain of them (see, e.g., Gauld, 1968, 1982, Gauld and Cornell, 1979, Eisenbud, 1979, Stevenson, 1968) are willing to entertain and defend the evidence for the more peculiar phenomena mentioned in the literature. Representing the less radical contingent is a recent paper by S. A. Schouten (1979), which in part purports to take up the gauntlet for spontaneous case material. Schouten's detailed study is interesting and valuable. But I am struck by the extreme modesty of his defense of this portion of the parapsychological literature. Although he claims to defend the study of spontaneous cases, he discusses this material only insofar as it is evidence for ESP. I realize that Schouten attempts to *analyze* only those spontaneous cases where ESP seems to have occurred. But his defense of spontaneous case material needn't have been restricted just to that portion selected for analysis. Because of this limitation, Schouten's paper is redolent of the spirit of some of the founders of the British S.P.R., who (like Frank Podmore and Richard Hodgson) were willing to entertain the evidence for ESP, but who could not believe that the phenomena allegedly produced by the physical mediums of their day were anything but fraudulent, no matter what the evidence. Moreover, by restricting his defense to the evidence for ESP, Schouten ignores some of the most important reasons for studying non-experimental evidence generally.

According to Schouten, spontaneous cases merit our attention because (a) the analysis of such cases might help us construct theoretical models and testable hypotheses, and (b) these cases are what motivated laboratory research in the first place. Now I agree these are reasons for studying spontaneous cases. But they strike me as relatively superficial. One can offer deeper justifications than (a) for the claim that spontaneous cases are of theoretical value. The first is the aforementioned possibility that psi can only be understood adequately in its natural setting, like most human capacities. The second is that many, if not most, human abilities or capacities are best studied *in extremis*. Our various

13

powers, skills, or personality traits are, of course, possessed or manifested in degrees. Most often, though, they exist in positions falling well between relevant poles, where their characteristic features do not stand out especially clearly. For that reason, usually the best way to understand or analyze a given human ability or trait is to study its extravagant manifestations, so that we later will be able to discern its more moderate occurrences as instances of the appropriate extreme. That is why William James's *Varieties of Religious Experience*, with its penetrating survey of advanced forms of religious behavior and sentiments, affords such insight into their less dramatic manifestations. Similarly, it may well be that PK on random event generators, thermistors, or compass needles, are modest forms of a phenomenon whose more extreme instances are, e.g., levitations, materializations, and apports (see Chapter 4 for further discussion of this point).

Nevertheless, I imagine that most of us can empathize with those who recoil from the more bizarre spontaneous phenomena just because they seem so weird. Some go so far as to maintain – usually off the record – that reports of materializations, etc., *by themselves* discredit those reporting the phenomena. For others, however, the response takes a milder form. And it is not merely critics of parapsychology who are inclined to dismiss the more dramatic phenomena as *prima facie* less credible than the tamer laboratory variety. Even parapsychologists willing to entertain the more bizarre cases tend to find run-of-the-mill ESP easier to swallow than a levitation or apport.

But while this reaction may be understandable, I doubt that it is defensible. The refusal to consider the wilder phenomena of parapsychology is abetted by the prevailing view (mentioned earlier) that non-experimental evidence can *never* be as good as that for the admittedly more humdrum phenomena of the lab. And behind this view lurk various assumptions about the nature of science and the evidential value of human testimony, along with more specific assumptions about what the parapsychological evidence really is. These are matters which must now be examined in detail.

1.3 SCIENCE AND THE ALLEGED IMPROBABILITY OF PSI

A good place to begin is to consider the issues and errors attending the claim that psi phenomena *generally* are improbable. Then we may consider the parallel issues and errors involved in claiming that a certain *subset* of the set of psi phenomena is improbable.

A person who claims that psi phenomena generally are improbable, usually means one of two things – namely, (a) that psi phenomena are initially improbable relative to some well-supported background theory, or (more radically) (b) that psi phenomena are empirically impossible. Let us consider these in turn.

Even if we were to concede that psi phenomena (including small-scale ESP and PK) are initially improbable relative to the accepted background theory, we are hardly compelled to deny their reality. We need only show that the direct evidence in their favor overrides their initial and conditional improbability. This, I believe, is easy to do, and the evidence presented later constitutes a major part of the case.

But I see no reason, from the start, to concede that psi phenomena are improbable relative to any well-entrenched background theory. As I have mentioned elsewhere ('The Meaning of "Paranormal",' in Braude, 1979), no well-supported global scientific theory (e.g., quantum physics, or the general or special theories of relativity) has any implication at all regarding the possibility of ESP or PK. Not even theories of perception in psychology are incompatible with the existence of ESP, since the theories are concerned only with the familiar sense modalities, and do not forbid other forms of information acquisition or organic interaction. I may have been too cursory or timid when I voiced this objection before. So let me now be more explicit and blunt.

Many people believe (and even fear) that the existence of ESP and PK would pose a threat to the very fabric of science, or at least to fundamental laws of physics. But as far as I can see, this position is far from obvious and may well be false. First of all, even if we were to accept at face value all the decent evidence for ESP and PK (large- or small-scale), no fundamental physical laws – including conservation laws – seem to be violated. For one thing, so little is understood about the phenomena that it is not which laws (if any) would apply (see also Stewart, 1886). ..vertheless, as Dobbs (1967) correctly observed, even if ESP is mediated by a kind of radiation, there is no reason to suppose (as many have claimed) that the phenomenon violates the inverse square law. In fact, no evidence available now or in the foreseeable future could possibly establish that claim.[4] Moreover, some facts concerning physical mediumship suggest that, to the extent that PK is a physical process, some conservation laws may actually be obeyed. Among these facts are the cold breezes preceding physical phenomena, and the measured increase in the weight of certain mediums by the amount of force needed to raise a levitated table. Besides (as I mention in more detail below), to the extent that ESP and PK are intentional or cognitive phenomena, the laws of physics may not apply to them at all, and the phenomena would pose no more of a threat to the laws of physics than would the phenomena of ordinary volition.

Psi phenomena *do* seem to be proscribed by various philosophical theses, like Broad's *basic limiting principles* (see Broad, 1962a, and the discussion in Braude, 1979). But the basic limiting principles are not at all universally accepted, even among educated members of Western industrial society. More importantly, however, the basic limiting principles are neither presupposed nor implied by *any* fundamental scientific theory. For example, even if consciousness should turn out to survive bodily death, the main body of scientific theories, and certainly the global theories of physics, would remain largely unaffected. As far as I can see, biology would continue to describe the workings of the body pretty much as it did all along. Only the brain sciences are likely to be affected by the reality of survival; and even then, the casualties would only be those areas attempting to analyze consciousness in conventional physical terms. (Of course, I and many others believe that those branches of science should be scuttled right now – independently of the data of parapsychology – simply in virtue of the incoherence of their mechanistic presuppositions.) But even if the only genuine psi phenomena are humdrum ESP and PK, it is still unclear why those phenomena should deal a fatal blow to the foundations of science. No fundamental scientific theory will obviously need to be rejected if it turns out that persons can affect remote physical systems or receive information bypassing usual sensory channels. Naturally, certain philosophical theses will have to be discarded, and certain scientific theories will find their domains somewhat more restricted. But once again, the only outright casualties will be in certain branches of the already restricted areas of cognitive science and physiological psychology. Interestingly, the majority of scientists who accept (or are willing to theorize about) psi phenomena tend to analyze them in conventional scientific terms – i.e., in terms of the background theory (usually physics). For different reasons (see below) I happen to think that is not such a good idea. But the important point is that practicing scientists do not believe that psi phenomena spell the end of science as we know it.

More importantly, however, it is not clear to me why physics *should* have anything of great interest to say regarding psi phenomena, because it is unclear why physics should have anything of great interest to say about organic activities generally. Although few philosophers (I think) would go this far, many parapsychologists have remarked to me that since humans are complex physical systems, physics may be expected to describe and explain every human organic function (including interactions between humans). This argument is really an egregious example of blind reductionism. Let us ignore for the moment the claims of Cartesian dualists and spiritualists, and grant that human beings are physical systems. Even so, it is specious to argue that the language of physics is (or will be) able to express all the important facts of human functioning. For one thing, it seems to me that the laws of physics (including conservation laws) strictly speaking apply only to impersonal or mechanical forces – i.e., to physical systems and interactions *abstracted* from the realm of intention. There is no reason to think that physics must have anything at all to say about the ranges of phenomena ignored in, or simply not susceptible to, that particular process of abstraction. Similarly, the fairly procrustean set of logical connectives permits us to analyze language and reasoning abstracted from a great many factors that make up human discourse. But those connectives (and their associated formal systems) are completely impotent to describe and analyze the linguistic phenomena (or aspects of language use) overlooked in or resistant to the process of abstraction. So if there are vital or intentional processes in nature not analyzable into or describable in terms of impersonal or mechanical forces, those processes would not *violate* the laws of physics

17

any more than certain 'if—, then—' constructions, unanalyzable in terms of the material conditional (or any other formal conditional), violate the laws of logic. Those vital processes would simply be *outside* the domain of physics, as part of language is beyond the domain of formal analysis.

In fact, it is commonplace to consider exceptions to formal laws as demonstrating, not that the laws are literally violated or false, but rather that the domain of the laws is limited. Not even the simple truths of arithmetic apply without limit or restriction to the world of experience. '7 + 5 = 12', for instance, should not be interpreted to mean that any time one adds 7 things to 5 things, one gets a total of 12 things as a result. The addition of 7cc of water to 5cc of alcohol yields less than 12cc of liquid. Of course, the chemical reaction of water with alcohol reveals no defect in arithmetic. It shows merely that the formal system of arithmetic is not properly interpreted as applying to the addition of water to alcohol – i.e., that it is simply the wrong formal system for describing the process. Similarly, the properties of objects in curved space do not violate or falsify the principles of Euclidean geometry. They reveal merely that the system applies only to plane surfaces. Analogously, I suggest, the principles and equations of physics are bound to have their limitations. However useful the formal systems in mathematical physics may be for some states of affairs, they may be inapplicable to a great many others – quite possibly including every situation in which volitions or intentions have observable consequences.

Furthermore, even if humans are physical systems, persons and their activities may be characterized and analyzed on many different levels of description, none of which must be translatable into any other. For example, humans may be described on levels at which their intentional or vital properties are ignored; hence, they may be described as if they were inert or non-living systems like sticks and stones. Here, physics may indeed have something to say about humans, although what it describes will not be anything distinctively human or organic. After all, both humans and rocks, if thrown from a building, will obey the laws of gravitation. But humans may also be described with respect to psychological regularities, such as manipulativeness, optimism, the tendency to be intimidated by intellectuals, and the inability to sustain a meaningful relationship. In these cases, there are totally persuasive reasons for thinking that the associated levels of description have no further analysis or underlying structure, and that the regularities lie beyond the domain of physics (I discuss this issue in more detail in Chapter 4, and in Braude, 1979, 1983). But since it seems as if a great deal of psi functioning concerns phenomena or regularities that must be characterized intentionally, it is moot (to say the least) whether psi phenomena pose any threat to physics. Physics may be as irrelevant to parapsychology as it is to psychology (see also J. Fodor, 1975, 1981).

Moreover, as Nancy Cartwright (1980a, 1980b) has recently observed, many, if not most, scientific laws are approximations, based on ideal cases and oversimplified boundary conditions (including single causes), and as such do not strictly apply to real-life situations (which at very least usually include multiple causes). So even if vital, volitional, or cognitive phenomena fall within the domain of physics, the laws of physics may still apply (strictly speaking) only to cases far less complex than any into which those organic phenomena enter.

The only way I can see parapsychology threatening the fabric of science is the way in which practically any cognitive or intentional phenomenon poses a threat. The most that would happen, I think, is that physics would no longer be regarded as the fundamental branch of science, or even as prime contender for that position. In fact, if clear thinking were to reign, we would witness the abandonment of the view that *any* branch of science is fundamental. Physics would be regarded as neither more nor less fundamental than biology or psychology (now considered to have laws and descriptive categories not reducible to the language of physics). Granted, this would require a substantial and important change in thinking for many people. But the field of physics would not be undermined. All that would be affected is the faith in the reducibility of all other sciences to physics, not the laws of physics themselves. So neither volition and memory on the one hand, nor ESP and PK on the other, should force the rejection of, say, the theory of relativity, or undermine the accuracy and utility of the mathematics of quantum physics. What *would* happen is that global physical theories would need to be embedded within a different philosophical nexus.

It seems to me, then, that psi phenomena are *not*, after all, clearly incompatible with any existing received scientific theory,

19

especially theories in physics, and that even if they were, their initial improbability would be outweighed by the direct evidence in their favor.

It hardly looks promising, then, to make the stronger claim that psi phenomena are empirically impossible. To say that a phenomenon P is empirically impossible is to claim that P is incompatible with the laws of this world (though there may be possible worlds in which P occurs). But what *are* the laws of this world? All we ever have to go on are the scientific theories of the day. But of course, science may undergo minor or substantial theoretical revision, and some future scientific theory may countenance phenomena not embraced by current science. So the claim that psi is empirically impossible presumably means that psi phenomena violate principles, not just of current scientific theory, but also of any rational evolution of current science. (I say 'rational' because it is presumably possible that the scientific community comes to be dominated by lunatics whose theorizing is insensitive either to the data or to the canons of rationality, such as the laws of logic.) The claim, therefore, seems to rest on a personal intuition about the future course of scientific development – specifically, that future science will never countenance psi phenomena. But there is little reason for according much respect to this intuition. Indeed, the history of science cautions us against treating it as anything more than a member of a set of many competing intuitions, or perhaps as a parochial or undernourished belief concerning the limits of the empirically possible.

Not surprisingly, parapsychologists have long been wary of this kind of metaphysical smugness. F. W. H. Myers, lamenting the lack of dispassionate scientific curiosity among critics of parapsychology, remarked,

> let certain of our correspondents note that 'intuitions and deep perceptions' can cut both ways, and that while their own intuitions as to the truth of certain tenets may be so cogent that they deem it superfluous to aid our plodding inquiry, other people's intuitions may make for just the opposite view; and where is the intuitive umpire who shall settle it between them? (Myers, 1890, p. 250)

And Ducasse, paraphrasing C. D. Broad, once wrote,

scientists who regard the phenomena investigated by psychical researchers as impossible seem . . . to confuse the Author of Nature with the Editor of the scientific periodical, *Nature*; or at any rate they seem to suppose that there can be no productions of the former which would not be accepted for publication by the latter! (Ducasse, 1956, p. 147)

Finally, William Crookes remarked, after noting that parapsychology is in an embryonic stage of development (a fact still true),

the prudent man shrinks from dogmatizing on the egg until he has seen the chicken. (Crookes, 1897, p. 338)

It seems to me, then, that nothing we knew about the physical world forbids, or even renders implausible, the existence of psi phenomena. Quite apart from the fact that I regard the evidence in favor of such phenomena coercive, I consider the standard normal counter-explanations to be seriously inadequate. (That topic, however, is what I shall discuss at length in the remainder of this chapter.) Furthermore (as I argued above), most branches of science (certainly the 'hard' sciences) seem to proscribe nothing in the psi domain. Granted, no body of received scientific knowledge seems able at present to explain psi phenomena, especially along the mechanistic lines currently in vogue. But that is no reason to declare the phenomena improbable or impossible. The theories may simply be irrelevant to them, as physics is irrelevant generally to behavioral phenomena. For that matter (and contrary to the conceits of some neuropsychologists and workers in the field of artificial intelligence), no body of scientific knowledge comes even close to explaining how ordinary cognitive phenomena such as volition and memory work. Indeed, there are good reasons for thinking that no mechanistic theory *can* explain the phenomena (see Braude, 1979, and Chapter 4). Yet no one doubts their existence. In fact, as with many initially puzzling phenomena eventually incorporated into the standard scientific world view (e.g., tides, magnetism), the existence of memory (say) has never depended on the vagaries of scientific theory. If science has any contribution to make to our understanding of memory, it would be to explain (if possible) *how* it is that we remember – not to establish *that* we remember. Similarly (one would think), we should be able to determine whether PK occurs even if we cannot explain how it occurs.

Scientific theories, we must remember, are human artifacts, and are not inscribed by God in granite. They are, in the first place, descriptive and not prescriptive. Moreover, like any empirical statement, scientific laws are always open to revision. The fact that we hold some empirical (and even some non-empirical) statements more dear than others reflects no more than what J. W. Swanson (1967) once called a 'rational preference ranking' that *itself* is capable of revision. But once we admit that scientific laws are fallible, we will have to concede that we simply do not know, and have no grounds for asserting confidently in advance, which laws will eventually need to be amended or abandoned, and hence which phenomena are or are not possible.

Consider, now, whether it is justifiable to claim that a materialization (for example) is less probable than (say) laboratory ESP or small-scale PK. Here, the issue concerns the probability of a subset of the set of psi phenomena, rather than psi phenomena generally. But the claims seem to have a similar underlying structure. A person who maintains that a subset P of the set of psi phenomena is improbable, usually means one of two things – either (a) that P is initially improbable relative to some relevant and well-supported background theory, or (more radically) (b) that P is empirically impossible.

Regarding (a), even if there *were* a well-supported parapsychological theory relative to which materializations, levitations, and other large-scale phenomena were initially improbable, the direct evidence in favor of the phenomena greatly overrides it (as I shall try to show later on). But in fact, there simply is no background theory, in or out of parapsychology, relative to which large-scale psi phenomena are less probable than small-scale phenomena. There is not even a well-confirmed background theory in parapsychology. Although parapsychologists continue to generate theories that purport to deal with various laboratory phenomena (e.g., the 'observational' theories – see the discussion in Braude, 1979), none of these proscribes the existence of larger-scale phenomena outside the lab. In fact, the scandal of many of these theories is that they have nothing at all to say about large-scale phenomena.

Nevertheless, some parapsychologists have gone so far as to

22

claim that large-scale phenomena are improbable relative to the modest laboratory evidence, which (on the surface, at least) suggests the existence only of limited and small-scale psi events. (To my surprise, even C. D. Broad seems to adopt this position. See Broad, 1962b, p. 232.) But there is no reason at all for taking laboratory evidence as a guide in such matters. Apart from the fact (which I document at length in the next chapter) that there is persuasive non-experimental evidence for large-scale phenomena, the reliance on laboratory data alone is simply foolish. It rests on the assumption that genuine psi phenomena must all be reproducible experimentally; only then could experimental evidence tell us how extensive or varied psi phenomena may be. Of course, that assumption is as ridiculous as the assumption that other human abilities (such as the ability to be funny, or conciliatory, or the ability to be hopeful in the face of adversity) must be reproducible experimentally. Indeed, the inflexible dependence on laboratory data would make it virtually impossible to frame psi hypotheses applicable to non-laboratory conditions, since the dynamics of real-life situations cannot be reproduced (much less controlled) in the lab. For that matter, considering that laboratory experiments in parapsychology were originally conducted in order to study kinds of events that occurred initially outside the lab, it seems more bizarre still to suppose that we can discuss psi only in connection with conditions appropriate to formal experimentation. But then if we are not entitled to claim that certain psi phenomena are initially improbable relative either to any background theory or to the laboratory evidence, *a fortiori* we cannot claim that they are empirically impossible. That latter claim would amount to little more than a transparent display of hubris over one's subjective probability assessments.

I see no justification, then, for regarding some particular subset of psi phenomena as being more improbable than another. As a matter of fact, absolutely nothing we know about psi (assuming it exists) indicates that it has any limits at all. In fact, contrary to the popular wisdom, I think (and shall try to show) that the data actually suggest that psi may be quite refined and extensive. But as I mentioned earlier, given the present state of our knowledge we must (at the very least) entertain the possibility of extensive psi once we entertain the possibility of limited psi. Whether one is a skeptic or a believer, it is methodologically indefensible to open the door to the paranormal (even as a mere thought experiment), and then rule, independently of supporting evidence, that the door may be opened only a crack. If even modest ESP and PK indicate that the usual constraints on information-acquisition and influence on physical systems may be bypassed, then as far as we know, anything goes. We then have no grounds for insisting that those constraints may be bypassed only slightly. For example, if we are willing to admit or entertain that people can affect remote physical systems, and if we have no idea how this might be accomplished, we have no grounds for supposing that such influence must be confined to minor or crude changes in small or medium-sized objects, and not extended to translocations or levitations, or an apparently refined achievement like the playing of an accordion without touching it. (See Chapter 4 for further remarks on this issue.)

Eisenbud is one of the few parapsychologists to have taken this point seriously. In fact, he has developed an interesting case for thinking that the scope of psi may transcend that suggested in this book, and that it may conceivably include, among other things, efficacious death wishes, the psychokinetic production of great disasters, and extrasensory omniscience (see Eisenbud, 1970, 1982a). No doubt few (including Eisenbud) find this view appealing, and most would prefer that it turn out to be false. Nevertheless, we have no grounds at present – empirical or *a priori* – for rejecting it. Whether we like it or not, we simply have no idea what the limits of psi might be. That is why Eisenbud once wryly protested,

> if [psi] exists at all it very likely exists all the way and . . .
> from the standpoint of the sheer existence of the
> phenomenon, nothing is more inherently improbable . . . than
> anything else. At the most some things occur less frequently
> and are for this reason psychologically more difficult to
> swallow. I have a feeling that if there were a psi God, his
> first commandment would be 'Thou shalt not set my limits in
> vain'. (Eisenbud, 1979, p. 147)

It would appear, then, that we are not entitled to dismiss reports of the more extreme and apparently outlandish phenomena of parapsychology just because the phenomena seem so weird. But of course the neglect of the non-experimental evidence is not due simply to the weirdness of much of it. For one thing, what counts as weird or bizarre varies from culture to culture, and epoch to epoch. More importantly, even if we accept current Western criteria of weirdness, many cases (e.g., some reports of apparitions or precognitive dreams) are not especially weird at all, at least by comparison to the phenomena of physical mediumship. A more general objection to non-experimental case reports (whether of ESP, poltergeists, or materializations) appeals to the unreliability of human testimony, particularly as compared to the results of formal experimentation. I want, now, to examine this objection. In my view it is greatly overrated.

1.4   THE RELIABILITY OF HUMAN TESTIMONY

One notorious problem with evaluating the semi-experimental and anecdotal evidence of parapsychology – especially the more bizarre reports – is that many cases have fallen victim to the gnawing tooth of time. We can no longer interrogate witnesses or study the ostensible psi agents for ourselves. We cannot determine first-hand that all reasonable precautions were taken against trickery on the part of mediums, or see for ourselves whether investigators of poltergeist disturbances overlooked some means of fraudulently (or unwittingly) producing the phenomena. We are forced to rely on eyewitness accounts at best (some written considerably after the event) and follow-up investigations at worst – not to mention numerous assumptions concerning the integrity and reliability of those whose depositions serve as evidence. And unlike most scientific experiments, we can't simply re-create the conditions (including the provision of superstar subjects) under which the phenomena occurred. Can there really be anything here for the serious researcher to sink his teeth into?

I propose to answer this question by considering an array of arguments against the reliability of the kinds of reports that comprise most of the non-experimental evidence in parapsychology. If these arguments fail, then I suggest we have *no choice* but to pay serious attention to the amazing phenomena reported in the days before parapsychology turned almost exclusively experimental, as well as those that continue to be reported outside the lab.

Before proceeding, however, we should consider an important terminological point. In his discussion of spontaneous cases, Stevenson made the useful distinction between the *authenticity* and *evidentiality* of an eyewitness report of an ostensibly paranormal event (Stevenson, 1968). Elaborating somewhat on Stevenson's use of the terms, I propose the following definitions.

(D1) A report of an ostensibly paranormal event is *authentic* if and only if the reliability of the testimony is such that the event probably occurred as reported.

(D2) A report of an ostensibly paranormal event is *evidential* if and only if the report is authentic and the event is plausibly interpreted as paranormal.

I do not wish to discuss here the highly problematic meaning of 'paranormal' (see Braude, 1979), and the issue of what justifies interpreting an event as paranormal. Rather, I want to observe that most of the skeptical arguments we shall now consider attempt to undercut claims of paranormality by attacking the *authenticity* of eyewitness reports. In fact, the prevailing distrust of non-experimental evidence seems primarily to be a distrust of its authenticity. Lab reports, by contrast, are usually assumed (even by skeptics) to be authentic. When experimental studies are challenged, it is usually on the grounds that the results are not plausibly interpreted as paranormal.

With this distinction in mind, let us now turn our attention to six more or less standard arguments regarding human testimony. (The issue of outright *fraud* will be dealt with in Chapter 2.)

(1) The most radical argument would be a sweeping indictment of all human testimony. Some might argue that observation and testimony are inherently fallible, and that what is inherently fallible cannot be trusted. But of course the matter is not this simple. The possibility of error exists equally with respect to sources of evidence on which we rely all the time – for example, laboratory studies in science, which are based on various sorts of observation, notation, and instrument readings – all far from incorrigible.

Skeptics might concede that human testimony generally *is* suspect, but that some cases are better documented than others, *especially* scientific laboratory reports. After all, they might say, many scientists, on the same or on different occasions, report the same results; and such collective and repeated testimony is more credible than the isolated and untestable reports found in the semi-experimental and anecdotal literature of parapsychology. I have heard this argument in conversation numerous times, and in my view it merely displays its proponent's ignorance of the evidence. To be sure, some non-experimental case reports are isolated and unique. But there exist numerous *collective* eyewitness accounts of phenomena, and reports of unusual sorts of phenomena occurring on more than one occasion. Such accounts may be found in many cases of physical mediumship, poltergeist disturbances, and apparitions.

Moreover, as Gauld and Cornell's recent survey of poltergeist and haunting cases demonstrates, non-experimental case reports frequently agree on peculiar and unexpected details, despite the fact that the reports are made independently of one another, and often under quite different social and cultural conditions (Gauld and Cornell, 1979). Among these details are: the slow and gentle trajectories of airborne objects, the apparent passage of levitated objects through walls and closed doors, and the poltergeist bombardment with human excrement. Since until recently victims of poltergeist disturbances have tended to be unfamiliar both with the literature on the subject (*if* any existed)[5] and with other contemporaneous cases of the same kind, it seems to me that such convergence of independent testimony cannot easily be brushed aside. Furthermore, when close examination of poltergeist cases suggests strongly that those involved share no common underlying needs to experience or report phenomena of this sort (especially in their details), and in the absence of any reasonable proposals as to what such needs might be, we simply have to entertain seriously the hypothesis that the phenomena occurred largely as reported.

The literature on apparitions also displays an impressive degree of internal coherence, and perhaps most importantly, not of the sort one would have expected (see Gurney, Myers, and Podmore, 1886; and Tyrrell, 1942/1961). One might argue, following West (1948), that similarity in reports of apparitions might be explained in much the same way as we account for similarity in descriptions of ghosts found in popular fiction – namely, as due to widely-diffused ideas about what ghosts should be like. But first-hand reports of apparitions tend to differ strikingly from the apparently popular conception of ghosts. For example, apparitions tend not to engage the subject in prolonged conversations, and they tend *not* to leave behind physical traces or produce other physical effects. Now it is easy to see how, in the 19th century, the printed word might have spread the general conception of a ghost. But, in the case of apparitions (especially apparitions of the living), such channels of communication did not exist – or at least were not exploited – by the time the S.P.R. conducted its survey of hallucinations. Not only was there no popular literature on apparitions, but apparently only a very small number of the percipients surveyed knew each other or had heard about another's experience of an apparition. Many, in fact, had been reluctant to mention their experiences to anyone. Therefore, it seems rather unlikely that the classic apparitional type emerging in *Phantasms of the Living* (Gurney, Myers, and Podmore, 1886) can be explained away by appeal to common mechanisms for disseminating ideas or myths. (See Chapter 3 for a fuller discussion of apparitions.)

(2) Nevertheless, some might protest that witnesses of ostensibly paranormal phenomena are disposed to see the miraculous, or to see what they want, and thus are prone to misperceive or deceive themselves, and perhaps even lie or exaggerate (possibly unconsciously) in order to protect their preconceptions. Therefore, they would conclude, it is more reasonable to suppose that some process of motivated misperception, self-deception, or dishonesty is at work, than to treat such eyewitness testimony as serious evidence for paranormal phenomena. But this rejoinder, which we may call 'The Argument from Human Bias', is still unsatisfactory, and for two main reasons.

(a) Even if witnesses of ostensibly paranormal phenomena *were* biased or predisposed to see such things, this would not explain why the biased misperceptions or reports should be similar in so many peculiar details. One would need a rather elaborate psychological theory (to say the least) to explain why people of dissimilar backgrounds and cultures, with apparently no common needs to experience bizarre phenomena of any sort (much less the same sort), should, independently of one another, report (say) 'raining' stones inside a house or the intense heat of apports.

Moreover, it is not clearly to the skeptic's advantage to rely heavily on the Argument from Human Bias. That argument cuts two ways, against reports by the credulous *and* the incredulous. If our biases may lead us to malobserve, or misremember, or lie, then we should be as suspicious of testimony from non-believers as from believers. If (on the basis of their favorable dispositions) we distrust reports by the apparently credulous or sympathetic that certain odd phenomena occurred, we should (by parity of reasoning) be equally wary of reports by the incredulous or unsympathetic that the alleged phenomena did *not* occur (or that cheating occurred instead). And in that case, the implications of the argument extend clearly beyond the boundaries of parapsychology. For example, we would be entitled to doubt every scientific lab study based on instrument readings and ordinary human observation. Scientists, one would think, have at least as much at stake, and hence at least as many reasons for perceptual biases, as do witnesses of psi phenomena. In fact, they may have more, given the intimate connection between their lab work and career interests. Although philosophers and scientists who fancy themselves to be tough-minded and impartial are often reluctant to concede this point, there have been exceptions. For example, Ducasse wrote,

> allegations of detection of fraud, or of malobservation, or of misinterpretation of what was observed, or of hypnotically induced hallucinations, have to be scrutinized *as closely and as critically* as must the testimony *for* the reality of the phenomena. For there is likely to be just as much wishful thinking, prejudice, emotion, snap judgment, naiveté, and intellectual dishonesty on the side of orthodoxy, of skepticism, and of conservatism, as on the side of hunger for and of belief in the marvelous. The emotional motivation for irresponsible disbelief is, in fact, probably even stronger – especially in scientifically educated persons whose pride of knowledge is at stake – than is in other persons the motivation for irresponsible belief. (Ducasse, 1958, p. 22)

Ducasse's caveat about irresponsible disbelief is buttressed by a wealth of evidence. For one thing, according to Stevenson (1968, p. 112), experiments have revealed a number of interesting ways in which peer pressure and other contextual factors can apparently influence a person's perceptions or perception reports. But even apart from the experimental evidence, the history of parapsychology chronicles an astounding degree of blindness, intellectual cowardice, and mendacity on the part of skeptics and ardent non-believers, some of them prominent scientists. Since the foibles and sins of the opponents of parapsychology are rarely given the attention lavished on those of its supporters, a few words on the topic seem in order.

We could begin by citing Robert Browning's somewhat famous change of heart regarding D. D. Home. (The case of Home is discussed in detail in the next chapter.) Browning had initially been impressed by Home. At the Ealing residence of London solicitor John Rymer, he had been given the opportunity to observe the medium levitate a table in good light, with Home's hands visible above the table. He had also been allowed to look under the table to determine that Home was not using his legs or feet. Browning also observed, among other things, the playing of an accordion that nobody was touching (one of Home's regular phenomena). At the time, Browning admitted that he was unable to explain what he had observed. A month later, however, he was arguing passionately (suspiciously so, in my opinion) that Home had been cheating – but *not* as the result of any further first-hand experiences with Home. And although the poet never again attended a Home séance, he continued his emotional denunciations of the medium.

The reasons for Browning's sudden about-face are not altogether clear, and seem to be rather complicated. It is not simply that he *deliberated* after the fact and concluded that what he observed could only have been due to trickery, although ratiocination may have played a part in the process. Indeed, it would hardly be surprising if Browning harbored philosophical or religious objections to psychokinesis, mediumship, or spiritualism generally. But it seems that his antipathy toward Home was fueled primarily by more down-to-earth matters. For one thing, according to Jenkins (1982, p. 39), Browning 'abhorred Home's gentle, effeminate bearing', and the 'childishly caressing behaviour' he displayed toward the Rymers (who had more or less appointed themselves Home's British 'family'). Jenkins also suggests that Browning so strongly desired total spiritual union with his wife Elizabeth, that he could not bear their differing sympathies toward spiritualistic phenomena in general, and her endorsement of Home in particular. And no doubt Browning was rankled further by Home's fascination with and attention toward Elizabeth, and perhaps also by the Rymers' refusal to grant Browning a second séance. Others have suggested that Browning's ego was bruised by the fact that at the Rymer séance a garland was placed on Elizabeth's head rather than his own. But whatever the cause, it is clear enough that Browning circulated numerous falsehoods about events at the séance. Fortunately for historians, in a letter dated two days after that occasion, Browning wrote a detailed description of the events, contrasting sharply with accounts he began spreading soon afterward. Moreover, the malice he displayed toward Home was so disproportionate to anything that transpired at or after the séance, that one cannot help but feel that the poet was moved by something far deeper and more personal than detection of trickery. (See Jenkins, 1982, pp. 37–49; and Dingwall, 1962a, pp. 101–8.)

Of course, Browning was neither a scientist nor a philosopher; and although he was a celebrity, he certainly was not widely regarded as an authority on the empirically possible. His behavior, then, is perhaps less reprehensible than that of some of his prominent scientific contemporaries, who unquestionably abused, not only their influence as public figures, but also the power and prestige of their positions within the scientific community. Possibly the best documented case of this sort concerns Scottish physicist Sir David Brewster (see N. Fodor, 1966, pp. 37f; Mme. Home, 1888/1976, pp. 36–43, 203–4; Inglis, 1977, pp. 227–9; Jenkins, 1982, pp. 32–6; Podmore, 1902/1963, vol. 2, pp. 142–4; Zorab, 1975; and especially Home, 1863/1972, appendix). Its essentials are as follows. In 1855 Brewster attended two of Home's séances, first (at the invitation of Lord Brougham) in the home of William Cox, and then at the Rymers'. After the Cox séance, Home wrote to a friend in the United States, claiming that Brewster and the others had admitted their inability to explain his physical phenomena by any normal means. The letter was subsequently published in some newspapers, and before long the story of the Cox séance travelled back to London, where Home's letter was reprinted in the *Morning Advertiser*. Brewster then wrote to the *Advertiser*, denying that he had found the phenomena inexplicable, and charging, 'I saw enough to satisfy myself that they could all be produced by human hands and feet, and to prove that some of them, at least, had such an origin' (Home, 1863/1972, p. 241).

Brewster's letter sparked an intense exchange in the *Advertiser* (a relatively accessible source for the correspondence is Home, 1863/1972, pp. 237–61). Cox wrote and reminded Brewster that he had remarked at the time, 'This upsets the philosophy of 50 years' (Home, 1863/1972, pp. 243, 252). Brewster also alleged that he had not been permitted to look under the table. Cox denied this, as did T. A. Trollope, who had attended the Rymer séance. Trollope pointed out that Home and Rymer had encouraged Brewster to look under the table, which Brewster did, and that while he looked under the table, it moved apparently without Home's agency, and that Brewster admitted to having seen the movement (Home, 1863/1972, p. 253). Brewster refused to retract his claim, and then added, somewhat revealingly,

> Rather than believe that spirits made the noise, *I will conjecture* that the raps were produced by Mr Home's toes . . . and rather than believe that spirits raised the table, *I will conjecture* that it was done by the agency of Mr Home's feet. (Home 1863/1972, p. 247)

It was not until 1869, a year after Brewster's death, that the controversy was settled and Brewster's dishonesty revealed. Brewster's daughter published in that year *The Home Life of Sir David Brewster* (no pun intended), in which she unwittingly included an account by her father of the séances, written at the time. Of the Cox séance he writes.

> [Lord Brougham] invited me to accompany him in order to assist in finding out the trick. We four sat down at a moderately-sized table, the structure of which we were invited to examine. In a short time the table shuddered, and a tremulous motion ran up all our arms; at our bidding these motions ceased, and returned. The most unaccountable rappings were produced in various parts of the table; and the table actually rose from the ground when no hand was upon it. A larger table was produced, and exhibited similar movements.
> . . . a small hand-bell was then laid down with its mouth on the carpet, and, after lying for some time, it actually rang when nothing could have touched it. The bell was then placed on the other side, still upon the carpet, and it came over to

me and placed itself in my hand. It did the same to Lord
Brougham.

   These were the principal experiments; we could give no
   explanation of them, and could not conjecture how they
   could be produced by any kind of mechanism. (Gordon, 1869,
   pp. 257–8)

After these revelations, the *Spectator* remarked, rather lamely,
'The hero of science does not acquit himself as we could wish or
expect'.

Another such episode from the same period is physiologist
William Benjamin Carpenter's anonymously-authored denunci-
ation of three prominent scientific investigators of mediums:
William Crookes, Cromwell Varley, and William Huggins, all
Fellows of the Royal Society. His unsigned article, 'Spiritualism
and its Recent Converts', in the *Quarterly Review* of October
1871 mixes innuendo and distortion of the facts with outright
dishonesty. Yet even after the Council of the Royal Society, in a
special resolution, admitted that statements in the article were
false, Carpenter was not censured, and in fact the British A.A.S.
elected him president the next year. (For details, see N. Fodor,
1966, p. 70; Inglis, 1977, pp. 256ff; and Podmore 1902/1963, vol.
2, pp. 141–2, 151–2.)

   Still another example from the same period is the treatment of
William Crookes by an Official of the Royal Society, physicist
George Stokes (see Chapter 2.2). But of course reprehensible
behavior on the part of skeptics is not restricted to the latter part
of the nineteenth century. As far as the case of Home is
concerned, there exists a tradition of shoddy evaluations,
continuing to this day. A typical approach is to attempt to discredit
the phenomena by focusing on hazy or questionable – and irrelevant – details of Home's personal life, such as his involvement
with Jane Lyon and his alleged homosexuality. Another is to
examine the weakest evidence (such as Home's alleged levitation
out the window at Ashley House) and ignore the strong cases or
the sittings held expressly for the purpose of careful investigation
(rather than the informal sessions held for friends or other
convinced spiritualists). For two recent examples of these tactics,
see Brandon, 1983, and Hall, 1984. These books will appear to
the novice to be unbiased and scholarly; but in my opinion they

are to serious psychical research what the *National Enquirer* is to serious news reporting. Inglis (1983) reviewed Brandon and quite rightly called her book 'deplorable'. Hall's work is equally shoddy (see Braude, 1985).

A different sort of contemporary example is a doubled-barrelled offense: the combination of (a) magician James Randi's hollow challenge, mis-reporting, and evasive dialectic aimed at Eisenbud's study of Ted Serios, and (b) the support of Randi's account by scientists and others who have made no direct study of the evidence. For instance, in an inexcusable act of misrepresentation and abuse of his position of influence, Martin Gardner claims (*Nature* v. 300, Nov. 11, p. 119) that Randi 'regularly' duplicates the Serios photographic phenomena. Now it is not clear whether Gardner has simply and unwisely taken Randi's word on this; but the claim, nevertheless, is patently false. Randi has never even *attempted* to duplicate the Serios phenomena under the most stringent – and most relevant – conditions in which Serios succeeded. The story is too complicated to be presented here, and Randi has (sagely) not granted permission to publish his revealing correspondence on the matter. I refer the interested reader to Fuller, 1974, for a partial (and unfortunately, the only accessible) account of the matter.[6]

(b) In the first part of my response to the Argument from Human Bias, I was willing to grant that witnesses might in some way be biased or predisposed to experience the phenomena they report. But that concession is by no means necessary; it is often *false* that witnesses are biased in favor of the phenomena. It would be ludicrous, for example, to attribute such biases to the skeptics who reluctantly admitted, after careful study of the mediums D. D. Home and Eusapia Palladino, that their physical phenomena were not produced fraudulently (see Chapter 2.2 and 2.3). Charles Richet, for example, says of his own belief in the physical phenomena of Palladino,

> It took me twenty years of patient researches to arrive at my present conviction. Nay – to make one last confession – I am not yet even absolutely and irremediably convinced! In spite of the astounding phenomena I have witnessed during my sixty experiments with Eusapia, I have still a trace of doubt; doubt which is weak, indeed to-day, but which may

perchance be stronger to-morrow. Yet such doubts, if they come, will not be due so much to any defect in the actual experiment, as to the inexorable strength of prepossession which holds me back from adopting a conclusion which contravenes the habitual and almost unanimous opinion of mankind. (Richet, 1899, p. 157)

Moreover, the careful and detailed accounts of many poltergeist cases suggests strongly that witnesses often neither hoped nor expected to experience the phenomena. Indeed, as Rogo observes in his review of Gauld and Cornell, 1979,

Most people who initially confront the poltergeist, as Gauld shows. . . , do not usually assume that anything paranormal is occurring. Their first reaction is to find a normal explanation for the events in question. On this basis, such a witness would not be expected to malobserve a PK event in such a way as to exaggerate the unusualness of the event. He would tend to normalize it. *That* would be consistent with his motivation. (Rogo, 1979, p. 334)

Rogo therefore suggests, quite sensibly,

if a witness were to malobserve a poltergeist antic, he would actually be more likely to misperceive it in *such a way as to make the incident more amenable to a natural explanation*. (Rogo, 1979, p. 334)

Rogo may be somewhat optimistic about the proportion of cases fitting his description.[7] Nevertheless, his observation seems quite right for many cases – including some of the best.

Granted, the belief-systems of many witnesses allow for the *possibility* of poltergeist and other physical phenomena. But a person's merely being open to the possibility of a phenomenon would not explain why the person should actually report having observed it. Being open to the possibility of phenomenon P is quite a different matter from being biased or predisposed to observe P or believe that P occurs. For example, many would concede that it is possible that alien spaceships will visit or have visited the Earth, while nevertheless assigning to such an event a probability approaching 0. As a matter of fact, one can be open to the possibility of P but be biased *against* observing or believing in *P*. This is undoubtedly why many parents fail to register clues indicating that their children have been smoking marijuana, even though they would admit that such an event is empirically possible. Interestingly, many poltergeist victims display a similar attitude or bias. They would grant that such events might occur, while feeling strongly that they would never happen to *them*.

Furthermore, the probability of misperception through motivated seeing (as Gauld and Cornell, 1979, correctly observe) increases as conditions of observation deteriorate. But many of the more bizarre spontaneous phenomena have been observed collectively, near at hand, in good light, with clear heads, etc. In this category belong many of the phenomena of Home and Palladino, as well as some of the more spectacular poltergeist manifestations, such as the slow and apparently deliberate movements of objects through the air and (in the E. Zugun case – see Gauld and Cornell, 1979, pp. 127–42) the sudden appearance of bite and scratch marks on the hands and face of an ostensible poltergeist agent/victim.

(3) Let us waive, then, issues concerning reporter bias and motivated misperception. There are still good reasons, my opponent might continue, for distrusting human testimony of the sort comprising most non-experimental case reports. We know from 'staged incident' cases in legal contexts that people are often guilty of outright malobservation. In some experiments, a group of people unexpectedly witness a carefully pre-arranged confrontation or dispute, and their subsequent reports of the incident tend to differ in many details from what actually occurred. For example, witnesses may fail to observe that one participant said something designed to provoke another, or they might report that one participant said something rather different from what was actually said.

I tend to agree with Gauld and Cornell (1979, pp. 256–8) and Stevenson (1968, pp. 106ff.) that these studies have little relevance to the assessment of non-experimental case reports in parapsychology, though they are clearly important in legal contexts. The magnitude of error demonstrated in the studies – while no doubt relevant to determining matters of guilt and innocence in a court of law – is quite small as compared to the errors we would have to posit to explain away many semi-experimental and anecdotal case reports. As far as I can ascertain, there is no evidence that observers in good light, often collectively and from near at hand, make perceptual mistakes as gross as those needed to discredit eyewitness accounts of objects moving *slowly* through the air with nobody touching them, or from parts of the room where no one is present (and where prior and subsequent investigation reveals no hidden machinery or apparatus capable of producing the phenomena), or (say) of accordions playing melodies while held keys downward, in one hand, and enclosed in decent illumination in a cage.

But even if we forget about the evidence from staged incident studies, many simply assume that malobservation is more probable in the case of ostensibly paranormal events than in cases of normal events. It seems to me, however, that this is just another prejudice about non-experimental evidence which a sober reading of the material makes difficult to sustain.

As far as apparitions are concerned, many occur when subjects are relaxed; and witnesses frequently remark how natural and non-startling the occurrences are. In fact, apparitions are typically recognized as such only *after* subjects realize that the object apparently perceived had to have been elsewhere. Experiences of apparitions, then, although certainly unexpected, often lack the gut-wrenching element of surprise that might undermine the credibility or reliability of accounts of many normal phenomena. Furthermore, the apparitions tend not to be particularly action-packed; frequently they do no more than merely appear for a brief time, and on rare occasions utter something. Witnesses of apparitions, then, are seldom confronted with the dizzying array of events which witnesses of crimes and staged incidents must remember. It would seem, therefore, that many witnesses of apparitions are in at least as good a position to give accounts of what they experience as are witnessess of ordinary events.

Of course, it is with regard to the physical phenomena of the séance room and poltergeist cases that the possibility of malobservation is most frequently invoked. It is well-known that outlandish observation reports have issued from darkened séance rooms. And in fact there is also semi-experimental evidence showing that under certain (rather poor) séance conditions, and for certain kinds of small-scale ostensibly paranormal phenomena (e.g., slate-writing), subjects often err in their observations, and sometimes report events that never occurred (see Besterman,

1932a; Hodgson, 1892; and Hodgson and Davey, 1887). But the conditions of these tests were considerably more conducive to malobservation than those in the best studies of mediums, and the magnitude of error in the former (as in staged incident cases) is again much smaller than what we would have to posit in the latter.

Also, as Stevenson (1968) observes, in many poltergeist and mediumistic cases, the unusual events reported occur more than once, either on the same or on different occasions. Furthermore, the phenomena often persist far longer than the brief incidents typically overlooked in staged incidents or in the studies of Besterman, and Hogdson and Davey. Therefore, unlike witnesses of staged incidents, participants in poorly-lit séances, or observers of small-scale phenomena easily producible by sleight-of-hand, witnesses of apparent large-scale PK are frequently able to lavish sustained and repeated attention on the occurrences in question. And as Loftus notes in her recent study of eyewitness testimony, a number of experiments have confirmed the commonsense observation that memory reports are more reliable when the perceived events or objects are observed repeatedly or for extended periods (Loftus, 1979, pp. 24–5).

Moreover, in the studies of mediums and poltergeists where the conditions of observation were good, reports of unusual phenomena are not *inherently* more problematical – *qua* observation reports – than reports of ordinary phenomena under similar conditions of observation. In the best studies of mediums – e.g., the famous 1908 Naples sittings with Eusapia Palladino (see Chapter 2.3; Feilding, 1963; and Feilding, Baggally, and Carrington, 1909) – the observers were highly skilled in and knowledgeable about the art of conjuring. In some cases they did not believe in genuine physical phenomena, and in fact were sent to debunk the medium. In any event, they were certainly *on the lookout* for phenomena of the sort they observed and for the employment of conjurers' tricks. They were thus prepared to make relevant sorts of observational checks while the phenomena were occurring (e.g., being sure to ascertain that the medium was not raising the table with her legs or with an apparatus concealed beneath the table or in her clothes). Investigators of poltergeist disturbances have likewise often been prepared in advance for the phenomena they observed, and were ready to make crucial sorts of on-the-spot checks. Of course many historical poltergeist cases were not investigated by trained observers. But the diaries of the victims or other amateur observers who kept records of the incidents reveal that they were often level-headed and scrupulous in their observations. However unpleasant the phenomena may have been, after a while they became rather commonplace to those involved, and not very likely to upset them in a way that would weaken their powers of observation. Indeed, they were often psychologically well-prepared to observe and study the phenomena while they occurred, and occasionally their observational skills appear to improve as time goes on.[8]

In fact, given the preparedness and occasional skepticism of the observers, as well as the large-scale nature of some reported phenomena, there is reason to think that witnesses might be *less* liable to malobserve than are witnesses of more ordinary events. One would need to posit a magnitude of error for these cases considerably greater than that generally required to undermine eyewitness accounts of ordinary events (e.g., crimes, domestic squabbles, or occurrences during military campaigns). Normal events are often observed and reported under conditions at least as conducive to error as those encountered by psychical researchers, and sometimes more so. We could easily cast doubt on reports concerning the behavior of military commanders by appealing to the psychological pressures affecting witnesses – e.g., the tension and perhaps panic of retreat, the fear of imminent surrender or defeat (combined with anger at the officers for bungling their jobs, or the petty jealousies of soldiers regarding their superiors), or the effects of lack of sleep and other forms of battle-fatigue. But it is more difficult to cast doubt on the reliability of reports of psychologically and methodologically well-prepared and often skeptical observers of apparent large-scale PK, and even reports of ordinary victims of poltergeist phenomena who have grown somewhat accustomed to incidents of that kind. In fact, eyewitness reports in parapsychology may even be less suspect than many scientific laboratory reports. The collecting of experimental data often requires great alertness, and is easily subverted by a momentary relaxation of attention. Thus, the soporifically routine and painstaking observations of some scientific studies may be more conducive to (minor but critical) error than the immediate and unusual experience of a large-scale paranormal event, as in poltergeist cases or the levitations of Joseph of Copertino. (See also Eisenbud, 1979, pp. 147–8, and Stevenson, 1968, pp. 96ff. on this point.)

Therefore, if malobservation is no more probable in the case of large-scale ostensibly paranormal phenomena than in the case of many normal phenomena, it would seem that reports of the former are no more inherently unreliable than reports of the latter. But then to reject eyewitness accounts of large-scale phenomena simply because the phenomena reported seem paranormal is to hold an indefensible double standard with respect to eyewitness testimony.

Furthermore, skeptics have little to gain by appealing to the fallibility of memory. For one thing, reports from poltergeist cases and séances are often written on the spot or shortly thereafter, and not after a considerable lapse of time. And as Stevenson (1968, pp. 100ff.) observes, in many experiments concerning the fading of memory, subjects are presented with ordinary or simply boring material (including nonsense syllables and dull stories). But non-experimental cases frequently concern events that are far more easily remembered. They are often emotionally intense and highly interesting, and the subject (either for these reasons or from an interest in the paranormal) is frequently highly motivated to remember what occurred. Therefore, it seems likely that witnesses of ostensibly paranormal occurrences will remember what took place. In fact, this conclusion seems to have independent empirical support. After discussing an experiment suggesting that witnesses are best able to remember salient features of an observed event, Loftus, in her book on eyewitness testimony, approvingly quotes D. S. Gardner's observation that

> The extraordinary, colorful, novel, unusual, and interesting scenes attract our attention and hold our interest, both attention and interest being important aids to memory. The opposite of this principle is inversely true – routine, commonplace and insignificant circumstances are rarely remembered as specific incidents. (Loftus, 1979, p. 27)

Also, according to Gauld and Cornell, experimental evidence concerning change of memory reports over time shows that subjects tend to tone down rather than embroider their stories, especially in contexts where accuracy is demanded – for example, where witnesses are placed on oath (see Gauld and Cornell, 1979; also Stevenson, 1968, pp. 103ff.). In addition, there are cases where witnesses of ostensibly paranormal occurrences have given accounts many years apart, and discrepancies between the different accounts are minimal. Assuming (plausibly) that the subjects found these incidents important or otherwise impressive, the similarity in their accounts is consistent with Gardner's observation above, and pretty much what one would expect (see Gauld and Cornell, 1979, pp. 254–6, and Stevenson, 1968, pp. 101ff.).

(4) Should we suppose, then, that non-experimental case reports demonstrate no more than a natural (if reprehensible) desire for publicity or notoriety, especially when it might spice up an otherwise humdrum existence? I think not. At best, this approach to explaining away phenomena reported in non-experimental cases might be appropriate to a small proportion of the total number. But in many cases, eyewitnesses clearly have nothing to gain from making depositions about the odd phenomena they believe they observed; nor have they attempted to capitalize on their experiences (e.g., many cases of apparitions – see Gurney, Myers, and Podmore, 1886, and Tyrrell, 1942/1961; also the many reports of the levitations of Joseph of Copertino – see Chapter 2.5; also Dingwall, 1962a, Eisenbud, 1979, 1982b, and Inglis, 1977). In fact, the notoriety likely to be achieved in most cases is predictably unpleasant. For example, once their plight becomes known, victims of poltergeist disturbances are frequently subject to harassments of other kinds – in particular, the invasion of privacy by curiosity-seekers, publicity-hungry debunkers, and (especially in times past) the scorn or ridicule of those who attribute the disturbances to the work of the devil or something comparably unsavory. Similarly, prominent defenders of physical mediumship have usually had to endure a good deal of public and professional derision, and often their careers have suffered for their interest in the paranormal. In the eyes of many, the reputations of both William Crookes and Alfred Russel Wallace were permanently tainted by their interest in spiritualistic phenomena. (For a recent example of this attitude, see Hyman, 1980, and the reply by Braude, 1980.) In fact, Crookes's devotion to mediumistic investigations seems to have earned him, on the whole, more aggravation than public reward.

For that matter, we now know that observers of ostensibly

paranormal phenomena have sometimes *witheld* information, for fear of ridicule or loss of professional prestige and credibility. Of particular interest in this connection are the unreported exhibitions of ESP and bizarre physical phenomena apparently observed in some early French studies of hypnotism (see Dingwall, 1967, vol. 1, pp. 220ff; and Inglis, 1977, pp. 255–6). And despite the very promising results of certain nineteenth-century experiments in hypnosis and ESP, scientists showed a marked reluctance to pursue the matter (see Eisenbud, 1970, pp. 54–60), and turned their attention to more conservative areas of investigation. Thus, Richet admitted, in his disarmingly candid address to the S.P.R.,

In the course of these studies [in somnambulism] I had here and there observed certain facts of lucidity, of premonition, of telepathy; but since these facts were denied and ridiculed on every side, I had not pushed independence of mind so far as to believe them. I deliberately shut my eyes to phenomena which lay plain before me, and rather than discuss them I chose the easier course of denying them altogether. Or, I should rather say, instead of pondering on these inexplicable facts I simply put them aside, and set them down to some illusion, or some error of observation. (Richet, 1899, pp. 153–4)[9]

(5) Still, even when there is evidence that more than one person, on the same or on different occasions, observed an apparently large-scale paranormal event under good conditions, some might continue to insist that their converging testimony carries little weight. They would argue that it is more reasonable to explain away the apparent paranormality of such cases by appealing to one of two closely related hypotheses: (a) *collective hallucination* – i.e., that each of those reporting the phenomenon in reality experienced a non-veridical apparent perception produced by processes internal to the subject (i.e., auto-suggestion), and (b) *collective hypnosis* – i.e., that each of those reporting the phenomenon in reality experienced a non-veridical apparent perception induced externally (and presumably intentionally) through a process of suggestion or hypnosis. Thus, in the first case, some might suggest that sitters at a séance or witnesses of poltergeist disturbances each suffered an internally-generated apparent

perception, and that their resulting peculiar non-veridical subjective experiences agreed in small and highly unusual detail. Or, in the second case, they might suggest that a medium exerted a kind of hypnotic trance over all the sitters at a séance, so that they all had the same or similar peculiar and detailed non-veridical apparent perception.

Now I confess that I find a retreat to this position rather desperate. Its flaws, however, are instructive. To begin with, as far as I can ascertain, there simply *is* no evidence – apart from the ostensibly paranormal cases, apparent UFO sightings, and some biblical stories where the hypotheses of collective hallucination and hypnosis are advanced as explanations – that such collective, concordant, non-paranormal, and non-veridical experiences ever occur. We know, of course, that people are susceptible to hypnotic suggestion and hallucination. But if we have no evidence, apart from the peculiar cases in question, that the proposed sort of *collective* hallucination or hypnosis occurs, then these counter-hypotheses are extremely weak indeed.

Some might argue that the success of the Indian Rope Trick demonstrates that concordant, collective, non-veridical experiences do in fact occur. In these cases, allegedly, a magician induces nearby observers to experience (among other things) a boy climbing a rope and then disappearing, although people outside the magician's vicinity (and thus, presumably, outside his range of suggestion) see merely the other onlookers gazing skyward. It turns out, however, that appeals to the Rope Trick do *not* bolster the skeptical position. For one thing, even if the Rope Trick was genuine, and therefore even if the appropriate sort of collective hypnosis had been performed, the cases in which the trick was apparently produced differ crucially from many of the best mediumistic and poltergeist cases, where there were no obvious preliminaries or opportunities for suggestion. But more importantly, there is no reason to think that the Rope Trick *is* genuine. As far as I can discover, there is no good evidence that any such trick has ever been performed (see Dingwall, 1974, for a good survey of the defects in the testimony). The evidence for it is far less persuasive than the evidence for many second-rate spontaneous cases in parapsychology. Indeed, if the evidence for the Rope Trick were subjected to the intense critical appraisal accorded experiments and spontaneous case reports in parapsychology, it would have to be dismissed as inconclusive at best, and probably worthless. The trick, in fact, seems to be no more than a collection of fanciful (and occasionally intentionally fraudulent) anecdotes, reported so often as to create a legend. Therefore, there still seems to be no decent evidence – apart from the curious cases under consideration – that the relevant sorts of concordant, collective, non-paranormal, and non-veridical experiences occur.

There is, I should add, a substantial body of evidence for the occurrence of collective *apparitions*, some of which – as in certain cases of apparent hauntings – appear to recur at a particular location, or strongly resemble or relate to previous or subsequent apparitions occurring at or near that location. But these cases are of no help to those hoping to explain away the apparent paranormality of poltergeist or mediumistic physical phenomena. For one thing, it would be question-begging to assume that these cases are non-paranormal. In fact, it is their *prima facie* peculiarity that places them in the class of spontaneous case material in parapsychology. We must explain, for instance, why in many cases people apparently experience the *same* apparition. And one serious hypothesis (certainly one that cannot be dismissed out of hand) is that one person hallucinates an apparently externally-localized apparition and telepathically or psychokinetically communicates it to (or infects) others. Another is that the apparition is a localized *objective* entity of a peculiar and scarcely understood sort, created paranormally either by the individual of whom it is an apparition, or by one of the percipients (see Broad 1962a, pp. 224–38; also Chapter 3, for a discussion of apparitions).

Moreover, some cases of collective apparitions (e.g., certain crisis and haunting cases) have proven to be veridical – that is, they represented a remote individual as being in some outstanding (as opposed to trivial or universally predicable) state identical or very similar to an actual state of the individual at or about that time.[10] But of course the primary reason skeptics appeal to collective hallucination or hypnosis in connection with physical phenomena is to maintain that what appeared to be veridical experiences were in fact *non*-veridical. And clearly, they cannot assume from the start that the veridicality of apparitions is explicable in terms of processes we already understand. We would have to explain, without an appeal to ESP or something even less familiar, why (say) more than one person should experience an apparition (often the only such experience of their lives) that accurately corresponds to a more or less concurrent state of affairs whose existence they had no reason to expect – for example, the critical condition of a remote individual. Or, we must explain why (say) more than one person should experience, in a certain room of a house, an apparition of an individual in some way formerly connected with that room or house, and of whom those experiencing the apparition were totally ignorant. Of course, as with most non-experimental material in parapsychology, various non-paranormal explanations have been offered to account for the features of these cases. Nevertheless, the fact remains that cases of collective apparitions are far from clear-cut cases of non-paranormal phenomena. So the evidence for collective apparitions appears to be evidence of the wrong kind. It seems implausible to regard it as – and it certainly cannot be *assumed* to be – evidence for non-paranormal, non-veridical, collective and concordant subjective experiences.

Furthermore, reports of physical phenomena from séances and poltergeist cases are often reports of phenomena affecting more than one sense simultaneously. D. D. Home's séances sometimes included the production of something dubbed the 'earthquake effect,' wherein sitters would see, hear, and feel the rocking or shaking of the entire room and the accompanying movement of objects in the room. In other cases, sitters would see and hear untouched musical instruments play, and they would agree on what was being played and that it was played beautifully. Now as far as I know, there is no experimental or other independent evidence of the simultaneous production, in a group of people of varying degrees of suggestibility, of a combination of visual, auditory, and tactile non-veridical experiences, much less experiences produced so thoroughly or expertly that all present agreed as to the nature of the extra-subjective phenomena they apparently witnessed. In poltergeist cases, too, there is often total agreement among those present as to the simultaneous auditory, visual, tactile, and sometimes olfactory, characteristics of the phenomena reported.

The hypotheses of collective hallucination and hypnosis seem, therefore, to be on an even weaker footing than some paranormal hypotheses. If, for example, we attempt to explain cases of apparent paranormal foreknowledge as cases of ESP (rather than, say, purely accidental correlations between one person's mental states and some future state of affairs), at least ESP is a phenomenon for which we have independent experimental evidence.

Besides, even if there *were* independent evidence (from ostensibly *non*-paranormal cases) for the occurrence of collective hallucination or hypnosis, these counter-hypotheses face additional serious obstacles. First, as far as physical phenomena are concerned, the hypotheses are rather limited in scope. Collective hallucination, for example, seems inapplicable to mediumistic phenomena; at best, the hypothesis might work for some poltergeist cases. If we appeal to collective hallucination (rather than hypnosis) to account for cases of apparent physical mediumship, we would have to explain why subjects *internally* generate (i.e., by auto-suggestion) concordant non-veridical experiences *without* implicating the medium. Otherwise, the medium would presumably be responsible somehow for the sitters' experiences. To consider that possibility, however, is to entertain a version of the hypothesis of collective hypnosis. But presumably the medium *is* connected causally to the experiences of the sitters. Why else would the sitters' concordant experiences concern things allegedly done by the medium, and why would the experiences occur only in the medium's presence? The hypothesis of collective hallucination thus seems to ignore completely the crucial role played by the medium, whatever precisely that role is.

The hypothesis of collective hypnosis, on the other hand, is difficult to apply to some poltergeist cases, especially those in which the phenomena are observed in the absence of the presumed poltergeist agent. Of course, once we allow for PK, we can argue that the agent produced the poltergeist phenomena remotely. But it is not open to the skeptic to claim that the agent practiced *suggestion* at a distance – when, that is, we take the suggestion to be of a non-paranormal sort. The history of hypnosis contains many reports of remote suggestion (see Dingwall, 1967). But these cases are typically (and plausibly) regarded as evidence for telepathic influence, and for enhanced telepathic sensitivity under hypnosis. Apparently, then, the appeal to suggestion-at-a-distance would succeed merely in replacing one paranormal phenomenon with another.

But even if we heed these limitations on the hypotheses of collective hallucination and hypnosis, it is still doubtful that they can be made plausible. Those favoring collective hallucination would have to explain (a) why people, at different times and places (often centuries and oceans apart), independently of one another, and with different biases and predispositions relative to the alleged phenomena, should have, spontaneously, the same sorts of detailed and peculiar non-veridical experience; (b) why people, with apparently no previous history of visions or hallucinations, should suddenly undergo a series of such experiences, at the same time as this occurs to others who likewise have demonstrated no such tendency in the past; and (c) why these hallucinations should occur in situations of a sort ordinarily considered unfavorable to hallucination – e.g., waking, alert states, as opposed to hypnagogic states which *are* conducive to hallucinations.

But the hypothesis of collective hypnosis is also not especially promising. Its proponents would have to explain (a) the sheer multiplicity of apparently untrained but prodigiously gifted mesmerists; (b) how subjects could be induced to report concordant visual, auditory, and tactile impressions in the absence of standard or obvious preliminaries to suggestion; (c) how this might be accomplished in an environment ordinarily considered unfavorable to hypnosis – e.g., where sitters at a séance (some of whom had already been found insusceptible to the suggestions of trained hypnotists) were wary, skeptical, sometimes familiar with hypnotic techniques, and (perhaps most importantly) biased against the phenomena they claimed to observe, or where they took specific precautions against suggestion (e.g., by purposely engaging in loud and jocular conversation or other activities considered unfavorable to hypnosis – see, e.g., Zorab, 1970); (d) how, in such an environment, several (and often substantial numbers of) people could – often without exception – be induced to report the *same* experience; and (e) why the alleged hypnotists, independently of one another, should induce their subjects to report the same peculiar non-veridical experiences. Granted, around the turn of the century, mediums were often familiar with one another's work; and for these cases the last problem does not arise. But it remains an intractable puzzle when we turn to poltergeist disturbances, where often the relevant persons were completely ignorant of the details of other such cases.

And this is not all. As Beloff observed in connection with the phenomena of D. D. Home, even if we suppose that Home was a super-mesmerist, we would have to suppose that he could use his power

> with 100 per cent efficacy. If even one witness for even part of the time failed to succumb to it, the game would have been up. Yet there is no record of even one such witness failing to see, say, a table-levitation, which every one else present claimed to observe, and this is the more telling inasmuch as investigators were well aware of the danger of falling victim to Home's charisma and took strenuous precautions against it. (Beloff, 1977b, p. 10)

In fact, the supposition that Home could successfully and continually mesmerize *all* his sitters (sometimes groups of more than a dozen) so that they all report the same phenomenon, seems difficult to square with the well-founded observation that people differ in their degrees of suggestibility. Not only would Home have had to mesmerize all the sitters, and do it in a manner escaping detection by people specifically on the lookout for it and familiar with hypnotic techniques, but he would also have had to do this in a way bypassing the different sorts of preliminaries ordinarily required to hypnotize people of different levels of suggestibility (some of whom, remember, were taking specific precautions against being hypnotized). And then he *still* would have to get them to agree on what they observed.

Barrett and Myers (1889) noted, in addition, that Home's sitters frequently observed phenomena despite the fact that Home never spoke to them and (in some cases) never even moved. This makes it all the more difficult to defend the hypothesis that Home resorted to some process of suggestion. It is true that he sometimes directed the proceedings at séances and announced what phenomena would occur. But this seems to have been the case primarily during informal sittings for laypersons and convinced spiritualists (see Dunraven, 1925), not at sittings with inquisitive and skeptical scientists. In the latter cases, phenomena tended to occur unannounced and unexpected (see Medhurst, *et al.*, 1972).

Now if Home *had*, by some process of suggestion, been able to induce so many people to report concordant experiences under these various circumstances, that ability would arguably be as paranormal as the one the appeal to suggestion was intended to explain away. In fact, if suggestion was the key to Home's success, it would seem to be *telepathic* suggestion or influence, not ordinary (or virtuosic) hypnosis. But even the counter-hypothesis of tele-pathic influence seems less plausible than the hypothesis that Home directly altered the physical environment around the sitters. The most direct explanation of the agreement between the sitters' experiences still seems to be that Home psychokinetically provided them with the same extra-subjective phenomena to observe. This is not to deny the possibility of extensive telepathic influence. One would think, though, that telepathic suggestibility, like hypnotic suggestibility – or for that matter, the normal ability to influence a person's thoughts – would vary from one person to another, and from one situation to another. Telepathic influence, then, seems to be a less parsimonious paranormal hypothesis than the appeal to straightforward, but large-scale, PK.

Granted, some of Home's phenomena (e.g., materialized hands) were not visible to all sitters (see Medhurst , *et al.*, 1972). But many were, and since those cases are clearly the most trouble-some, I submit that the hypothesis of collective hypnosis should be tested against them first. Besides, as Perovsky-Petrovo Solovovo (1909a) noted in his review of the hallucination and hypnosis hypotheses, even when only some sitters reported seeing material-ized hands or spirit forms, they usually *all* agreed on the nature of the object movements apparently produced by the forms, and the object movements seem undoubtedly to have been genuine. Thus, even if the experience of materialized forms resulted from suggestion, the reports of objects movements are still difficult to account for in this way. And the implausibility of applying the hypothesis of collective hypnosis to these latter phenomena makes it less plausible or less urgent to apply it to the former.

Still another relevant fact about physical mediumship is that the reported phenomena often seem to leave lingering physical effects. In some cases, for example, the perceived displacement of objects was measured or found to be correlated with other physical phenomena measured mechanically. For example, during some table levitations by Eusapia Palladino and Kathleen Goligher, under conditions when any physical contact between the medium and the table would have been detected, it was found that the medium's weight increased as if she were lifting the table herself (see Courtier, 1908, p. 441; Crawford, 1918, 1919; Inglis,

1977, p. 424, and Perovsky-Petrovo Solovovo, 1909c, p. 572; see also Chapter 2.4). And in both mediumistic and poltergeist cases, tables and other levitated objects have been broken by what was apparently a rapid descent. These various findings only increase the implausibility of the view that observers were merely having non-veridical experiences.

They do not, however, conclusively rule it out, provided we suppose (rather implausibly, in my opinion) that the presumed hypnotist kept the sitters mesmerized long enough to (a) tamper with the measuring devices and (b) break the objects (including massive pieces of furniture) manually. But regarding the former, experimenters discovered no foul play with their instruments. And regarding the latter, the objects in question were often large dining room tables, which ordinarily required the effort of several people to raise them. The skeptic would therefore have to suppose that a woman or a frail consumptive like Home would single-handedly have been able to raise and drop (from a height sufficient to break the table) an object too large, substantial, and unwieldy for even a normally strong person to handle in that manner.

Finally, just as we observed earlier that the Argument from Human Bias applies not only to reports of the sympathetic or credulous, the appeal to collective hallucination likewise cuts two ways, against those who apparently observe that phenomenon *P* occurs, and against those who apparently observe that *P* does not occur (Eisenbud also makes this point; see 1967, pp. 149ff.). In fact, if the non-veridical experience is attributed to motivated auto-suggestion, the appeal is simply a special case of the Argument from Human Bias. And considering just the possibility of hallucination for the moment, it is hard to see what other reason could be advanced for having the hallucination in the first place. It is not as though sitters at séances or poltergeist witnesses had been ingesting hallucinogens, and were thus *bound* to have some kind of hallucinatory experience, no matter what their motivation or bias. Granted, if we instead consider the possibility of hypnosis, it is considerably more difficult to explain why witnesses should be hypnotized (say, by a medium) *not* to see something paranormal. But the appeal to collective hypnosis is implausible anyway, for reasons already mentioned, and would apply at best only to some of the spontaneous cases.

The hypotheses of collective hallucination and hypnosis seem, therefore, to be plagued by an overwhelming number of difficulties. Even if one or two could be dealt with plausibly, an imposing array of obstacles would remain. To use a familiar philosophical image, the considerations weighing *against* the hypotheses do not form a chain, which would only be as strong as its weakest link. Rather, they resemble the structure of a cable, made strong by its numerous overlapping fibers, however slender some may be individually. The same point, in fact, applies to most of the anti-skeptical arguments considered in this chapter. Even if no one of them is independently conclusive, they tend to reinforce one another impressively.

(6) What arguments remain, then, for those opposed to treating the non-experimental case material as serious evidence for paranormal occurrences? For those still intent on challenging the authenticity of the case reports and eyewitness accounts, the only remaining option, as far as I can see, would be to maintain that the testimony results from some *combination* of those factors already discussed: motivated perception, self-deception, exaggeration, naiveté, outright misperception or dishonesty, and perhaps even fraud and conspiracy among witnesses or investigators eager for publicity or notoriety. This would clearly be a last-ditch attempt to discredit the non-experimental evidence, and I propose that we call it, somewhat disdainfully, *hodge-podge skepticism*.

The most moderate form of this position is that, given a choice between treating the evidence as authentic or as the result of some combination of the aforementioned factors, the latter course is always more reasonable. But as Broad (1962a) observed, this position is plausible, at best, only when we consider the cases *one at a time*. Even when a skeptical hypothesis works on a case-by-case basis, this does not thereby support a *general skepticism* with regard to the total corpus of cases. Broad writes,

Provided that one is prepared to stretch the arm of coincidence far enough, to postulate sufficient imbecility and dishonesty on the parts of investigators who are known to be in other respects intelligent and truthful, and to suppose that the narrators have gone to considerable trouble in falsifying diaries and forging letters with no obvious motive, it is always possible to suggest a normal, or at worst an abnormal, explanation for any story of an ostensibly paranormal sporadic event. This procedure, which has a certain amount of plausibility when applied to each of the best-attested cases taken severally, becomes much less convincing when applied to the sum total of them taken collectively. For it then has to postulate imbecility and dishonesty on a very large scale in a large number of mutually independent reporters and investigators. (Broad, 1962a, p. 15)

Broad's argument concerns the weaknesses of hodge-podge skepticism when applied to the anecdotal evidence in parapsychology. But that body of evidence is generally more vulnerable to skeptical objections than the semi-experimental material. When dealing with recurrent rather than sporadic psi phenomena – especially in the strongest cases – it would be outrageous to make the sorts of assumptions about imbecility and dishonesty mentioned in the passage just quoted. In the next chapter we will examine the phenomena of Home and Palladino in detail; and there we will see how hodge-podge skepticism may have no force even on a case-by-case basis.

At any rate, despite the soundness of Broad's observation, some might still protest (in the spirit of Hume's *Essay on Miracles*) that we must weigh the reasonableness of positing misperception, dishonesty, etc., against the reasonableness of accepting the authenticity of reports of ostensibly paranormal events, events that apparently do not fit comfortably (if at all) into the received scientific framework. Since it is highly improbable (they would argue) for events to occur that so strongly appear to violate well-confirmed scientific principles, it is therefore always more reasonable to suppose that some combination of the above sorts of non-paranormal events occurred instead (even if, as Broad notes, we must posit dishonesty, etc., on an enormous scale).

To this, it should suffice to repeat certain points made in section 1.3. First, it is moot whether psi phenomena violate any important scientific theory. Only from an already suspect reductionistic perspective would they seem to pose a threat to received science. It seems more plausible to me that psi phenomena, like organic phenomena generally, simply fall outside the domain of physics. Second, even if psi phenomena *did* violate some major scientific law(s), there is nothing sacred about received science. Like the received science of days past, much of it may require modification or rejection, even just to countenance ordinary phenomena (such as volition and memory). Third, intuitions about which scientifically anomalous phenomena are or are not probable or possible carry little weight, as the history of science amply demonstrates.

Moreover, I would add that since we know very little about ostensibly paranormal phenomena (especially, I suppose, if they are genuinely paranormal),[11] but a great deal about misperception, naiveté, fraud, etc., our assessments of the probability of the latter should be given greater weight than our assessments of the probability of the former. We often have a solid basis for judging the likelihood of misperception, etc., occurring in spontaneous cases. But we have virtually no basis for deciding the likelihood of an event occurring – in the absence of fraud, misperception, etc. – that at least appears to violate some fundamental scientific law or metaphysical assumption. We do know, of course, that phenomena have been discovered in the past that have deeply changed the course of science, and we know that phenomena which have been thought impossible or highly improbable on received scientific principles were found to be possible or not so improbable after all. We know, in other words, that genuine scientifically anomalous phenomena may occur. But precisely because the phenomena are not ordinary, and so long as they remain not well understood, we lack the kind of information customarily needed to assess the probability of such events having occurred. To judge whether a given event is likely in a particular circumstance, we must first know something of the event's nature and limits. After all, this is how we determine the likelihood of misperception, fraud, etc. We know why and under which conditions they tend to occur, and we have some idea about their possible extent or limits in given circumstances. For example, we know what sorts of situations might motivate fraud or encourage misperception, and we can make quite reasonable judgments about how much of either would have been possible or likely in the circumstances in question. But it is just this sort of information that we lack in the case of ostensibly paranormal events. With these considerations in mind, then, it seems to me to be quite a good procedure to decide the likelihood of an ostensibly paranormal event having occurred on the basis of the evidence *against* the occurrence of misperception, fraud, etc.

To this we could add Ducasse's observation that

assertions of antecedent improbability always rest on the tacit but often in fact false assumption that the operative factors are the same in a presented case as they were in superficially similar past cases. For example, the antecedent improbability of the things an expert conjurer does on stage is extremely high if one takes as antecedent evidence what merely an ordinary person, under ordinary instead of staged conditions can do. The same is true of what geniuses, or so-called arithmetical prodigies, can do as compared with what ordinary men can do. And that a man *is* a genius or a calculating prodigy is shown by what he *does do*, *not* the reality of what he does by his being a genius or prodigy. This holds equally as regards a medium and his levitations or other paranormal phenomena. (Ducasse, 1954b, p. 823)

It would be almost transcendentally foolish to maintain that the unprecedented mnemonic abilities reported by Luria (1975) are unlikely to be genuine, due to their antecedent improbability (based on the population of normal human beings). With reasoning such as this, we could forever avoid countenancing exceptional human abilities. But then it is presumably equally indefensible to distrust nearly a quarter-century's worth of reports of decently-illuminated table levitations by D. D. Home, on the grounds that the antecedent improbability of that ability is over-whelmingly high.

At this point, the skeptical diehard appears to have only one move left. He might point out that it is nevertheless (empirically) *possible* (though perhaps not probable) that some combination of the aforementioned non-paranormal factors does indeed explain away the total body of non-experimental evidence. And this may well be true. But for those who take comfort in this observation, and find in it a basis for resisting the conclusion that there is serious evidence from spontaneous cases for paranormal events, I can do no better than to quote from Gauld and Cornell's incisive comment with regard to the evidence for poltergeists.

Such a position is, in a sense, quite impregnable. But, paradoxically, it is its very impregnability which undermines it. One cannot deny that . . . undetected trickery, undetected natural causes, undetected malobservation and undetected lying *may* lie behind all reports of poltergeist phenomena. But

54

to assume without supporting evidence, and despite numerous considerations . . . to the contrary, that they *do* lie behind them, is to insulate one's beliefs in this sphere from all possibility of modification from the cold contact of chastening facts. It is to adopt the paranoid stance of the flat-earther or the religious fanatic, who can "explain away" all the awkward facts which threaten his system of delusions. At its worst, such a stance borders on insanity; at best it constitutes an unhealthy and unprofitable turning away from the realities of the world. (Gauld and Cornell, 1979, p. 262)

1.5 ON MAINTAINING PERSPECTIVE

Even if it is true, as I have been urging in the previous pages, that the non-experimental evidence of parapsychology is a serious and substantial body of data, I do not want to be misunderstood as claiming that the various cases are equally valuable as evidence. Naturally, some are better documented and more scrupulously reported (i.e., more compellingly authentic) than others, and sometimes cases are found to be fraudulent well after the events have been reported favorably. But the best cases are so good, in my opinion, that we are justified in adopting a somewhat more charitable or sympathetic attitude toward the rest of the material than would otherwise be defensible. For example, were there not such convincing evidence for the physical phenomena of Home and Palladino, we would find it easier, perhaps (though not necessarily justifiable), to disregard the less well-documented studies of mediums and poltergeists. Similarly, the reports of Joseph of Copertino's levitations gain credibility when viewed in the light of more recent evidence of object levitations. (But even on its own, the evidence for Joseph's levitations can't be dismissed as the mere ravings of religious zealots; see Chapter 2.5).

On the whole, in fact, the best semi-experimental work lends credibility to the rest of the non-experimental evidence. Even the best anecdotal cases (e.g., some poltergeist reports, and accounts of collective apparitions) likewise not only stand rather well on their own, but reinforce the less thoroughly documented cases. For that matter, the best non-experimental evidence should also lend some credibility to the results of laboratory experiments.

Had these experiments been more consistently and dramatically successful, such assistance might have been superfluous. As it is, however, good semi-experimental or anecdotal evidence of large-scale PK, and well-documented cases of spontaneous ESP, can only lend support to a charitable interpretation of the positive results of laboratory experiments. Of course, good non-experimental evidence might also be marshalled in support of the claim that most laboratory tests for psi are profoundly misguided, as their often underwhelming results tend to suggest.

This last point brings me to perhaps the most important reason for paying careful attention to non-experimental evidence. I must begin by making – in a somewhat different way – an observation made earlier about the current state of parapsychological research. Many (though certainly not all) parapsychologists assume that if psi functioning is genuine, it will yield its secrets to the quantitative experimental techniques of the physical and biological sciences. They assume, in other words, that major insights into the nature of psi will most likely be obtained by studying psi functioning the way we study measurable forces or purely physiological processes (e.g., cortical arousal or wave propagation). Parapsychologists often assume, therefore, that the ability to manifest psi is more like the ability to digest food or the ability to produce vocal sounds than, say, the ability to make clever retorts or the ability to empathize, which resist quantitative analysis. Psi, then, is often assumed to be a *process*, first of all, and a particular kind of process at that – namely, one whose salient features are quantitatively describable.

But perhaps psi is not like this. Perhaps psi can be described, in part at least, in quantitative terms. But perhaps the quantitative aspects of psi tell us as little about psi as a knowledge of the physiology of the larynx or the physics of sound propagation contributes to our understanding of communication (see the discussion of the energy-transfer theory of telepathy in Braude, 1979). And perhaps the failure of decades of laboratory research to yield little more than moderately reliable (but not especially informative) evidence for the mere existence of psi is a symptom of the fact that we have been studying and conceptualizing psi in the wrong way.

Now how can we decide whether modern experimental psi research is generally misguided, or at least severely limited in its utility? One very promising source of help, I suggest, is the semi-experimental and anecdotal evidence of parapsychology. By placing the laboratory phenomena in the wider context of all the phenomena of parapsychology for which there exists good or suggestive evidence, we are bound to get a more well-rounded picture of what sort of thing psi really is. We might then be in a position to determine if the major features of psi, like those of artistic abilities, or the ability to be resourceful, mediate disputes, or tell interesting stories, can only be described qualitatively. In fact, to take matters even further, a careful study of the evidence for materializations and apports may suggest that psi is not a familiar kind of *process* at all, and that it is more akin to bringing things about instantaneously by waving a magic wand (see Chapter 4).

I don't mean to endorse this last suggestion. Nor am I ready to dismiss it. But it is difficult to see how we can reach a responsible decision one way or the other without placing laboratory evidence in the larger context of the entire body of evidence for psi. After all, the value or utility of laboratory studies of the function of our internal bodily organs is bound up in a critical way with our knowledge of how those organs function systemically, and how the behavior of the whole organism is connected with systemic changes. That is why it would be ridiculous to think we could understand the operation and importance of, say, the stomach, by examining nothing more than processes internal to the stomach, or even just internal to the human body. But perhaps the relationship of psi-in-the-lab to psi-in-life is equally intimate. If so, it would be foolhardy and indefensibly myopic to develop theories of psi based solely on the evidence from one small corner of the psi domain (that of the lab). That would seem to be analogous to developing a theory of humor based entirely on a study of slap-stick. Or (perhaps more relevantly) it might be analogous to developing a theory of nutrition based exclusively on data pertaining to physiological processes, while ignoring the effects of diet on behavior (both individual and social) and the effects of behavior on diet.

The pioneers of psychical research had a great deal of semi-experimental and anecdotal evidence to theorize about, but little or nothing in the way of laboratory evidence. Today we have an abundance of laboratory evidence, and are ignoring centuries –

not just decades – of non-experimental evidence (including present-day cases). The former situation was unavoidable; the latter is not. Parapsychological research may proceed simultaneously along two broad areas of inquiry: experimental on one hand, and non-experimental on the other. It would not be surprising, to say the least, if the results in one area did not bear critically on those of the other.

2

PHYSICAL MEDIUMSHIP

2.1 INTRODUCTION

The evidence for physical mediumship differs in some interesting ways from the evidence for poltergeists and apparitions. Although the best evidence for all three tends to fall within the late nineteenth century to the present, the evidence for physical mediumship is largely confined to a period of about 80 years, from the 1850s to around 1930. To be sure, the quantity and quality of evidence for all sorts of paranormal phenomena improved in the latter part of the nineteenth century, as scientists became more actively involved in the study of the paranormal. That increased activity resulted, finally, in the establishment of the British, and then the American, societies for psychical research. But whereas poltergeist and apparitional phenomena continued to occur rather steadily from this period to the present, physical mediumship seems for the most part to have flourished as a kind of fad, accompanying the enormously popular spiritualist movement beginning around the middle of the nineteenth century. During this period, séances in the home became as widespread a form of entertainment as bridge or poker games today. The serious side to the phenomena, of course, concerned their apparent connection to the survival of human consciousness after bodily death, and the associated phenomena of mental mediumship. The topic of survival, however, must be reserved for a subsequent volume. In any case, many devotees of séances, and many physical mediums, proclaimed the physical phenomena as yet another kind of evidence for survival, rather than a manifestation of large-scale PK on the part of the medium. Others, however, could not accept this construal of such phenomena as table rappings and object levitations. In their eyes, the phenomena were simply beneath the dignity of surviving spirits, and certainly incompatible with the morally and religiously elevated nature of (at least some) ostensible communications from departed spirits.

The popularization – indeed, the commercialization – of spiritualism accounted both for the rise and fall of physical mediumship. The speed with which spiritualistic séances seized the public attention was nothing short of astounding. Almost overnight it seemed as if the world abounded in mediums. Suddenly they emerged from every corner of society, many aspiring toward, and some achieving, genuine celebrity. Not surprisingly, the spiritualist movement was also a boon to opportunists. The lure of fame and fortune seduced many blessed with little more than a dynamic personality and a modest ability to practice sleight-of-hand or other forms of deception. And before long, with the inevitability of economic law, others began to cultivate reputations as debunkers of mediums and defenders of metaphysical sobriety. As it turned out, their successes were so legion and well-promoted that the very business of mediumship became critically tainted. Finally, public interest and trust in mediums eroded, and the spiritualist movement, like fads of all kinds, suffered an inexorable decline. Parapsychologists, too, had been disappointed (and sometimes embarrassed) by their investigations of mediums, and eventually turned elsewhere for clear evidence, many going so far as to eschew the study of any form of physical phenomena.

I regard this state of affairs as unfortunate, since a great deal of outstanding evidence seems to have been lost in the shuffle, or erroneously catalogued with the considerable evidence for fraudulent mediumship. Although I argued in the last chapter that a substantial body of evidence remains that is extremely difficult to account for in terms of familiar processes, I did not address in detail the topic of possible fraud. The discussion in Chapter 1.4 was devoted to the alleged defects of human testimony and observation. In order to deal satisfactorily with the issue of fraud, we must examine the evidence in detail. I want to argue that – at least for the best cases – the skeptic's charge of fraud is forceful only so long as one remains ignorant of the facts.

But before embarking on our survey of the cases, we must consider two sweeping skeptical objections concerning the possibility of fraud in physical mediumship. These raise the spectre of fraud, not in connection with particular phenomena, kinds of phenomena, or particular mediums, but rather in connection with certain general features of physical mediumship and the spiritualist movement.

To begin with, skeptics sometimes note that physical mediums have virtually disappeared from the parapsychological scene. The current paucity of mediums, they argue, suggests strongly that their earlier abundance was due mainly to (a) the lack of adequate scientific techniques for exposing fraud, and (b) the innocence and gullibility of past generations. In other words, they maintain that physical mediumship declined (a) because modern technology and experimental techniques rendered the detection of fraud highly likely, and (b) because the public simply got wise to the mediumistic racket, once the exposure of frauds began in earnest.

This point of view, however – like many of the skeptical positions considered in the previous chapter – enjoys only a surface plausibility. Several key observations count against it.

(1) Fraudulent mediums *were* exposed during the late nineteenth and early twentieth century. In fact, they were exposed by the hundreds. Obviously, then, the detection of mediumistic chicanery did not have to await the advent of modern technology. Nineteenth-century knowledge of conjuring techniques seems to have been sufficient to expose the bag of tricks possible during that era.

Moreover – and more important – the technological primitiveness of nineteenth-century methods for exposing fraud had to be part of an *overall* technological primitiveness of the period. But then the skeptical appeal to the state of scientific technology is a double-edged sword. The lack of technological sophistication limited not only the means for debunking mediums, but also the means for perpetrating fraud. This is particularly important in cases of (a) phenomena produced in locations never before visited by the medium, or in other settings where no opportunity existed for preparing a trick, planting an apparatus, or concealing a confederate, and (b) phenomena that seem simply to be beyond *any* technology of the period – e.g., dissolving or melting materialized hands, and massive objects levitated in good light and with ample opportunity to inspect them before, during, and after the levitation.

61

Of course, decent conjuring needn't rely on technological razzle dazzle. Often it requires nothing more than a competent magician's ability to divert attention and practice sleight-of-hand. And no doubt we are better able today (e.g., with movie and video cameras) to reveal tricks of this sort than we were in days past. But these considerations, however apt, still fail to cast suspicion on the best mediumistic phenomena. For one thing, it takes more than diversion techniques and fast hands to produce the more dramatic phenomena for which there exists good evidence.[1] And for another, the lack of modern technological safeguards can be largely offset by means of admittedly cumbersome controls (such as those enforced in the 1908 Naples sittings with Palladino – see section 3).

(2) There is simply no justification for claiming that people were more gullible around the turn of the century than they are now. Granted, spiritualism is no longer a major social force. But widespread 'occultist' fads and movements continue to flourish, and all along skeptics and believers existed side by side. Moreover, it may well be that the scientific community is *more* sympathetic to parapsychology than ever before. Serious parapsychological research is being conducted at major universities and independent research centers all over the world, and the ranks of the Parapsychological Association (an affiliate organization of the A.A.A.S.) currently number about 300. Furthermore, a recent survey has shown that the academic community, on the whole, is rather sympathetic or open-minded with regard to parapsychological research, and that the percentage of sympathizers seems to be on the rise (see Wagner and Monnet, 1979). It appears, then, that skepticism may have been weakening in the very community where one would have expected it to thrive.

(3) It is far from clear that there *are* fewer physical mediums today. Certainly they are not so visible. The alleged datum about the current paucity of mediums must be stated with some care. We know that there are now fewer practising *professional* mediums in Western industrial society. And we know that mediumship flourishes in less industrialized cultures – that is, in social environments where physical mediumship is not automatically suspect or at odds with the prevailing or official world view.

Skeptics might reply that mediumship survives *only* in primitive or scientifically unsophisticated cultures or subcultures – environments, in other words, in which mediumistic duplicity is most easily practiced. But this would be a shallow response. A better explanation of the current dearth of physical mediums in technologically advanced settings rests on the following points.

(i) The exposure of fraudulent mediums in the late nineteenth and early twentieth century has undoubtedly given physical mediumship bad press. Although emerging from the mediumistic closet is not quite on a par with admitting that one is a child molester, many would nevertheless view it as an admission of moral bankruptcy, and it certainly is a way of asking for trouble. Few today would care to risk the almost certain scorn, derision, or imputations of dishonesty they would encounter in going public. But herein lies a clue to the former abundance of physical mediums.

(ii) In the past it *was* easier to be a public medium, but not simply (if at all) because people were more gullible. We must go deeper. The spectacular rise in physical mediumship which began in the mid-nineteenth century was not due to a sudden corresponding increase in scientific naiveté. There simply was no such increase, and so the degree of credulity regarding mediumistic phenomena is not merely a function of the degree of scientific sophistication. Rather, it had to do with the social and psychological conditions that permitted the spiritualist movement to gain momentum in the first place. During that period, psychological conditions in the West *were* similar, in crucial respects, to those of more 'primitive' cultures where mediumship flourishes today. For one thing, in the mid 1800s there was not yet a history of exposing fraudulent mediums. The very business of mediumship, in other words, was not yet automatically suspect. Conditions were ripe, then, for mediums – dishonest *and* honest – to go public, and for spiritualism to gain a foothold.

Even more important, the spiritualist movement nourished and was nourished by attitudes or belief systems that were clearly favorable to the production of dramatic phenomena. To begin with, all the great nineteenth- and early twentieth-century mediums had complete faith (whether naive or sophisticated) in the reality of survival. But of course a genuine and deep belief in the possibility of mediumship may well be essential – or at least unusually favorable – for the production of the phenomena. At very least one would expect it to be conducive to their occurrence.

Furthermore, once people *truly* believed they were mediums, psychologically they were absolved of any responsibility for what happened during séances. When no phenomena occurred, people did not automatically attribute the failure to the medium. Nor did they assume it was a sign of probable fraud. The absence of phenomena could instead, and quite naturally, be accounted for in terms of an inept communicator, or perhaps a 'weak connection' between the medium and the other side. Equally important, when phenomena *did* occur, the medium had no need to fear the extent of her powers. Only a small minority of people considered physical phenomena to be examples of paranormal ante-mortem agency. Spiritualists and non-spiritualists alike viewed the phenomena as effects of post-mortem agency, of a power not available to flesh-and-blood creatures. Dramatic physical phenomena, then, did not inspire the fear of what Freud called the 'omnipotence of thought'. Mediums had no need to worry about the possibility of exerting dramatic or extensive paranormal influence over day-to-day events – especially effects inspired by their hostilities or other negative (and presumably unconscious) feelings and drives. This last point, I feel, should not be underestimated. The possibility of PK, and the corresponding role of ante-mortem paranormal agency in the production of physical phenomena, was not the live option during the heyday of spirtualism that it is now. Even parapsychologists of the period gave little credence to the idea. But as the scientific and especially the popular conceptions of paranormal physical phenomena shifted their locus from spirits to humans, the psycho-dynamics of physical mediumship changed considerably, and in ways that were probably unfavourable to the production of the phenomena.

(iii) The trend in parapsychological research became more conventionally experimental, partly in order to emulate recent trends (however ill-conceived) in orthodox psychology, and partly to avoid the apparent looseness of experimental conditions in the séance room (see Mauskopf and McVaugh, 1980).[2] Also, due in part to the proliferation of fraudulent mediums, and in part to a growing belief in the reality of telepathy (and a corresponding belief in the immaterial nature of the spirit), physical phenomena seemed to many to be intrinsically implausible. And some regarded the study (and production) of physical phenomena as a frivolous diversion from the loftier investigation of the possibility of survival.

So, even in parapsychology there was a growing prejudice against the study of physical phenomena, either because of the apparent difficulty of conducting it experimentally (Rhine's dice tests were not published until the 1940s), or because of its alleged impossibility or irrelevance. The attention of the parapsychological community was accordingly shifted from the séance room to the lab. Parapsychologists, for the most part, and for a variety of reasons (whether justifiable or not), simply stopped looking for mediums to investigate. Parapsychological fashion had changed.

Skeptics must be wary, then, of arguing from the present paucity of physical mediums. Not only may the dearth of mediums be only apparent, but the overall psychological climate has changed so profoundly since the turn of the century that few today even try to discover whether they have mediumistic abilities. Certainly, the current social atmosphere is not one in which such attempts would be encouraged. And (a few exceptions notwithstanding) parapsychologists stopped looking seriously for mediums decades ago. In my view, it behoves parapsychologists to begin the search anew. No amount of fiddling with random event generators promises the insights that could be gleaned from a medium the calibre of Home or Palladino.

The second general skeptical objection concerns the theatrical and apparently trivial nature of the phenomena. Why, one might wonder, would mediums do such things as levitate tables and make hands appear? Not only do the phenomena seem on the surface like stage tricks, but they seem to be useless. If mediums had such great paranormal abilities, why didn't they cure disease, obtain military secrets, control roulette wheels, and get rich?

The answer to this objection, like the last, has several parts.

(1) Not all the phenomena were trivial or stagey. Home, for example, produced an array of phenomena, including healings, messages from spirits, and trance impersonations. And on some occasions, his materialized hands reportedly resembled those of dead persons known only to the sitters, and were allegedly identified by their characteristic deformations.

(2) It is not clear how justified the charge of staginess is, even in the case of raps and object levitations. We must remember that the physical phenomena of spiritualism were viewed by most

people as attempts – by spirits – to make their survival or presence known. Raps and object levitations – the original physical phenomena of spiritualism – were not produced, at least initially, either for amusement, profit, or for their scientific interest. Rather, they were handy vehicles for communication with the deceased. But considered as devices for communication or physical evidence of survival, table levitations (say) do not seem particularly stagey. After all, the attempts at communication were typically conducted in homes (not on stage), with groups of hopeful sitters seated around tables, often touching or holding hands. In general, it seems that the primary purpose of object movements was to facilitate communication. Spiritualists viewed raps and object movements as attempts by spirits either to impart a particular message, or to demonstrate that life continues after bodily death, or to display the power of a liberated spirit. And as far as they were concerned, these were plausible forms for the communications to take. Most considered them to be rudimentary – and relatively uncomplicated or easy – attempts to bridge the two worlds, certainly easier than controlling the body of a medium, especially in the fine-grained way necessary for trance imperson-ations. But in the context of a sincere séance, not even trance impersonations or full-form materializations seem particularly theatrical, much less inherently suspicious. Granted, the phenomena are dramatic; but they are appropriate – and not artificial or contrived – forms for attempted communications with the deceased. In the context of an impartial scientific investigation of PK, the phenomena would no doubt seem stagey. But physical phenomena were not initially objects of theoretical interest and study. That development took place only later, when spiritualists and non-spiritualists alike began to wonder about their impli-cations for science and philosophy (independently of their relevance to the issue of survival).

(3) The objection fails to take seriously the psychological atmos-phere prevailing during the spiritualist movement. The great physical mediums were sincere spiritualists. Even if they were not deeply religious as a way of life, they were at least firmly convinced of the non-corporeal origin of the phenomena. Those who were religious would have considered opportunistic uses of the power of the spirit to be morally inconceivable or repugnant. And as for the rest, psychic opportunism would still have been an implausible

use of that power, since at the very least they believed it to be a matter over which they had no control. Mediums (as the term suggests) believed they were merely vehicles through which the production of phenomena might be facilitated. They believed that spirits determined the course of the phenomena for their own purposes, with respect to which material wealth and military superiority presumably had little relevance. The mediums considered it either presumptuous, reprehensible, or at least simply futile to enlist the spirits' help for their own earthly aims, no matter how appealing the prospect might have been.

(4) The topic of psychic opportunism concerns the exercise of ESP as well as PK. Not only do skeptics wonder why mediums fail to use their PK for a variety of obvious practical interests, but they also ask why apparent ESP virtuosi don't paranormally obtain information relevant to a wide range of goals in everyday life. The question is reasonable; and an adequate response proceeds along the following two general lines.

(i) As Eisenbud (1966b) has argued, people regularly fail to utilize even their *ordinary* aptitudes, abilities, and readily available information to secure goals that they consider desirable. With regard to the general goals of wealth and health, for example, people frequently fail to act in their own best interest, even though they have both the ability and available information to do so. And in more pathological cases, people unconsciously use their abilities and information to act *contrary* to their professed interests and goals, all the while insisting that they are victims of external forces. Similarly (as far as we know), not only might psi operate unconsciously, beyond voluntary control, but

> the goals it serves, as is the case also with the rest of the functions in the cognitive spectrum, may be often at variance with those which are consciously espoused and which we all too unthinkingly imagine to be the 'natural' or 'normal' goals of the individual. (Eisenbud, 1966b, p. 649)

Certainly we are in no position to rule out this possibility. We cannot ignore the fact that mediums, like the rest of us, are complex creatures concealing an extensive network of needs, desires, fears, interests, and purposes. And of course, our hidden or unconscious agendas might be quite different from – even incompatible with – those apparent only on the surface. One might argue, then, that mediums – like the rest of us – may simply fail to use their abilities in ways that contribute to their material welfare, or for any goal that is valued relative to superficial concerns. In fact, since there is no reason to think that mediums are less self-destructive than the rest of humanity, a more cynical position might be justified. We might reasonably *expect* mediums to be as unsuccessful as most people at achieving life's more obvious surface goals, and that they might even enlist the service of their psi abilities to help them fail. That would simply be a large-scale real-life analogue of *psi-missing* in the lab (see Braude, 1979, for a discussion of psi-missing).

But whether or not the lack of psychic opportunism among mediums can be traced to deep-seated self-destructiveness or other unconscious drives, Eisenbud is nevertheless directing attention to a fact of life that must be taken seriously in this context. Whatever the reason may be, people often seem unable to use their abilities or special skills to their own best advantage. For example, therapists and counselors frequently make a shambles of their personal lives, even while they sagely guide those of their clients. And similar disparities obtain in the health and legal professions. I see no reason to assume that mediums should be any more likely to use for their everyday interests the paranormal abilities they exercise in other contexts.

(ii) It is not clear what we should *expect* a psychic superstar to be able to do. Quite apart from considerations of our general ineptitude or destructive tendencies, there may simply be practical limits to a superstar's influence over ordinary immediate physical surroundings and ability to obtain relevant information. Skeptics must be careful here. In all honesty, I think we must admit that we have no idea at all how extensive or diverse a medium's powers may be. Perhaps Eisenbud and others are correct in maintaining not only that psi is fundamentally need-determined, but that it is the sort of thing that operates on a grand and refined scale all the time, and usually in ways that do not attract our attention. In fact, if grand psi occurs, it may well be in our interest that its operation be inconspicuous (see Chapter 4.2). In that case, mediums like Home and Palladino would be remarkable for the frequency with which they could function psychically in overt ways – i.e., in ways deeply uncharacteristic of psi functioning. (I suppose Home and Palladino would then be analogous to persons who could do high-level mathematics in situations not usually conducive to such an activity – say, while making love or awaiting execution.)

But even if psi occurred only on a more modest scale than that envisioned by Eisenbud, it might nevertheless still be subject to certain limitations. For example, its range, variety, and reliability might be connected in deep ways to the agent's belief system (e.g., whether the agent feels responsible for or fears the phenomena, how the agent integrates psi into an overall world view). But apart from those possible constraints on psi functioning, psi might simply be the sort of thing that is exceedingly difficult to harness in clearly detectable ways. If the best a PK superstar can do is what D. D. Home or Carlos Mirabelli did, then – for now, at least – that is simply one more datum to be digested.

Furthermore, I don't see any reason for assuming that an accomplished physical medium *must* have certain abilities – trivial or otherwise – just because he has certain others. We hardly know enough about psi, or just PK, to have a competent opinion about what a medium's range or repertoire of phenomena ought to be. For all we know, mediumistic abilities might be limited in any number of ways, especially if psi functioning is basically need-determined. In our present state of ignorance, we are not entitled to assume that a medium who can levitate tables or materialize hands should also be able to heal the sick. One would think, in fact, that (like musical or athletic abilities) mediumistic abilities would vary from person to person, and in characteristic ways. Of course conjuring abilities (one's bag of tricks) will vary from magician to magician. So the different repertoires of different mediums is compatible with the hypothesis that they were merely conjurors. But conjuring abilities are hardly the only ones that vary from person to person and display characteristic limitations. It seems perfectly plausible that mediumistic abilities would have similar features.

Moreover, it seems as if no medium (not even Home) had full control of his powers. (In fact, the spirits allegedly deprived Home of his abilities for an entire year.) From the medium's point of view, phenomena occurred when the spirits made them happen. Alternatively, one could say they occurred when the medium believed the spirits made them happen, or when the medium simply allowed them to happen. But then psychic virtuosi seem not to be like musical or athletic superstars, who can summon their powers with considerable regularity. And I see nothing inherently suspicious in this. It is suspicious only when we assume that psi abilities are easily controllable. But we have absolutely no grounds for making that assumption. For all we know, mediumistic abilities might very well be more situation-sensitive than musical or athletic abilities. They might be as fragile as the ability to be objective, or the ability to be sensual. That might just be the way things are, and another fact we must accept and integrate if we are to understand the place of psi in the scheme of things. An honest and open-minded inquiry into physical mediumship should be alert to the possibility of fraud, malobservation, etc. But there is no reason (at this stage in the game, especially) to assume that the evidence must take one form rather than another.

2.2 DANIEL DUNGLAS HOME (1833–1886)

a. Biographical remarks

Home was born in Edinburgh, in March, 1833. Not long thereafter he was adopted by his maternal aunt, a Mrs Cook. According to Jenkins (1982), the reason was that Home's parents, who had only a very modest income, also had six sons and three daughters. At this point, accounts diverge. According to Zorab (1975), Home's parents emigrated to the United States in 1837, and Daniel remained behind with Mrs Cook. Then in 1842, when Daniel was nine, he and Mrs Cook followed suit, settling near Home's parents in Connecticut. Jenkins, on the other hand, claims that Home's parents moved to New England *after* Daniel and Mrs Cook had emigrated there.

In any case, psychic experiences were not unprecedented in Daniel's family. His mother was frequently subject to clairvoyant (often precognitive) visions, and Daniel himself was apparently somewhat precocious in this respect. He tells us that, according to Mrs Cook, his own visions began occurring at the age of four. But Home's first recollection of any such incident is from his thirteenth year. He and Mrs Cook had moved from Norwich, Conn., to Troy, N.Y., and one night Daniel's close friend Edwin appeared to him as a luminous cloud in his darkened room. Daniel knew then that Edwin had died, and was keeping a solemn promise he had made. Back in Norwich, the boys had spent many hours together reading the Bible, and one day they had made a pact, agreeing that the first to die would appear to the other. Home's next important vision came four years later, this one announcing the death of his mother and the hour at which she died.

Not long after his mother's death, physical phenomena began occurring in Home's presence. One night he heard 'loud blows on the head of [his] bed, as if struck by a hammer' (Home, 1863/ 1972, p. 5), and the next morning at breakfast, to the horror of his aunt, loud raps sounded all over the table. Mrs Cook believed the noises were manifestations of the devil, and promptly sent for two ministers to attempt an exorcism. But the raps continued, and in the days ahead the phenomena escalated. Soon objects were moving about the room, and before long the neighbors got wind of the peculiar goings-on. Eventually, Mrs Cook could no longer tolerate the apparent affront to her religious sensibilities, and she turned Daniel out of the house at the age of eighteen.

Daniel, unlike his aunt, felt that the manifestations were expressions of God's goodness. During the attempted exorcism, it seemed to him as if the raps and object movements displayed God's participation in his prayers. And once, when Mrs Cook tried to subdue a moving table by placing a Bible upon it, 'the table only moved in a more lively manner, as if pleased to bear such a burden' (Home, 1863/1972, p. 7). Apparently, then, the phenomena which so appalled his aunt only reinforced Home's already deep religious convictions.

In any case, Daniel was now on his own. Although he apparently neither asked for nor received direct payment for his activities, from this time until his death he survived on the hospitality and generosity of those attracted to and intrigued by his visions, trances, healings, and assorted other physical phenomena. For several years Home travelled throughout New England, holding séances in the homes of his benefactors, and attracting considerable attention among laypersons as well as academics. Numerous published accounts survive of Home's phenomena during this period, some apparently quite careful and detailed (see Home,

1863/1972; Jenkins, 1982; Zorab, 1975; and Zorab/Inglis, unpublished).

Evidently, Home was not originally interested in making a name for himself as a medium. Rather, he aspired to be a physician. As a matter of fact, one of his benefactors even sent him to medical school, although he undoubtedly would have been equally (if not more) pleased to finance a career for Daniel as a spiritualist missionary. Home's health, however, which had been delicate since childhood, interfered with his studies. His persistant and debilitating cough was diagnosed as consumption, and his physicians recommended (inscrutably) that he move to England. Armed with little more than this questionable medical advice and a few letters of introduction to English spiritualists, Daniel left America in 1855.

The most important phase of Home's career as a medium now began. Before long, his reputation spread throughout Europe, and Home quickly became an international celebrity and friend of both royalty and common folk (albeit mostly upper class). Among his acquaintances and admirers were Napoleon III, the German Emperor, the Queen of Holland, and many members of the Russian royal court.

Home's life is filled with fascinating incidents, some of the more acrimonious of which were sketched briefly in the previous chapter. Rather than dwell on these, I prefer now to consider important details about his phenomena. I should mention, however, that during the entire period of Home's mediumship – a period of almost 25 years – he was never detected in fraud of any kind. Naturally, allegations of fraud were lodged against him from time to time. But most were second or third hand, and none were substantiated. As Eisenbud remarks (1982a, p. 127), the charges seem mostly to have been cries of outrage. Home's keenest and most persistant critic was Podmore (1910/1975, 1902/1963). But Podmore's attempts to explain away Home's most carefully studied manifestations are quite inadequate and transparently contrived (suggesting, for example, that Home might have used thin and nearly invisible horsehair threads for moving massive pieces of furniture from a distance). In fact, as we will soon see, given the technological limitations of the period, it is difficult to imagine what sort of legerdemain Home could possibly have been practicing. Actually, Podmore reluctantly conceded this point. As far as Home's best phenomena are concerned, he had to fall back on the the hypothesis of collective hypnosis, the weaknesses of which have already been surveyed.

b. *Catalogue of phenomena*

It seems that most of Home's extensive palette of phenomena had been revealed before his move to England in 1855. Focusing just on physical phenomena (and excluding numerous apparent healings and trance-impersonations of deceased persons), the list of manifestations is quite mind-boggling. The major items are as follows:

(1) Raps, or knocking sounds, heard not just in the séance table, but in all parts of the room, including the ceiling.

(2) Object levitations and movements, including the movement and complete levitation of tables with several persons on top, and the complete levitation of pianos.

(3) Tables would tilt or move sharply, although objects on the table would remain stationary. Sometimes the objects would alternately move and remain in place in response to sitters' commands.

(4) Alteration in the weight of objects. On command, objects would become heavier or lighter. Before Crookes measured the phenomenon with instruments, its typical manifestation was that a table would become too heavy for one or more persons to tilt or lift, or at least more difficult to move than before.

(5) The appearance of lights or luminous phenomena in various parts of the room.

(6) The appearance of partially or fully materialized forms in various parts of the room.

(7) Touches, pulls, pinches, and other tactile phenomena occurring while the hands of all present were visible above the table.

(8) Auditory phenomena (e.g., voices, sounds), and also music occurring without instruments in various parts of the room.

(9) Odors, produced in the absence of any visible object with which they might be associated.

(10) Earthquake effects, during which the entire room and its contents rocks or trembles.

(11) Hands, supple, solid, mobile and warm, of different sizes,

shapes and colors. Although the hands were animated and solid to the touch, they would often end at or near the wrist and would eventually dissolve or melt. Sometimes the hands were reportedly disfigured exactly as the hands of a deceased ostensible communicator (unknown to Home) had been.

(12) The playing of an accordion, guitar, or other musical instrument, either totally untouched (and sometimes while levitated in good light), or while handled in such a way as to render a musical performance on the instrument impossible.

(13) The handling of hot coals, and the transfer of incombustability to other persons and objects.

(14) Elongations, in which the medium grew from several inches to more than a foot.

(15) Levitation of the medium. This is perhaps the least well-documented of Home's major phenomena, occurring (according to Home himself) only once in daylight (Home, 1863/1972, p. 39).

Clearly, this repertoire of phenomena is impressive, and presents an imposing challenge to the skeptic. While some phenomena may appear to admit of simple normal explanations (e.g., elongations and the production of odors), others seem to allow none. And counter-explanations which have a certain degree of plausibility in some cases fail miserably for others. To explain the entire array as due to conjuring or fraud, we must (as should become clear) endow Home with an implausible degree of conjuring skill, or else with access to technology known to no scientist of his day (or even of today).

Reliable documents concerning Home's phenomena come from many sources, domestic and foreign. The best known – if not always the best documented – are from the investigations of Sir William Crookes, and it is these on which I shall concentrate. But one of the reasons Home's case is so important is that good evidence for his phenomena comes from many different sources during a period of nearly 25 years. In fact, the reader cannot hope to assess the evidential weight of the case without appreciating the full range of conditions under which phenomena apparently occurred, and the sheer length of time during which alleged frauds would have gone undetected, despite careful efforts to expose or prevent them. It would be counter-productive, then, to concentrate only on Crookes's investigations. So let us first consider other important sources of information about Home, and examine some sample eyewitness descriptions.

c. Early documentation

The first decent description of Home's phenomena concerns a séance held early in 1852 in Springfield, Mass. Some distinguished guests arrived at the home of Rufus Elmer, where Home was staying, for the purpose of testing Home's powers. Among them were poet William Cullen Bryant and Prof. David A. Wells of Harvard. After several sittings they published a signed statement (see Home, 1863/1972, pp. 22–23; Mme Home, 1888/1976, pp. 14–15) concerning the results of their investigation.

> The undersigned . . . bear testimony to the occurrence of the following facts, which we severally witnessed at the house of Rufus Elmer, in Springfield . . .
>
> 1. The table was moved in every possible direction, and with great force, when we could not perceive any cause of motion.
>
> 2. It (the table) was forced against each one of us so powerfully as to move us from our positions – together with the chairs we occupied – in all, several feet.
>
> 3. Mr. Wells and Mr. Edwards took hold of the table in such a manner as to exert their strength to the best advantage, but found the invisible power, exercised in an opposite direction, to be quite equal to their utmost efforts.[3]
>
> 4. In two instances, at least, while the hands of all the members of the circle were placed on the top of the table – and while no visible power was employed to raise the table, or otherwise move it from its position – *it was seen to rise clear of the floor, and to float in the atmosphere for several seconds, as if sustained by some denser medium than air*.
>
> 5. Mr. Wells seated himself on the table, which was rocked for some time with great violence, and at length, it poised itself on the two legs, and remained in this positions for some thirty seconds, when no other person was in contact with it.
>
> 6. Three persons, Messrs Wells, Bliss and Edwards assumed positions on the table at the same time, and while thus seated, the table was moved in various directions.

7. Occasionally we were made conscious of the occurrence of a powerful shock, which produced a vibratory motion of the floor of the apartment in which we were seated – it seemed like the motion occasioned by distant thunder or the firing of ordnance far away – causing the table, chairs, and other inanimate objects, and all of us to tremble in such a manner that the effects were both seen and felt.

8. In the whole exhibition, which was far more diversified than the foregoing specification would indicate, we were constrained to admit that there was an almost constant manifestation of some intelligence which seemed, at least, to be independent of the circle.

9. In conclusion, we may observe, that Mr. D. D. Home, frequently urged us to hold his hands and feet. During these occurrences the room was well lighted, the lamp was frequently placed on and under the table, and every possible opportunity was afforded us for the closest inspection, and we admit this one emphatic declaration: *We know that we were not imposed upon nor deceived.*

Wm. Bryant
B. K. Bliss
Wm. Edwards
David A. Wells

Subsequent reports of Home's phenomena, drawn from numerous sources (including reports by skeptics), allow us to construct a profile of a typical Home séance. Sometimes Home was in a trance state, in which he referred to himself as 'Dan' or 'Daniel', and in general talked as if another were speaking through him. But in many instances he remained more or less in a normal waking state, sometimes conversing with sitters about ordinary matters, and other times sitting silent and still. Séances usually began with sitters feeling a cold breeze, and then loud raps would be heard in various locations about the room. Then more spectacular phenomena would occur, sometimes beginning with the earthquake effect.

Before offering sample descriptions, I must remind the reader that the phenomena reported were frequently produced in locations never before visited by Home. Sometimes the séances were arranged on the spur of the moment, so that there can be no question of Home knowing beforehand where he would need to produce phenomena, or of his being able to plant an apparatus or an accomplice in those locations. Moreover, the objects moved during the séances (e.g., large tables, bookcases, and pianos, as well as personal items belonging to the sitters) were certainly not props carried by Home from place to place, nor items he had access to before the séance began.

Consider, now, some sample reports, and keep in mind that this is a very modest selection from hundreds of private and published accounts.

I begin by quoting from a paper by Zorab (1970) on an enquiry made in Amsterdam in 1858. The tests were conducted by members of a somewhat hard-nosed Protestant society, decidedly unsympathetic to spiritualist claims (as well as to claims of Biblical miracles), but with an avowed interest in seeking out the truth. Three sittings were held in Home's hotel room in a period of just over 24 hours. Although the séance room was Home's own, the reader will be hard-pressed to explain what sort of advance preparation could have produced the phenomena that occurred during the séances. The number of investigators ranged from 7 to 10 for the sittings described below (and 5 for the middle sitting, not excerpted). They were held around a massive round mahogany table, 80 cm. (32 ins.) high, resting on a heavy central column, and capable of accomodating 14 people easily. Four bronze candelabra with wax candles were placed on top of the table, and two beneath. The tablecloth was folded up toward the center of the table, leaving a free space of about 18 ins. wide around the table for the sitters' hands, and to allow an unobstructed view under the table.

> Mr Home, who talked very little himself, urged us, in order to remain in a normal state, to go on talking freely among ourselves. This we did, continuing our conversation now in Dutch and then again in French. He also insisted that we should observe him and all his manipulations as closely as possible. . . . (p. 52)
> [In order to frustrate any possible attempt by Home to hypnotize them] everyone present talked freely with his neighbors, making all kinds of comments and, laughing mockingly concerning the matter at hand, gave expression to

his disbelief, especially in reference to the dogmatic [i.e., spiritualistic] beliefs connected with the phenomena. . . . (p. 53)

. . . the table started to make a sliding movement toward the place where Mr Home was sitting. Those sitting at Mr Home's side of the table were requested to try to stop this movement; this, however, they could not do. At the other side of the table (i.e., our side) the same maneuver was attempted, but without any more success. . . . (p. 54)

The table now started to rise up on one side. . . . [T]he rising up . . . took place in spite of the fact that some of us tried very hard to prevent the table from going up and that [one of the sitters] took his hands off it and, with a light in his hand, squatted on his haunches under the table to investigate.

We then ordered the table to become as light as possible so that we should be able to lift it with one finger. And so it came to pass. When the order was reversed (i.e., to increase the table's weight) the table could hardly be lifted at all in spite of our utmost efforts.

[At the final sitting], hardly had we seated ourselves – within ten seconds – than we heard soft rappings that soon changed into loud knocks. These raps were heard to come from all sides of the large room. They were accompanied by a complete rocking movement of the ceiling which became so violent that, together with the chairs on which we were seated, we felt ourselves going up and down as if on a rocking-horse. We experienced the same sensation and movement as when sitting in a carriage on springs while driving along the highroad.

The table behaved more or less in the same manner observed in the former two sittings, i.e., rising high and then descending smoothly to the floor without any abrupt movements. (p. 55)

And now phenomena were produced that would make those who possessed weaker nerves than we had believe that there indeed existed a world of spirits. Here are the facts. One of us suddenly asked his neighbor if *he* had touched him, a question the latter answered in the negative. The gentleman who had been touched declared that he felt something

78

touching his cheek. The unbelievers loudly laughed at him, and all these men wanted also to be touched. Their desire was at once gratified. The one was touched on his arm, another felt something touching his knee, a third one was contacted on his cheek, etc. This went on to such an extent that one only needed to think of a limb or of some other part of one's body to be touched and at the very same moment this wish would be fulfilled. In the case of one of us, this touching and contacting went on continuously during twenty minutes and the touching took place on various parts of his body. Another man was so violently clutched at all of a sudden that he jumped from his chair.

Then one of us took out his handkerchief and threw it onto the floor in front of himself. He then requested that it be put into the hand of the man sitting opposite to him. The gentleman indicated laid his opened hand upon his knee, while the sitter next to him kept his eye constantly upon it. After a few moments the handkerchief flew into the hand on the knee; but as the owner of the hand did not close his fingers quickly enough, it dropped again onto the floor, and in the next instant it returned to the spot from where it had departed, viz., at the feet of the gentleman who had made the request. This gentleman then picked up the handkerchief and wound it around his little finger. Thereupon he placed his hand on the table and asked that the handkerchief be taken away from him. Immediately a force started to tug at the handkerchief, continuing to do so all the time until the handkerchief was slipped off the gentleman's little finger. All of us – some of us looking on above the table while others were watching under the table – saw all this happening. Other persons were keeping a constant eye on Mr Home in order to see if he was exercising some influence on the phenomena.

I myself then pulled out my handkerchief, wound it around the whole of my right hand, and requested that it be taken away from me. Within a few seconds I had the sensation as if an invisible hand was trying to wrench the handkerchief off my hand. But I was holding on so firmly to the handkerchief that, after some repeated unsuccessful attempts lasting several minutes, the force could not succeed in getting the handkerchief off. I then took hold of the handkerchief between my thumb and one of my fingers; and at my request, it was immediately pulled away from my fingers.

. . . nothing could be observed that could give rise to even the slightest suspicion that Mr Home was acting in a fraudulent manner. (pp. 55–57)

In 1889 Barrett and Myers published a review of *D. D. Home, His Life and Mission*, written by Home's second wife (Mme Home, 1888/1976). To their lengthy and generally favorable appraisal of the evidence, they appended a series of additional testimony, solicited on behalf of the S.P.R. For reasons discussed by the authors, the descriptions which follow are decidedly above average as evidence – e.g., because of independent corroborating testimony, or because the accounts were written immediately after the event, or because the phenomena occurred in locations never before visited by Home, and (in every case) because the descriptions are not supplied by Home's wife. But as far as the phenomena reported are concerned, they are remarkably typical of accounts written over the entire extensive period of Home's mediumistic activity.

Home arrived at our house shortly before dinner. After dinner we agreed to sit in the drawing room at a square card table near the fire. . . . In a few minutes, a cold draught of air was felt on our hands and knockings occurred. . . . My gold bracelet was unclasped while my hands were on the table and fell upon the floor . . . I think I asked if the piano could be played; it stood at least 12 ft. or 14 ft. away from us. Almost at once the softest music sounded. I went up to the piano and opened it. I saw the keys depressed, but no one playing. I stood by its side and watched it, hearing the most lovely chords; the keys seemed to be struck by some invisible hands; all this time Home was far distant from the piano. Then a faint sound was heard upon my harp [a few feet from the piano, and across the room from Home], as of the wind blowing over its strings. . . . Later on in the evening, we distinctly heard two voices talking together in the room; the voices appeared to come from opposite corners, from near the ceiling, and apparently proceeded from a man and child, but we could not distinguish the words. They sounded far off. Home was talking the whole time the voices were heard, and

gave as his reason that he might not be accused of
ventriloquism. (Barrett and Myers, 1889, pp. 127–8).

Another witness, a veteran of several Home séances, writes,

The séances begin by sitting round Mr Home's table, which
is rather large, as it holds 10 people sitting round it. We lay
our hands flat on the table before us. After a while there is
usually a trembling of the table and often a strong tremulous
motion of the floor and chairs, and loud raps sound about the
room and under the table. Then the table usually heaves up
with a steady motion, sometimes clear off the floor, sometimes
on one side to an angle of about 45 deg. Mr Home makes a
practice of asking anyone present, usually the last comer, to
sit under the table to be enabled to assure his friends that
no trickery was possible. I have sat so several times and heard
raps about my head, some loud, some soft, and have seen
the table rise from the floor and have passed my hand and
arm clear through between the floor and the pedestal of the
table while it was in the air. It has happened several times
when we have been sitting in this way that some one of the
company has been drawn back in his chair from the table, and
once Mrs Parkes, who was sitting next to me, was drawn at
least a foot back and then sideways about six inches. A bell,
bracelet, or pocket-handkerchief, or anything taken in one
hand and placed under the table is taken by the 'spirit' hands,
which are palpable warm fingers of various sizes and feeling,
but which when attempted to be grasped always seem to
dissolve in a curious manner and leave airy nothing.

Mr Home has an accordion; it is not a mechanical one, for
he left it by accident at Mrs Parkes' house one day, and I
carefully examined it. He takes this in one hand by the side
of it which is furthest from the keys and places it just beneath
the edge of the table. In that position I have watched it
attentively as I stooped with my head and shoulders thrust
under the table, and have seen the bellows begin to rise and
fall, and then faint sounds to issue which, gaining in strength,
at last swell out into the most beautiful spiritual airs of a
strange and fantastic character. On any particular air being
called for it is played, sometimes beautifully, sometimes in a
very fitful uneven manner. . . . I have several times sat next

81

to Mr Home when 'the spirits' are playing the accordion, and
he always holds one hand on the table and supports the
accordion with the other. Sometimes 'the spirits' remove the
instrument from his hand and carry it to some other person,
when the same result is the consequence. . . . All these
phenomena . . . have been done *not in the dark*, which some
people say is necessary in a séance, but in bright light. I should
also say that I have seen them in Mrs Parkes' own house,
where she invited Mr Home one evening and I was present;
it was the first time he had ever put foot in her house, and
the tilting and rapping and music was just the same, and the
table travelled along the floor, turning and pushing chairs
and stools about, right up to one side and along the side of a
sofa. Mr Home also stretched up his hands above his head,
and rose in the air 3 ft. from the floor. Mrs Parkes was sitting
next to him, and she looked at his feet and then he
descended. (pp. 129–30)

Still another witness writes,

The incident . . . took place at the home of Lady Poulett . . .
Mr Home was there. We all saw the supper table, on which
there was a quantity of glass and china full of good things,
rise, I should say, to an angle of 45 deg. without anything
slipping in the least, and then relapse to its normal position.
There was also a so-called centre-table in the room, round
which we were seated – it had nothing upon it – and as we
joined hands it moved and we followed it. There was Baron
Reichenbach, the discoverer of paraffin, present, who laughed
at us, and challenged us to move the table if we would let him
get under it and hold it. He was a rather tall and powerfully-
built man, and he got under the table and clasped it with
both his arms, but it moved as before, dragging him all round
the room. (pp. 133–4)

Next, the following excerpt from a letter written by a sitter to
his wife, concerning a séance held in Edinburgh in 1870. The
letter agrees, in important ways, not only with notes made at the
time by another witness, but with a subsequent account given
verbally to Barrett by the author of the letter. At the time the

verbal account was offered, the author did not know that his earlier letter was still in existence.

> Home . . . held [the accordion] in his right hand by the bottom, i.e., upside down under the table, and it began to play chords. By his desire I looked under the table, and distinctly saw it open and shut as if some one was playing upon it. It first played an air which no one knew, then 'Still so Gently' was asked for and played. Also, 'Home, Sweet Home.' Elizabeth then held the instrument and it played some beautiful chords.
>
> [Home then proposes to see what will happen if the company moves into the library.] The library opened into the landing, where there was a bright gaslight, but the room itself had no light. The door was, however, left wide open; we were round a little table, the rest seated, and I on my knees. In an instant the table began to rock, and a very weird sound was heard in the corner of the room. An immense shifting bookcase, that would require at least four men to move, began slowly to come toward us. (pp. 124–5)

And from testimony given orally to Myers by a sitter at another Home séance,

> I saw Mr Home take this [burning] coal from the fire, moving his hands freely among the coals. It was about the size of a coffee cup, blazing at the top, and red-hot at the bottom. While I held it in my hand the actual flame died down, but it continued to crackle and to be partially red-hot. I felt it like an ordinary stone, neither hot nor cold. Mr Home then pushed it off my hand with one finger on to a double sheet of cartridge paper, which at once set on fire.
>
> I have repeatedly taken Mr Home in my own carriage to the houses of friends of mine who were strangers to him, and have there seen the furniture at once violently moved in rooms which I knew he had never entered till that moment.
>
> I have seen heavy furniture moved. . . . Not horsehairs, but ropes would have been necessary to pull the furniture about as I have seen it pulled. (p. 136)

In connection with Home's apparent ability to handle burning coals and to transfer his incombustibility to others, consider this passage from a letter, dated July 5, 1868, written by a Mrs S. C. Hall to Lord Dunraven.

[Home] went to the fire-place; half knelt on the fender stool; took up the poker and poked the fire, which was like a red-hot furnace, so as to increase the heat; held his hands over the fire for some time, and finally drew out of the fire, with his hand, a huge lump of live burning coal, so large that he held it in *both* hands, as he came from the fire-place in the large room into the small room; where, seated round the table, we were all watching his movements. Mr Hall was seated nearly opposite to where I sat; and I saw Mr Home, after standing for about half a minute at the back of Mr Hall's chair, deliberately place the lump of burning coal on his head! I have often since wondered that I was not frightened; but I was not; I had perfect faith that he would not be injured. Some one said – 'Is it not hot?' Mr Hall answered – 'Warm, but not hot!' Mr Home had moved a little away, but returned, still in a trance; he smiled and seemed quite pleased; and then he proceeded to draw up Mr Hall's white hair over the red coal. The white hair had the appearance of silver threads, over the red coal. Mr Home drew the hair into a sort of pyramid, the coal still red, showing beneath the hair; then, after, I think, four or five minutes, Mr Home pushed the hair back, and, taking the coal off Mr Hall's head, he said (in the peculiar low voice in which, when in a trance, he always speaks), addressing Mrs Y—, 'Will you have it?' She drew back; and I heard him murmur, 'Little faith – little faith.' Two or three attempted to touch it, but it burnt their fingers. I said, 'Daniel, bring it to me; I do not fear to take it.' It was not red all over, as when Mr Home put it on Mr Hall's head, but it was still red in parts. Mr Home came and knelt by my side; I put out my right hand, but he murmured, 'No, not that; the other hand.' He then placed it in my left hand, where it remained more than a minute. I felt it, as my husband had said, 'warm'; yet when I stooped down to examine the coal, my face felt the heat so much that I was obliged to withdraw it. . . . When Mr Hall brushed his hair at night he found a quantity of cinder dust. (Dunraven, 1925, pp. 281–2)

For reasons mentioned earlier, I regard testimony like the above as serious evidence for the reality of physical phenomena. One may not dismiss such accounts on the grounds that human testimony is unreliable, biased, and so forth. Moreover, when the conditions of observation are not conducive to malobservation (especially gross malobservation), and when the phenomena apparently observed are extraordinarily impressive, appeals to faulty perception or memory are also of little utility. Likewise, last-ditch appeals to collective hallucination or hypnosis explain far too little. Finally, considering the nature and magnitude of the phenomena and the conditions under which they were observed – as well as the technological limitations of the period – and, in addition, assuming (plausibly) the accounts to be truthful, conjuring or fraud seems equally out of the question.

Nevertheless, many believe (quite naively) that the testimony of ordinary laypersons or academics in the humanities is inherently less reliable than that of prominent scientists. But this prejudice is remarkably stubborn, and consequently the investigations of Home by William Crookes constitute an especially valuable body of evidence. More importantly, however, Crookes carried out some unprecedented experiments with Home, experiments that undoubtedly strengthen the case even further.

d. William Crookes

As the reader may already know, Crookes was one of the nineteenth century's most prominent scientists. Early in his career he discovered the element thallium, and later invented the radiometer and the Crookes tube (a form of cathode ray). At the relatively early age of 31 he was elected a Fellow of the Royal Society, and in 1913 became its president. Not long after his election to the Royal Society, he assumed the editorship of the *Quarterly Journal of Science*, where some of his early articles on spiritualism first appeared.[4]

Initially, Crookes was skeptical about spiritualistic phenomena. But as he explained:

> I consider it the duty of scientific men who have learnt exact modes of working, to examine phenomena which attract the attention of the public, in order to confirm their genuineness,

or to explain, if possible, the delusions of the honest and to expose the tricks of deceivers. (Crookes, 1870, p. 3; Medhurst, *et al.*, 1972, p. 15)

Crookes adds,

Faraday says, 'Before we proceed to consider any question involving physical principles, we should set out with clear ideas of the naturally possible and impossible.' But this appears like reasoning in a circle: we are to investigate nothing till we know it to be *possible*, whilst we cannot say what is *impossible*, outside pure mathematics, till we know everything.

In the present case I prefer to enter upon the enquiry with no preconceived notions whatever as to what can or cannot be. (Crookes, 1870, p. 4; Medhurst, *et al.*, 1972, p. 16)

It was in this spirit that Crookes invited Home to submit himself for investigation in 1870. The studies took place either at ordinary séances (during which Crookes occasionally introduced measuring instruments or other devices), or at more formal experimental sessions in which Crookes imposed special test conditions. Crookes made notes on all these occasions, most of which he later published.

Regrettably, Crookes's accounts are often less detailed than one would wish. For example, he does not provide the kind of moment-by-moment description of the proceedings furnished in the 1908 Naples sittings with Eusapia Palladino (section 2.3). In that report, we know at each moment where each person was located, where each hand or foot was placed, etc. Crookes, by contrast, tended to describe only the outstanding features of the sittings. His neglect of minute particulars seems to have been due primarily to a combination of naiveté and arrogance. In part he simply failed to appreciate the number of details that a naturally skeptical reader would want to have furnished. And in part Crookes was vain enough to think that his word should be sufficient to convince skeptics of the adequacy of his test conditions. In response to a barrage of criticisms concerning his first published report on Home, he wrote,

Others – and I am glad to say they are very few – have gone so far as to question my veracity: – 'Mr Crookes must get better witnesses before he can be believed!' Accustomed as I am to have my word believed without witnesses, this is an argument which I cannot condescend to answer. (Crookes, 1871b, p. 22; Medhurst, *et al.*, 1972, p. 35)

We must be careful to view this remark in historical perspective. No doubt Crooks would have been more patient or gracious with his critics had he received a different sort of reception from the academic community. But by the time he wrote 'Some Further Experiments . . .' (1871b), he was already angry over certain of the criticisms lodged against him. Many were foolish and incompetent, amounting to little more than protests that Home's phenomena *had* to be impossible. In fact, at one point, regarding an experiment with a board and spring balance, Crookes writes in exasperation,

Will not my critics give me credit for the possession of some amount of common sense? And can they not imagine that obvious precautions, which occur to them as soon as they sit down to pick holes in my experiments, are not unlikely to have also occurred to me in the course of prolonged and patient investigation? (Crookes, 1871b, p. 43; Medhurst, *et al.*, 1972, p. 60)

Still, despite the superficial nature of many of the criticisms, the continuing dialogue between Crookes and his critics is valuable. Not only did it force Crookes to be more specific about some test conditions and to modify earlier experiments somewhat, but it also demonstrates that scientific skepticism has scarcely changed its method or tone in more than 100 years. It is both fascinating and frustrating to read letters reprinted by Crookes, in which prominent scientists clearly refuse to investigate or think seriously about his claims – and, in fact, decline invitations to attend formal experiments with Home. In reply to one such overture, an officer of the Royal Society, Prof. George G. Stokes, wrote,

I don't want to meet anyone; my object being to scrutinize the apparatus, not to witness the effects. (Crookes, 1871b, p. 28; Medhurst *et al.*, 1972, p. 42)

Stokes, however, found himself too busy even to examine the

apparatus. Nevertheless, he wrote Crookes a long letter about what *must* have been wrong with his experimental designs. And shortly thereafter, he bypassed the usual procedures for refereeing papers submitted to the Royal Society. Exercising the power of his office, he single-handedly rejected Crookes's report of his experiments with Home, despite the fact that he apparently had not even read the paper (see Crookes, 1871b, p. 32; Medhurst *et al.*, 1972, pp. 47–8). Worse still, Stokes then communicated the Society's refusal, not through the usual channel of providing a report from the editorial committee directly to the author, but by leaking the information to the *Spectator*, where Crookes first learned of the decision.

Eventually, Crookes became disheartened and discouraged by the behavior of his colleagues. Although his investigations of spiritualistic phenomena continued until his death in 1919, he rapidly lost his zeal for communicating with members of the scientific community. Writing to Sir Oliver Lodge in a letter dated October 20, 1894, Crookes lamented,

> It seems a cruel thing that Home was about London for years, asking for scientific men to come and investigate, and offering himself freely for any experiments they liked, and with one or two exceptions no one would take advantage of the offer. I tried my best to get men of science to look into it, but all I got for my pains was a suggestion of lunacy for myself, and insults for Home. (quoted in Medhurst and Goldney, 1964, pp. 140–1)

In any case, Crookes was undoubtedly less cynical when he first investigated Home at a séance on April 21, 1870. He conducted a number of additional informal séances after this, before initiating more careful experimentation in 1871. Presumably, his intention was to determine that Home was, indeed, worthy of serious investigation. Evidently, Crookes saw more than enough to satisfy himself that he would not be wasting his time. He observed, among other things, an accordion held by Home in one hand (at the end away from the keys), playing first in a vertical, and then horizontal, position. On one occasion the accordion floated around the room playing melodies, travelling far outside the circle seated at the table, and then gently returning to the table and moving about within inches of the faces of some of those present.

The first séance in which anything like an experiment took place was on the evening of May 9, 1871. Guests were seated around a 32 lb. table. Light was provided by one candle on the table, two on the mantelpiece, and one on a side table. Some extra light was emitted by a dull wood fire. After some table tilting, Home invited Crookes to attach a spring balance he had brought with him to the edge of the table, in order to measure the force required to tilt it. (In order not to disrupt the flow of the séance, Crookes postponed taking control measurements until the sitting had ended.) The command, 'Be light', was issued, and an upward pull of 2 lbs. was required to lift one of the feet off the ground. The table was then told, 'Be heavy'.

> As soon as this was said, the table creaked, shuddered, and appeared to settle itself firmly into the floor. . . . All hands were, as before, very lightly touching the upper surface of the table with their fingers. (Medhurst, *et al.*, 1972, p. 163)

Crookes found that a force of 36 lbs. was now required to lift the foot of the table from the floor. He lifted the table up and down several times to assure himself that the balance read properly; and indeed, it continued to hover around the 36 lb. mark. On one of these occasions Home removed his hands from the table, and his feet at all times were tucked back under his chair.

Crookes attempted several more trials. When told to be light, a force of 7 lbs. was required to tilt the table. When next told to be heavy, a 45 lb. force was required, and this time sitters placed their hands *under* the table top, so that any unconscious force applied to the table would tend to decrease its apparent weight. Then another 'heavy' trial was conducted with hands beneath the table. This time, although the table did not move, the index on the balance rose steadily to the 46 lb. mark. Finally, the table rose an inch, but then slipped off the balance's hook and fell to the floor 'with a crash.' When Crookes examined the iron hook, he found that it had become distended. After the séance ended, Crookes measured the table's weight, and found it to be 32 lbs. Tilting it in the manner adopted for the trials required 8 lbs. of force. (Crookes claimed that the balance was accurate to about ¼ lb.)

After some accordion phenomena, a table levitation, and other manifestations, Home

went to the candle on a side table (close to the large table) and passed his fingers backwards and forwards through the flame several times so slowly that they must have been severely burnt under ordinary circumstances. He then held his fingers up, smiled and nodded as if pleased, took up a fine cambric handkerchief belonging to Miss Douglas, folded it up on his right hand and went to the fire. Here he threw off the bandage from his eyes and by means of the tongs lifted a piece of red hot charcoal from the centre and deposited it on the folded cambric; bringing it across the room, he told us to put out the candle which was on the table, knelt down close to Mrs W.F. and spoke to her about it in a low voice. Occasionally he fanned the coal to a white heat with his breath. Coming a little further round the room, he spoke to Miss Douglas saying, 'We shall have to burn a very small hole in the handkerchief. We have a reason for this which you do not see.' Presently he took the coal back to the fire and handed the handkerchief to Miss Douglas. A small hole about half an inch in diameter was burnt in the centre, and there were two small points near it, but it was not even singed anywhere else. (I took the handkerchief away with me and on testing it in my laboratory, found that it had not undergone the slightest chemical preparation which could have rendered it fire-proof.)

Mr Home again went to the fire, and after stirring the hot coals about with his hand, took out a red-hot piece nearly as big as an orange, and putting it on his right hand, covered it over with his left hand so as to almost completely enclose it, and then blew into the small furnace thus extemporised until the lump of charcoal was nearly white-hot, and then drew my attention to the lambent flame which was flickering over the coal and licking round his fingers; he fell on his knees, looked up in a reverent manner, held up the coal in front and said, 'Is not God good? Are not His laws wonderful?' (Medhurst *et al.*, 1972, pp. 165–6)

The next sitting, on May 21, produced (among other things) some good accordion phenomena. As in the previous sitting, not only did sitters observe the accordion expand and contract, but they also witnessed the movement of the keys. This observation tends to thwart the tempting objection that Home had some mechanical means of making the accordion move. Even if Home had been able to rig an accordion to move in and out, this alone could not have produced the music apparently issuing from the instrument. Beside, as far as I can discover, no suitably small device in 1871 (or now) could have made the accordion play melodies *on request*, much less make the keys move mechanically in accordance with the music.

Crookes also records the following interesting episode.

Presently Mr Home asked me (Mr Crookes) to look under the table. I did so and saw the accordion opening and shutting and at the end where the keys were was a hand playing on them. So natural was the hand that for the moment I took it for granted that it was Mrs W. Crookes's hand, and upon Mr Home's asking me if I saw anything, I said 'No.' He seemed surprised at this and asked the same question again, the hand at the same time becoming more visible and the accordion moving nearer to me. 'No,' I replied, 'I do not see anything except Carrie's [Mrs W. Crookes] hand which has been there all the time.' As soon as I said this there was a general ejaculation from all at the table that Mrs W. Crookes had had both her hands on the table all the time, and that one of Mr Home's was also on the table. I then looked up and saw that this was the case. On looking down again I saw the hand still there, but it appeared to draw itself behind the accordion and disappear.

Had I reflected for a moment I might have known that from the position of the hand it could not have belonged to anyone *sitting* at the table, for they would have had to leave their chair to get sufficiently low down.

There was ample light under the table to see what was going on. (Medhurst, *et al.*, 1972, p. 168)

In the next sitting, on May 22, Alfred Russel Wallace also observed a hand playing 'Home, Sweet Home', which he had requested. Although Crookes fails to mention it, Wallace had been invited to check and see that Home was not manually playing the accordion. As Wallace records in his autobiography, the room was well-illuminated, and he could see that only one of Home's hands touched the instrument, at the end furthest from the keys. Then, Home took even that hand away, and 'the instrument went on playing, and I saw a detached hand holding it while Home's two hands were seen above the table by all present.' (Wallace, 1905, vol. ii, p. 286)[5]

The May 22 sitting also contained several complete table levitations, with ample opportunity for sitters to take candles underneath the table to examine Home's feet and legs. Crookes also conducted his spring-balance test again, with similar results.

So impressed was Crookes by the accordion phenomena that he devised a method for testing its genuineness without interfering greatly with its normal mode of production. Home's standard practice was to hold the accordion, at the end away from the keys, just under a table, with his other hand supporting him, resting on top of the table. Home claimed the 'power' was greatest under the table. Naturally, this appears suspicious, despite the fact that sitters were regularly invited to check under the table and never observed Home engage in any form of trickery. But Crookes hit upon a way of allowing Home to hold the accordion under the table, while ruling out the possibility of chicanery.

The accordion used in the experiment was new. Crookes purchased it for the occasion, and Home had not seen the instrument before the experiment began. Moreover, when Crookes had called for Home earlier in the day, Home

> suggested that, as he had to change his dress, perhaps I should not object to continue our conversation in his bedroom. I
> am, therefore, enabled to state positively, that no machinery, apparatus or contrivance of any sort was secreted about his person. (Crookes, 1871a, p. 11; Medhurst *et al.*, 1972, p. 24)

Nine witnesses were present on the occasion – among them Serjeant Edward Cox (an attorney), and a prominent physicist and astronomer (like Crookes, a Fellow of the Royal Society), William Huggins.

The apparatus designed by Crookes was a wooden cage, wound with insulated copper wire and netted together with string. The cage fit just under Crookes's dining table, leaving space for Home's hand to hold an end of the accordion under the table, but *not* enough room for Home's hand to dip inside the cage to manipulate the instrument. And since the cage rested on the floor, Home's feet also had no access to the instrument (since Home had his boots on, there wasn't much he could have done with his feet anyway). Home sat at the side of the table, holding the accordion between the thumb and middle finger of one hand at the end away from the keys, while his other hand rested on top of the table (Figs. 1 and 2).

the cage being drawn from under the table so as just to allow the accordion to be pushed in with its keys downwards, it was pushed back as close as Mr Home's arm would permit, but without hiding his hand from those next to him. Very soon the accordion was seen by those on each side to be waving about in a somewhat curious manner; then sounds came from it, and finally several notes were played in succession. While this was going on, my assistant went under the table, and reported that the accordion was expanding and contracting; at the same time it was seen that the hand of Mr Home by which it was held was quite still, his other hand resting on the table. (Crookes, 1871a, p. 12; Medhurst *et al.*, 1972, p. 25)

Then, while Home's feet were

being held by those next him, and his other hand resting on the table, we heard distinct and separate notes sounded in succession, and then a simple air was played. As such a result could only have been produced by the various keys of the instrument being acted upon in harmonious succession, this was considered by those present to be a crucial experiment. But the sequel was still more striking, for Mr Home then removed his hand altogether from the accordion, taking it quite out of the cage, and placed it in the hand of the person next to him. The instrument then continued to play, no person touching it and no hand being near it. (Crookes, 1871a, p. 13; Medhurst *et al.*, 1972, p. 26)

Crookes next found that the phenomena continued as before, even when an electric current was run from two Grove's cells in another room to the insulated copper wire around the cage. Then,

The accordion was now again taken without any visible touch

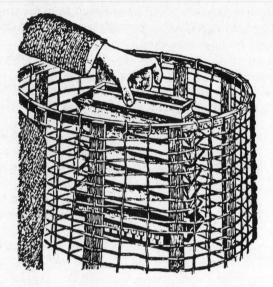

Fig. 1

Fig. 2

from Mr Home's hand, which he removed from it entirely and placed upon the table, where it was taken by the person next to him, and seen, as now were both his hands, by all present. I and two of the others present saw the accordion distinctly floating about inside the cage with no visible support. This was repeated a second time, after a short interval. Mr Home presently reinserted his hand in the cage and again took hold of the accordion. It then commenced to play, at first, chords and runs, and afterwards a well-known sweet and plaintive melody, which it executed perfectly in a very beautiful manner. Whilst this tune was being played, I grasped Mr Home's arm, below the elbow, and gently slid my hand down it until I touched the top of the accordion. He was not moving a muscle. His other hand was on the table, visible to all, and his feet were under the feet of those next to him. (Crookes, 1871a, p. 14; Medhurst, *et al.*, 1972, p. 27)

Crookes then took Home to an apparatus located in another part of the room. The device was supposed to test Home's apparent ability to alter an object's weight. It consisted of a mahogany board, 36 by 9.5 by 1 ins., onto whose ends had been screwed mahogany strips 1.5 ins. wide. One of these 'feet' rested on a 'firm table'; the other was supported by a spring balance hanging from a sturdy tripod. This apparatus was rigged so that the mahogany board lay horizontally between the table and the tripod. As in the case of the accordion, Home had never before seen the device. (A variation of this experimental set-up was successfully employed in a subsequent sitting. See Crookes, 1889, pp. 117ff; Medhurst, *et al.*, 1972, pp. 197ff.)

Home sat at the table where one end of the board rested, and placed his fingertips lightly on the end of the board. Crookes and Huggins sat on either side of the board. Almost immediately the board and spring balance began to oscillate up and down. Home then placed a nearby hand-bell and match box on the end of the board, one under each hand, in order to demonstrate (he said) that he was not producing the downward pressure (see Fig. 3).

The oscillations of the spring balance became more pronounced, and Huggins, who was watching the index, saw it descend to 6.5 lbs., and later to 9 lbs. The normal weight of the board as registered by the balance had been 3.5 lbs. prior to the experiment.

Fig. 3

Crookes adds,

In order to see whether it was possible to produce much effect on the spring balance by pressure at the place where Mr Home's fingers had been, I stepped upon the table and stood on one foot at the end of the board. Dr A. B. [i.e., Huggins], who was observing the index of the balance, said that the whole weight of my body (140 lbs.) so applied only sunk the index 1½ lbs., or 2 lbs. when I jerked up and down. Mr Home had been sitting in a low easy-chair, and could not, therefore, had he tried his utmost, have exerted any material influence on these results. I need scarcely add that his feet as well as his hands were closely guarded by all in the room.

This experiment appears to be more striking, if possible, than the one with the accordion. . . . The board was arranged perfectly horizontally, and it was particularly noticed that Mr Home's fingers were not at any time advanced more than 1½ inches from the extreme end, as shown by a pencil-mark, which, with Dr A.B.'s acquiescence, I made at the time. Now, the wooden foot being also 1½ inches wide, and resting flat on the table, it is evidence that no amount of pressure exerted within this space of 1½ inches could produce any action on the balance. Again, it is also evident that when the end furthest from Mr Home sank, the board would turn on the further edge of this foot as on a fulcrum. The arrangement was consequently that of a see-saw, 36 inches in length, the fulcrum being 1½ inches from one end; were he therefore to have exerted a downward pressure, it would have been in opposition to the force which was causing the other end of the board to move down.

The slight downward pressure shown by the balance when I stood on the board was owing probably to my foot extending beyond this fulcrum. (Crookes, 1871a, p. 15; Medhurst, *et al.*, 1972, pp. 28–29)

On a later occasion, Crookes successfully attempted a variant of the spring-balance test, as well as other experiments involving a still more complicated device (Crookes, 1871b). Although these experiments are also important and impressive, I shall turn briefly to some more informal sessions with Home in which very dramatic phenomena occurred. I shall dwell on these because they bear on the critical issue (discussed in Chapters 1, 4 and 5) of the conceivable range or limits of PK.

The experiments just described took place on May 31, 1871. On July 16, Crookes held another sitting in which

Mr Home took the accordion in the usual manner and we then were favored with the most beautiful piece of music I ever heard. It was very solemn and was executed perfectly: the 'fingering' of the notes was finer than anything I could imagine. During this piece, which lasted for about 10 minutes, we heard a man's rich voice accompanying it in one corner of the room, and a bird whistling and chirping. (Crookes, 1889, p. 116; Medhurst *et al.*, 1972, p. 196)

Another report of a man's voice accompanying the accordion appears in the description of a sitting held on Nov. 25 (see Crookes, 1889, p. 122; Medhurst *et al.*, 1972, p. 205).[6]

On July 30, in the light of two large spirit lamps, Crookes recorded the following remarkable series of incidents. I quote his remarks at length, not only because the phenomena are interesting, but also in order to convey a sense of the density of phenomena occurring at some sittings. The very proliferation of dramatic events involving objects not belonging to or prepared by

Home is another fact about his mediumship that skeptics are hard-pressed to explain away. (During the sitting, sitters were located as shown in Fig. 4.)

The accordion, which had been left by Mr Home under the table, now began to play and move about without anyone touching it. It dropped on to my foot, then dragged itself away, playing all the time, and went to Mrs I. It got on to her knees.

Mr Home got up and stood behind in full view of all, holding the accordion out at arm's length. We all saw it expanding and contracting and heard it playing a melody. Mr Home then let go of the accordion, which went behind his back and there continued to play; his feet being visible and also his two hands, which were in front of him.

Mr Home then walked to the open space in the room between Mrs I's chair and the sideboard and stood there quite upright and quiet. He then said, 'I'm rising, I'm rising'; when we all saw him rise from the ground slowly to a height of about six inches, remain there for about 10 seconds, and then slowly descend. From my position I could not see his feet, but I distinctly saw his head, projected against the opposite wall, rise up, and Mr Wr. Crookes [Crookes's brother], who

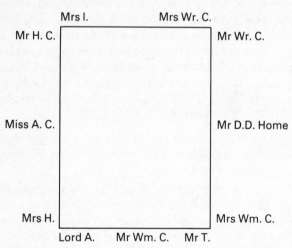

Fig. 4

was sitting near where Mr Home was, said that his feet were in the air. There was no stool or other thing near which could have aided him. Moreover, the movement was a smooth continuous glide upwards.

Whilst this was going on we heard the accordion fall heavily to the ground. It had been suspended in the air behind the chair where Mr Home had been sitting. When it fell Mr Home was about 10 ft. from it.

Mr Home still standing behind Mrs I. and Mr Wr. Crookes, the accordion was both seen and heard to move about behind him without his hands touching it. It then played a tune without contact and floating in the air.

Mr Home then took the accordion in one hand and held it out so that we could all see it (he was still standing up behind Mrs I. and Mr Wr. Crookes). We then saw the accordion expand and contract and heard a tune played. Mrs Wm. Crookes and Mr Home saw a light on the lower part of the accordion, where the keys were, and we then heard and saw the keys clicked and depressed one after the other fairly and deliberately, as if to show us that the power doing it, although invisible (or nearly so) to us, had full control over the instrument.

A beautiful tune was then played whilst Mr Home was standing up holding the accordion out in full view of everyone.

Mr Home then came round behind me and telling me to hold my left arm out placed the accordion under my arm, the keys hanging down and the upper part pressing upwards against my upper arm. He then left go and the accordion remained there. He then placed his two hands one on each of my shoulders. In this position, no one touching the accordion but myself, and every one noticing what was taking place, the instrument played notes but no tunes.

Mr Home then sat in his chair, and we were told by raps to open the table about an inch and a-half.

Mr T. touched the point of the [wooden] lath, when raps immediately came on it.

The planchette, which was on the table resting on a sheet of paper, now moved a few inches.

99

Sounds were heard on the accordion, which was on the floor, not held by Mr Home.

The corner of the paper next to Mrs Wm. Crookes (on which the planchette was standing) moved up and down. (These three last phenomena were going on simultaneously.)

I felt something touch my knee; it then went to Mrs I., then to Miss A. Crookes.

Whilst this was going on I held the bell under the table, and it was taken from me and rung round beneath. It was then given to Mrs I. by a hand which she described as soft and warm.

The lath was now seen to move about a little.

Mrs Wm. Crookes saw a hand and fingers touching the flower in Mr Home's button-hole. The flower was then taken by the hand and given to Mrs I. and the green leaf was in a similar manner given to Mr T.

Mrs Wm. Crookes and Mr Home saw the hand doing this, the others only saw the flower and leaf moving through the air.

Mrs Wm. Crookes held a rose below the table; it was touched and then taken.

The sound as of a drum was heard on the accordion.

The lath lifted itself up on its edge, then reared itself upon one end and fell down. It then floated up four inches above the table, and moved quite round the circle, pointing to Mrs Wm. Crookes. It then rose up and passed over our heads outside the circle.

The planchette moved about a good deal, marking the paper.

The cloth was dragged along the table.

Then, after several more phenomena,

The water and tumbler now rose up together, and we had answers to questions by their tapping together whilst floating in the air about eight inches above the table, and moving backwards and forwards from one to the other of the circle.

Mr H. Crookes said a hand was tickling his knee.

A finger protruded up the opening [between the leaves] of the table between Miss A. Crookes and the water bottle.

Miss A. Crookes, Mr H. Crookes, and Mrs I, were then touched.

Fingers came up the opening of the table a second time and waved about.

The lath, which on its last excursion had settled in front of the further window, quite away from the circle, now moved along the floor four or five times very noisily. It then came up to Mr T., and passed into the circle over his shoulder. It settled on the table and then rose up again, pointing to Wm. Crookes's mouth.

The lath then went to the water bottle and pushed it several times nearly over, to move it away from the opening in the table. The lath then went endways down the opening.

The tumbler moved about a little.

The lath moved up through the opening in the table and answered 'Yes' and 'No' to questions, by bobbing up and down three times or once. (Crookes, 1889, pp. 118–21; Medhurst *et al.*, 1972, pp. 199–203)

After a few more phenomena, the séance ended.

e. Comments

The case of D. D. Home merits a far more detailed examination than I can provide here. But before moving on to further impressive evidence, various remarks seem in order.

In considering the possibility of fraud with regard to table tilting and levitation, certain points should be kept in mind. First, when the medium's hands rest on top of the table, the tilting of large tables does not require an accomplice. But when the medium's feet are held or observed, it requires a device of some sort (e.g., hooks attached to the wrist and concealed under long sleeves). Such devices, however, are easy to detect when the light is good, and when observers are positioned under the table. Detection is easier still, when – as in some cases with both Home and Palladino – observers grasp the hands and wrists and make continual body checks. Complete levitation of a large table, on the other hand, requires at least an accomplice or an apparatus. But in the best cases this is usually out of the question. In Home's case, for instance, considering that table levitations occurred in hundreds of locations in Europe and America for nearly 25 years, not one, but an army of confederates would have been necessary, none of whom (we would have to suppose) ever later enjoyed the satisfaction of revealing the trick to the public. Moreover, (to reiterate points raised earlier), séances often occurred on the spur of the moment, in locations never before visited by Home. And of course no neatly concealable device or machine in the late nineteenth and early twentieth century could have produced the appropriate effect. Finally, if the levitation is conducted in good light, with opportunity *at any time* to physically inspect the goings-on, I think we must conclude that the phenomenon is genuine.[7]

Notice, also, that table movements in Home séances were often characterized as smooth and steady. This is difficult to reconcile with the hypothesis that Home was producing the phenomena manually, since in that case the movements would presumably have been abrupt or jerky, especially the table's descent. Not only is it difficult for one person (especially a weak person) to lift and lower a large, heavy table smoothly under the best of conditions, but Home was usually under continual observation during the phenomena. Therefore, the only movements likely to have escaped detection would have been sudden or rapid movements. But these would have produced sudden and unsteady movements of the table. A similar point applies to the slow and steady trajectories of other levitated objects, in connection with both physical mediums and poltergeist cases. The continuous, slow, and often graceful object movements reported seem impossible to produce by a quick undetected process (as in throwing an object). And certainly, no technology available to mediums of the nineteenth and early twentieth century would have enabled them to produce slow and smooth object movements while under continual observation in good light, much less in impromptu sittings.

One aspect of séances with Home (and Eusapia Palladino) that fuels skeptical suspicions is that only certain of the sitters claim to observe, say, an apparently materialized hand carrying an object, while others see a luminous cloud, and others see only the object movement. To some, this suggests that the experiences are *all* delusory – i.e., subjective constructs of some sort, perhaps induced by the medium's suggestion.

I think, however, that we should not make too much of such

discrepant testimony. For one thing (as I observed in the last chapter), many phenomena are reported by all present, and these are the ones that must first be explained. If no normal explanation does the job, then the divergent reports in the other cases are far less significant, and may even point to certain aspects of a *paranormal* process that are important to understand. Also, the object movements may be genuine and paranormal even if the spirit hands and luminous clouds are only subjective constructs. But we should remember that some quite ordinary non-delusory physical phenomena are perceivable (or perceivable in certain ways) only from certain vantage points – for example, rainbows and electromagnetic fields (which may appear luminous from certain positions). Even in the case of optical illusions (like mirages), which likewise are often not perceivable from all angles or positions, certain objective physical states of affairs account for the illusion. So the differing testimony from sitters located at different positions relative to the alleged phenomena, fails to show that the sitters' experiences are nothing more than subjective constructs. As with optical illusions, they might even afford important clues as to the nature of the underlying objective process.

The apparent materialization of hands is another phenomenon deserving of special comment. The hands appeared to be warm, soft, mobile, and flexible. Sitters claimed to see them move objects or play musical instruments. Yet they would melt or dissolve when grasped, or suddenly disappear. Apparently, they were never dragged away as they would be in the event that Home was trying to retrieve a previously concealed device. Considering that the hands were often associated with object-movements or other physical side effects that seem to have been genuine, skeptics face a formidable challenge. To account for the combination of physical effects along with tactile and visual impressions of the hands (including their mode of disappearance or dematerialization), one would presumably have to appeal to a complicated combination of hallucination (or hypnosis) and machinery. But for reasons discussed earlier, hallucination (or hypnosis) leaves too much unexplained. Moreover, it is certain that the production of warm, fleshy and mobile hands of varying colors, shapes, and sizes (much less hands that dissolve or melt) was beyond the technology of the period (and our own as well). The hypotheses that the hands were those of Home, or that they were stuffed gloves, are equally unsatisfactory. Home's hands were often visible while the spirit hands were seen, and often Home was located well beyond reach of the hands and their associated phenomena. Stuffed gloves, moreover, would not be warm, fleshy, or animated; nor do they dissolve or melt. And if the phenomena occur beyond the medium's reach, we must explain the means by which the hands and object movements were produced. Presumably, the skeptic would insist that Home resorted to a mechanical device to manipulate the hands and objects. But it is far from clear what mechanical contrivance of the period would have been both possible to conceal and capable of producing the additional associated physical effects.

Consider the following account. The narrator (Frank L. Burr, editor of the *Hartford Times*) had been describing some object movements, and had just reported the slow and deliberate movement of a piece of paper. At this point in the proceedings, light was furnished only by the glow from a coal fire near the table. However, given Burr's proximity to the hand and the minuteness of his examination, it seems to me that the lack of better illumination (although regrettable) does not undermine the value of the testimony.

> The quire of paper was placed upon the edge of the table, and so near my hand as to touch it. This was done slowly and deliberately, and this time at least I was permitted to see plainly and clearly *the hand that had hold of it*. It was evidently a *lady's hand* – very thin, very pale, and remarkably attenuated. The *conformation* of this hand was peculiar. The fingers were of almost preternatural *length*, and seemed to be set *wide apart*. The extreme *pallor* of the entire hand was also remarkable. But perhaps the most noticeable thing about it was the shape of the fingers, which, in addition to their length and thinness, were unusually *pointed* at the ends; they tapered rapidly and evenly toward the tips. The hand also *narrowed* from the lower knuckles to the wrist, *where it ended*. All this could be seen by as such light as was in the room, while the hand was for a few moments holding the paper upon the edge of the table. It suddenly disappeared, and in a moment the *pencil* was thrown from some quarter, and fell

104

upon the table, where the hand again appeared, took it, and *began to write*. This was in plain sight, being only shaded by one of the circle who was sitting between the paper on the table and the fire. The hands of each one present were upon the table, in full view, so that it *could* not have been one of the party who was thus writing. Being the nearest one to the hand, I bent down close to it as it wrote, to see the whole of it. It extended no farther than *the wrist*. With a feeling of curiosity natural under the circumstances, I brought my face *close* to it in the endeavor to see exactly what it was, and, in so doing, probably destroyed the electric or magnetic influence by which it was working; for the pencil dropped and the hand vanished. The writing was afterwards examined, and proved to be *the name, in her own proper handwriting, of a relative* and intimate lady friend of one in the circle, who passed away some years since. . . . That it was produced by no hand of any one bodily in that room I *know* and affirm.

The hand afterwards came and *shook hands* with each one present. I felt it minutely. It was tolerably well and symmetrically made, though not perfect; and it was *soft* and slightly *warm*. IT ENDED AT THE WRIST. (Home, 1863/ 1972, pp. 59–61)

This description is quite typical. Compare it to some of the brief descriptions collected by Barrett and Myers (1889, pp. 134–5). Burr describes how, 'in the full light of the lamp,' he shook hands with a hand apparently not attached to any arm. He continues,

When the hand found it could not get away it yielded itself up to me for my examination, turned itself over and back, shut up its fingers and opened them. It ended at the wrist.

Burr then pushed his finger through the hand. But the hole closed up, leaving a scar, and then the hand disappeared.

Another witness says of a large hand, 'I seized it, felt it very sensibly, but it went out like air in my grasp.' Another says of a 'little hand,'

I took hold of it; it was warm, and evidently a child's hand. I did not loosen my hold, but it seemed to melt out of my clutch.

Count Tolstoy reports, 'Hands laid themselves in my hands, and when I sought to retain one it dissolved in my grasp.' Still another witness writes,

> It was a summer's evening, about eight o'clock; and I sat near to a large window, against which stood a table, and on the table an ordinary large bell. Sitting very near to the bell, I distinctly saw a well-shaped hand appear on the table, and after resting there a short time the hand rose, grasped the bell, and carried it away, we knew not where. While the hand rested on the table, I rose from my seat, went to the table, and without touching the hand examined it by careful inspection. It looked like a grey, gauzy substance, exactly the form of a human hand, and it terminated at the wrist.

Yet another interesting passage is quoted by Gauld (1968, pp. 17–18). The account describes a sitting with Home in a private house, and is given in a letter to the *Hartford Times* in March, 1853.

> The gas light had been turned down, but sufficient light remained in the room to render ourselves, and most objects, quite visible, and the hands of the party, which rested on the table, could be distinctly seen. The spirits asked [by raps]:
>
> 'How many hands are there on the table?' There were six of us in the party, and the answer, after counting, was 'twelve'.
>
> *Reply* – 'There are *thirteen*.'
>
> And there, sure enough, on that side of the table which was vacant, and opposite to the medium, appeared a *thirteenth* hand! It faded as we gazed, but presently up it came again – a *hand and an arm*, gleaming and apparently self-luminous; and it slowly moved . . . toward the centre of the table! To make sure that we were not deceived or laboring under a hallucination, we counted our own hands, which were all resting in sight upon the table. There it was, however, an arm and a hand, the arm extending back to the elbow, and there fading into imperceptibility. We all saw it, and all spoke of it, to assure each other of the reality of the thing. It emitted a faint but perceptible *light*. Presently it vanished, but we were soon permitted to see not only the same thing again, but

the *process of its formation*. It began at the *elbow*, and
formed rapidly and steadily, until the arm and hand again
rested on the table before us. It was so plainly seen, that I
readily observed it to be a *left* hand.

After attempting to write, the hand picked up a bell, rang it about
six feet away from the circle, an then brought it to the writer,
who took the hand instead.

It was a real hand – it had knuckles, fingers, and fingernails,
and what was yet more curious. . . , it was soft and warm,
feeling much like the hand of an infant, in every respect but
that of size. But the most singular part of the strange
occurrence is yet to be told – the hand melted in my grasp!
Dissolved, dissipated, became annihilated, so far as the sense
of feeling extended.

Some of Crookes's observations are also worth quoting.

A beautifully-formed hand rose up from the opening in a
dining-table and gave me a flower; it appeared and then
disappeared three times at intervals, affording me ample
opportunity of satisfying myself that it was as real in
appearance as my own. This occurred in the light in my room,
whilst I was holding the medium's hands and feet.

The hands and fingers do not always appear to me to be
solid and life-like. Sometimes, indeed, they present more the
appearance of a nebulous cloud partly condensed into the form
of a hand. This is not equally visible to all present. For
instance, a flower or other small object is seen to move; one
person present will see a luminous cloud hovering over it,
another will detect a nebulous-looking hand, whilst others will
see nothing at all but the moving flower. I have more than
once seen, first an object move, then a luminous cloud appear
to form about it, and, lastly, the cloud condense into shape and
become a perfectly-formed hand. At this stage the hand is
visible to all present. It is not always a mere form, but
sometimes appears perfectly life-like and graceful, the fingers
moving and the flesh apparently as human as that of any in the
room. At the wrist, or arm, it becomes hazy, and fades off
into a luminous cloud.

To the touch, the hand sometimes appears icy cold and

dead, at other times, warm and life-like, grasping my own with the firm pressure of an old friend.

I have retained one of these hands in my own, firmly resolved not to let it escape. There was no struggle or effort made to get loose, but it gradually seemed to resolve itself into vapour, and faded in that manner from my grasp.
(Crookes, 1874, p. 92; Medhurst *et al.*, 1972, pp. 118–19)

If this book had been devoted solely to the amazing case of D. D. Home, I would pay closer attention to the evidence for the earthquake effect and the handling of coals, at the very least. As it is, we must move on to a case almost as remarkable.

2.3   EUSAPIA PALLADINO (1854–1918)

a. Background

This case contrasts dramatically with that of Home. Home's phenomena were highly refined, sophisticated, varied, and – when necessary – carefully controlled. And except for isolated and unsubstantiated charges of fraud, Home was never once detected in trickery. Eusapia, on the other hand, produced phenomena less startling than Home's, and even less impressive than those of some other mediums of the period. Also, whereas Home would give séances anywhere, at the drop of a hat, and would usually invite sitters to confirm that no trickery was in progress, Eusapia tended to impose séance conditions that were, at *best*, superficially suspicious. She often required the use of a 'cabinet', a curtain drawn behind her, which she would occasionally touch, and from which manifestations would issue. She also dictated many other séance conditions, frequently insisting on dim light and poor control of hands and feet.

Furthermore, not only had Eusapia actually been detected in trickery, but she even admitted that she would occasionally cheat (e.g., by substituting hands and feet) if not well-controlled. At the time, some debated whether these maneuvers were really fraudulent, and whether they cast serious doubt on Eusapia's character, or on the paranormality of her manifestations as a whole. Many of the apparent tricks occurred during trance, and

Eusapia would often twitch or move during the production of phenomena. Hence, some regarded the movements as involuntary, and the apparent tricks or substitutions as unconscious, or non-intentional by-products of her psychokinetic efforts.

In any case, Eusapia was hardly above reproach. For this reason, many refused (and still refuse) to take her case seriously, arguing that once a medium has been tainted by fraud, none of her phenomena can be trusted. Interestingly, the British S.P.R. even adopted an official policy along these lines. They refused to treat as evidential any phenomenon apparently produced by a medium once caught cheating (see H. Sidgwick, 1896; also Gauld, 1968 and Inglis, 1977, 1984). In my view, this stand is totally indefensible. That a person cheats in some cases does not show that he cheats in all cases. The issue is not whether there are instances in which the medium apparently cheated, but whether there are instances in which the indications are strong that cheating did not occur. Besides, lapses in honesty may make good sense when one takes account of the psychodynamics of the person's life (e.g., the strong pressure to produce phenomena when the 'power' is not forthcoming).

In fact, willingness to assist unreliable phenomena in this way is not limited to the domain of the paranormal. William James tells how, when he was assisting Newell Martin's physiology class at Harvard, he surreptitiously moved a needle that was supposed to have registered the beats of a turtle's heart. But the heart was uncooperative, and so James impulsively acted in the interests of 'a *larger* truth' (Murphy and Ballou, 1960, pp. 313ff.). And Richet relates an equally relevant anecdote about Ampère.

> A new electrical demonstration was being given before a scientific committee, and as the galvanometer needle failed to move at a critical moment, he gave it a touch with his finger. Repeating the experiment, successfully this time, he said triumphantly, pointing to the needle, 'This time it goes of itself!' (Richet, 1923/1975, p. 458)

Similarly, Richet suggested, when the pressure is great enough, a medium might 'give the push that he hopes will start the phenomena' (p. 458).

In any case, if one suspects that a medium might cheat under certain conditions, a resourceful researcher need only eliminate the conditions, and substitute test situations in which fraud may be ruled out. What matters is whether the performance of a medium in *particular cases* and under *specific conditions* can be explained as due to chicanery, no matter what the medium's transgressions may have been on other occasions. Granted, matters are slightly neater if the medium is indisputably honest (although no medium has ever been generally trusted; suspicion comes with the territory). But if doubts remain as to the medium's character, all one must do is design a set of séance conditions where his or her possibly dishonest proclivities are given no opportunity for expression. When test conditions rule out the possibility of conjuring or fraud by even the most highly-skilled magicians, it is simply irrelevant that the medium cheated on some other occasions.

Another difference between Home and Eusapia, which also worked to Eusapia's disadvantage (particularly in the disastrous Cambridge experiments of 1895), was that Home was a reasonably cultivated, articulate, and interesting man, while Eusapia was an illiterate peasant. Home could successfully hobnob with royalty and the European upper class. Eusapia, however, offended or repelled many (especially her Victorian investigators) with her unrefined behavior, and perhaps most of all with her earthy and crass sexuality. When emerging from a trance, she would often throw herself seductively into the arms of the nearest male sitter. Concerning Eusapia's character in general, Gauld remarks,

> [her] spiritual manifestations were not matched by any
> corresponding spirituality in Eusapia's character. She was
> vulgar, earthy, and addicted to bad company. There are even
> hints that during the séance sitters' purses and other valuables
> were rather too liable to dematerialise. (Gauld, 1968, p. 224)

Eusapia was born in January, 1854 in the province of Bari, Italy. Her mother died shortly thereafter, and Eusapia's father arranged that she be raised in the home of a neighbor. When Eusapia was 12, her father was killed by brigands, and Eusapia went to Naples to live with some foreigners who, according to Dingwall, wanted to adopt and educate a small girl. Dingwall writes,

> The plan was excellent, but the good people had counted

without Eusapia. The attempts to make her read and write, comb her hair, take a daily bath and behave like a little lady were disastrous. (Dingwall, 1962b, p. 178)

So Eusapia left the family, and moved in temporarily with another. It was at this time, when Eusapia was 13, that physical phenomena began to occur in her presence. Eusapia's reputation as a medium spread quickly. At first, séances assured her of continued lodgings with the family she had turned to. But in 1872 she was discovered by an active spiritualist, Mr G. Damiani, who thereafter apparently functioned as her self-appointed guardian and promoter. By the time scientists and other prominent persons began to investigate her – with varying degrees of competence and thoroughness – in the late 1880s, Eusapia had been a professional medium for some time.

One of Eusapia's earliest investigators was Cesare Lombroso, Professor of Psychiatry at the University of Turin; these days he is remembered primarily for his pioneering work in the science of criminology. Lombroso was a materialist, opposed to spiritualistic theories, and also fearful that participation in séances would jeopardize his reputation. But Lombroso had been impressed by something observed in one of his patients, an aristocratic girl suffering what he called 'hystero-epilepsy'; she was apparently able to 'read' with her eyes shut. And so Lombroso agreed to a challenge to study Eusapia. After a preliminary investigation, he arranged some sessions in Milan in 1892, to which he invited several well-known scientists, including Charles Richet, who eventually became one of Eusapia's principal investigators. Richet was not particularly impressed by the controls enforced at Lombroso's sittings, and was the only member of the investigating committee who refused to sign the report endorsing Eusapia's phenomena as genuine. But he was intrigued enough to arrange another series of sittings at a small island he owned off the south coast of France, the Ile Roubaud. More on that shortly.

Lombroso and company witnessed many of Eusapia's standard phenomena of the time, occasionally in good light. Tables levitated, objects beyond Eusapia's reach would move (sometimes in the air), objects looking like hands would appear, and the investigators felt frequent touchings. Although Lombroso recognized that controls could have been better, he was satisfied that

111

the light was often sufficiently good to determine that Eusapia was not using her hands, feet, or a contrivance, to produce the phenomena. But he was also fully aware of her tendency to resort to tricks.

> Many are the crafty tricks she plays, both in the state of trance (unconsciously) and out of it – for example, freeing one of her two hands, held by the controllers, for the sake of moving objects near her; making touches; slowly lifting the legs of the table by means of one of her knees and one of her feet, and feigning to adjust her hair and then slyly pulling out one hair and putting it over the little balance tray of a letter weigher in order to lower it. She was seen by Faifofer, before her séances, furtively gathering flowers in a garden, that she might feign them to be 'apports' by availing herself of the shrouding dark of the room. (quoted in N. Fodor, 1966, p. 272)

I find it curious, to say the least, that Lombroso would consider these tricks 'crafty'. Eusapia was, without a doubt, observed cheating; but she was never detected in sophisticated or clever trickery. Nothing about Eusapia was sophisticated or particularly clever. Her tricks were discovered precisely because they were clumsy and elementary. In fact, the evidence suggests that Eusapia cheated only when she felt she could get away with it – for example, when conditions were loose, or when investigators lacked adequate knowledge of conjuring techniques or experience testing mediums. But as far as I can determine, Eusapia was never caught cheating when phenomena occurred under good conditions, even when her investigators were magicians familiar with the varieties of fraudulent mediumship.

Consider, for example, Eusapia's celebrated 'exposure' at the 1895 Cambridge sittings. Not only were the tests conducted under poor conditions of illumination; but to make matters worse, Richard Hodgson deliberately passed himself off as an 'amiable imbecile' (Gauld, 1968, p. 238), intentionally relaxing controls in order to encourage Eusapia to cheat (see subsection c, below). Needless to say, under those conditions, Eusapia's cheating could hardly be considered adept. And the alleged exposures at the American séances in 1909–10 were even more farcical, with intentionally loose controls once again and inexperienced investigators

112

to boot (for summaries, see Dingwall, 1962; Inglis, 1977, pp. 429–32; 1984, pp. 26–7). By contrast, however, during the 1908 Naples sittings, under tight controls imposed by three trained observers familiar with the techniques of fraudulent mediums (two of whom were skilled magicians), no clever or sophisticated trickery (and, arguably, no trickery at all) was discovered (see subsection d, below).

In general, it seems to me that skeptics have not dealt honestly with two issues in the Palladino case: (1) the justification for supposing that Eusapia had ever executed a clever trick, and (2) the grounds for supposing that she even knew *how* to execute a clever trick. As far as (2) is concerned, there is no reason to think Eusapia had received an education in conjuring. Granted, some magicians develop idiosyncratic tricks or methods in their youth, independently of the mainstream of magicians. But, unlike the natural conjurer, Eusapia did not perform stage tricks, and permitted close hands-on investigations.

And regarding (1), the evidence falls far short of what one would require to discount the case as a whole – so much so, in fact, that the blindness of some prominent skeptics to the discrepancy is quite astonishing. The only cheating ever discovered, as Gauld recognized, was of 'a simple and well-known kind, and certainly not such as could have produced more than a fraction of the phenomena' (Gauld, 1968, p. 240). According to the Polish investigator, Ochorowicz, who conducted more than 70 séances with Eusapia, her tricks were easy to detect because they were 'invariably of an infantile character' (Hodgson, 1895, p. 77). Yet Hodgson claimed that Eusapia was a skilled trickster, despite the fact that neither he nor anyone else had observed anything more sophisticated than hand-substitution. Hodgson was certainly aware of this fact, just as he well knew that in his own case he had caught Eusapia apparently cheating only when he had made it easy and tempting for her. Dingwall, another skeptic, displays an interesting and revealing ambivalence on the matter. He admits repeatedly that many of Eusapia's phenomena could not be explained by a mere freeing of hands and feet, and 'rather clumsy tricks of the simplest kinds' (Dingwall, 1962b, p. 201). He also recognizes that Eusapia's alleged exposures in Cambridge and America took place under inferior (if not incompetent) conditions of control. And he even acknowledges in several places that

Eusapia's frauds were obvious. Furthermore, he never cites an example of Eusapia's skill at conjuring, or a reason for thinking she might somehow have learned the appropriate techniques. Nevertheless, rather than admit that Eusapia's phenomena appear to be genuine, he suggests that she resorted to 'clever' and 'adept' trickery.

Still, Eusapia did little to discourage suspicion. As a rule, she proved to be a difficult subject in her early investigations. Often, experimenters yielded to her demands for séance conditions, many of which were certainly suspect. For example, she frequently insisted on placing her hands atop those of her controllers, rather than within them, thereby making hand-substitution easy (and not, I must add, clever or adept). And on occasion she requested dim light, and sometimes refused to stand for the production of table levitations, demanding instead that she be allowed to sit in a chair by the table. Eusapia claimed this was because her knees and legs trembled violently when phenomena were produced. Admittedly, this seems suspicious. But much tougher sittings later confirmed that Eusapia indeed experienced frequent involuntary limb movements when phenomena were underway. Earlier in her career, however, experimenters seemed unable to work around Eusapia's demands. As a result, they were often unable to determine what was really suspicious, and what was only apparently so.

No doubt Eusapia sometimes insisted on loose controls for the purpose of cheating. But it would be hasty and insensitive to Eusapia's psychology to suppose this was always the case. Some of her specified conditions seem to have been due to her own – perhaps crude – beliefs about what was needed to make the 'force' work. Eusapia *did* have her own ideas about the nature of mediumship – or at least about her own. That is why she insisted on a cabinet, and her occasional need to touch it. Feilding, the principal investigator of the successful 1908 Naples sittings, wrote,

I cannot explain why she wished to do these things, any more than I can explain many other items in her procedure, such as why she should wish to have a table, or why she should require a curtain at all. I find, in talking with friends, that when I mention the curtain, they inevitably say, 'Ah, a curtain! Why a curtain? What a suspicious fact!' I agree that it may be suspicious, but it is not necessarily so. It is suspicious when used by a materializing medium who goes behind it, and, when a 'spirit' comes out, refuses to allow spectators to ascertain whether he is himself still there. But in Eusapia's case, where she sits outside it, I cannot see that, given certain obvious precautions, it is necessarily suspicious. She says it helps to 'concentrate the force.' Perhaps it does. I do not know what the 'force' is, nor what it requires to 'concentrate' it. Nor does anyone else. To a person ignorant of photography it is possible that the use by the photographer of a black cloth over his head would be suspicious. In dealing with an unknown force one can only judge empirically of the utility of certain conditions. That the curtain does have some bearing on the phenomena is clear. Eusapia appears to be *en rapport* with something within. And she constantly seems to experience the necessity of establishing this *rapport* by momentary contact with the curtain or by enveloping the table or part of herself in its folds. We never perceived, however, that the phenomena which followed this action had any normal relation to it whatever. (Fielding, 1963, p. 107; Feilding, Baggally, and Carrington, 1909, p. 397)[8]

Another factor influencing Eusapia's demands for séance conditions was her attitude toward the investigators. When she disliked them (as was probably the case in the Cambridge sittings), she would often try to cheat, possibly as a gesture of contempt. But when she liked and respected them (as in the 1908 Naples sittings), she was usually very cooperative, while still insisting on certain liberties. In the Naples sittings, for example, Eusapia usually asked permission before touching the curtain, allowed the room to be well-lit, and frequently urged the investigators to watch her execute the touch.

As Eusapia's health declined in her later years, her phenomena diminished in magnitude and quality. This is particularly regrettable, since her most careful séances were held only after the decline had begun. It is also unfortunate that the best of Eusapia's early phenomena occurred in the dark or in dim light. Of course, had no good phenomena ever been observed in decent light under good conditions, it would be easy to dismiss that fact as totally suspicious. But considering the success of later investigations, we must seriously entertain the possibility that for a medium of Eusapia's calibre – well below that of Home – darkness may really have been an aid to the production of genuine phenomena. In fact, recalling that Home often found the 'power' strongest beneath the table, we might even find a clue here to the conditions conducive to genuine physical manifestations.[9]

The above considerations raise a crucial methodological question concerning the study of physical mediums – namely: to what extent should experimenters comply with the medium's wishes regarding séance conditions? The obvious danger of insisting on rigid laboratory conditions, no matter how they conflict with the medium's preferred mode of operation, is that the phenomena may simply be snuffed out. On the other hand, the obvious danger of letting the medium dictate conditions is that the opportunities for fraud increase. The common wisdom, however, seems to be that the latter danger is the more serious of the two. After all, this is one reason – possibly the main reason – few today even bother to investigate mediums or non-spiritualistic PK 'superstars'.

I wonder, however, just how great this second danger is, especially when dealing with virtuosi the calibre of Home and Palladino. It seems to me that experimental ingenuity, under the circumstances, consists largely in yielding to the medium's idiosyncracies as much as necessary, while still maintaining sufficient control. Experimenters will thereby optimize the production of good phenomena, while keeping the evidence 'clean'. In fact, the success and importance of the 1908 Naples sittings with Palladino are due largely to their having struck such an ideal balance. Another virtue of this approach is that no other will yield a deep understanding of the dynamics of mediumship. Just as it would be counter-productive to study flirtatiousness or diplomatic skills in anything but the kind of setting in which the skills are actually manifested, it would seem counter-productive to force a medium to depart radically from standard operating procedures.

These days, for example, some alleged metal-benders often like to handle the objects. This makes control of the situation difficult, but not impossible, given additional obvious precautions such as a body search or change of clothes, and adequate recording techniques (e.g. continuous close-up filming). Similarly, if a 'psychic photographer' likes to handle the camera (and possibly work with it unobserved), the experimenter may introduce various controls compatible with the subject's wishes (e.g., sealing the camera and lens in some manner impossible to reseal without detection).

In the cases of Home and Palladino, however, the problem of submitting to the medium's idiosyncracies is far less serious, given the magnitude of the best phenomena and the impossibility of producing them by sleight-of-hand or easily concealable devices. For this reason I see no real problem in the fact that experimenters often yielded to Eusapia's preference for dim lights and a cabinet. Lodge made a very sensitive observation on this issue. He urged sitters to

> have the common sense to treat [Eusapia], not as a scientific
> person engaged in a demonstration, but as a delicate piece
> of apparatus wherewith they themselves are making an
> investigation. She is an instrument whose ways and
> idiosyncracies must be learnt, and to a certain extent
> humoured, just as one studies and humours the ways of some
> much less delicate piece of physical apparatus turned out by
> a skilled instrument-maker. (Lodge, 1894, p. 324)

b. *Catalogue of phenomena*

Eusapia's repertoire of phenomena is less varied and exciting than Home's. Still, it is quite extensive, and makes the productions of present-day 'superstars' such as Kulagina (Keil, *et al.*, 1976) seem like trifles. The major items are as follows:

(1) Rappings, on the séance table and other objects in the room.

(2) Table and object levitations and movements.

(3) Knots tied and untied in material either at a distance from or simply untouched by Eusapia, and sometimes in the rope or material used to restrain and bind her.

(4) Touches, pulls, pushes, hugs, and other tactile phenomena seemingly produced by hands and arms, but at a distance from Eusapia, or while her body is held by investigators.

(5) Billowing of clothing (usually Eusapia's skirt) and curtains.

(6) The production of scents.

(7) Cold breezes, in one instance (Naples, 1908) appearing to emanate from a scar on Eusapia's forehead.

117

(8) Lights or other luminous phenomena.

(9) Partial materializations, sometimes of hands felt through the cabinet's curtain, and other times of objects visibly or tactually resembling hands or feet (or stalks), either protruding or issuing from the cabinet, or appearing outside it. Sometimes rigid rods or thin thread-like protrusions (pseudopods) seemed to emanate from parts of Eusapia's body. Ochorowicz called them 'rigid rays'.

(10) Levitation of the medium.

(11) Writing on untouched objects, or writing without pen or pencil.

(12) Notes sounding on untouched musical instruments.

The best evidence for Eusapia's phenomena undoubtedly comes from the 1908 Naples sessions. But to appreciate what makes the sittings so persuasive, we must first consider the complex series of events leading up to them. The story begins with Richet's séances on the Ile Roubaud (see Lodge, 1894).

c. *Ile Roubaud*

Richet's house on the Ile Roubaud was the island's only dwelling. So when Oliver Lodge and F. W. H. Myers (members of the S.P.R.) joined Richet there on July 21, 1894, they looked forward to a tranquil atmosphere in which to study Eusapia's abilities. Furthermore, given their isolation, they could be certain that Eusapia had brought no accomplice with her to the island.

Séances were held in the evening, in a sitting-room on the ground floor. In most cases the door to the room was locked during the séance, and the shutters of the windows were fastened but partially opened. These precautions insured that no one could enter or leave the room unseen when the light was dim. A note-taker – either Richet's secretary, M. Bellier, or Ochorowicz – sat outside one of the two windows, and wrote down whatever the investigators called out to him. Eusapia and the sitters would assemble around a table, and although séances usually began under lamp light, later the light would be extinguished, leaving the room illuminated only by the moon and light from the note-taker's lamp outside the window.

Richet and company were treated to various of Eusapia's standard manifestations, including table levitations and assorted object movements, materialized hands, touches, and sounds played on musical instruments. Although the light was often dim, the room was not completely dark, and controls seem to have been good – certainly good enough to insure that Eusapia could not have produced many phenomena with a free hand or foot, or a concealed device (as Hodgson was later to insist).

Consider the following excerpts from the published account of the four July sittings:

First Sitting, July 21st, 1894

12.35 – Sittings at the small table were now resumed, with a change of positions. The table was moved considerably further from the window and

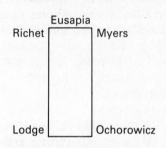

the positions were as shewn. The shutter was more widely opened so as to admit light from the bright moon outside. The candle from the recorder also gave some little light, but the lamp inside the room was not lighted. R. held both arms and one hand of E., while M. held both feet and her other hand. R. then felt a hand move over his head and rest on his mouth for some seconds, during which he spoke to us with his voice muffled. The round table now approached, R.'s head was stroked behind. R. held both E.'s knees, still retaining one hand while M. held the other, and the round table continued to approach in violent jerks.

12.49 – A small cigar box fell on to our table, and a sound was heard in the air as of something rattling. R. was holding head and right hand; M., holding left hand, raised it in the air holding it lightly by the tips of its fingers, but with part of his own hand free. A saucer containing small shot (from another part of the room), was then put into the hand of M. in the air. A covered wire of the electric battery came on to the table and wrapped itself round R.'s and E.'s heads, and was pulled till E. called out. Henceforth R. held her head and body, M. kept one hand and both feet, while L. held the other hand, and in this position E. made several spasmodic movements, each of which was accompanied or followed by violent movements of the neighbouring round table.

12.57 – The accordion which was on the round table got on to the floor somehow, and began to play single notes. Bellier counted 26 of them and then ceased counting. While the accordion played, E.'s fingers made movements in the hands of both M. and L. in accord with the notes as if she were playing them at a distance with difficulty. The lightly-touched quick notes were also thus felt by L. with singular precision. Sometimes the touch failed to elicit a response, and this failure was usually succeeded by an interval of silence and rest.

1.5 – E. being well held, M. heard a noise on the round table at his side, and turning to look saw a white object detach itself from the table and move slowly through the clear space between his own head and E.'s, visibly crossing the painted stripes of colour on the wall of the room. L. now saw the object coming past M.'s head and settling on the table. It was the lamp-shade coming white side first.

1.10 – The round table was moved further off and blows came upon it. L. was touched on the back, while R. saw both E.'s hands (which were still, as always, being held), and her body was also visible.

1.17 – The 'châlet,' [a music box] which was on the round table, now began to play, and then visibly approached, being seen by both M. and L. coming through the air, and settled on our table against M.'s chest. Shortly afterwards it moved away from M.'s chest on to the middle of our table and played there. Then it got on the floor between R. and E., and R. said 'enough of that music.' It stopped, probably because run down. M. was repeatedly and vigorously pushed on the back while L. was trying to see what was touching him [changing places with O. for the purpose]. L. could see M.'s back readily, but could not see anything upon it, though M. kept on calling out that he was being pushed, and that things which pushed like that must be visible. Soon afterwards the sitting was suspended and E. came out of the trance. During the latter half of the sitting, E. had taken one of M.'s fingers and drawn some scrawls with it outside R.'s flannel jacket, which was buttoned up to his neck. M. said: 'She is using me to write on you,' and it was thought no more of. But after the séance, when undressing, R. found on his shirt front, underneath both flannel jacket and high white waistcoat, a clear blue scrawl; and he came at once to bedrooms to shew it. (Lodge, 1894, p. 350–1)

Third Sitting, July 25th

The position of the three tables was altered so as to be more like what is here shewn; the second position of sitters being also represented (the first position was the same, except that R. and L. were interchanged): —

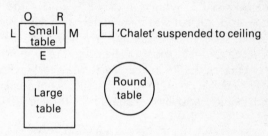

L. has suspended the 'châlet,' with its lowest point 5 feet from the floor, to a hook in the centre of the ceiling, by a bit of string, to see what would happen to it under these circumstances, and he had made sure that it was completely run down, so that it could not play till wound up. It hung at a distance distinctly beyond Eusapia's normal reach: at least two feet beyond. Lodge had entirely arranged the room as he wished, and kept special guard over it to see that no one entered or tampered with anything; locking the door immediately after the sitters were admitted. . . .

. . . The large table behind the medium now moved along the floor, while medium was under complete control; her hands, feet, and knees being held. Then an electric bell-push, which L. had arranged on round table, just within normal reach, was touched so as to ring the bell. The square table was violently dragged about, and loud bangs occurred on it. Then Richet and Lodge interchanged places [so as now to correspond with the above diagram], and several times during the next hour Lodge was touched, grasped, and pinched, while he distinctly held both Eusapia's hands and feet. . . . Also, while Lodge held both hands and feet, the large table was several times violently moved, and other clear movements of smaller objects occurred. . . .

While Lodge held *both* the medium's hands on the table, and also her head leaning over on to him away from the châlet, (see figure above), and while Richet held both her feet, the suspended châlet was heard to be wound partially up 3 times, with brief pauses, taking four seconds in all, as heard and recorded by Bellier. It did not now begin to play, but began to flap, as if its doors were trying to open. Soon it began to play and raps were heard on it. While it played Eusapia's hands waved L.'s hands in the air in time with the music. It soon stopped, but was immediately re-wound and went on playing some time. While this was going on, the châlet began to swing and the string was heard to break, but instead of dropping on the floor, the châlet was gently placed on M.'s head and thence on to the table. [This phenomenon occurred under quite satisfactory conditions.] (Lodge, 1894, p. 353–4)

Fourth Sitting, July 26th

. . . Ochorowicz took notes outside the window, Bellier having left the island; and the observers were Richet, Myers, and Lodge. The room was again arranged and guarded by Lodge, who again locked the door when the other two observers had entered with Eusapia. The first incident of note was some extremely loud and dangerous-sounding bangs on the square table and on the small table at which they sat. These bangs were louder than could be made with hand blows [and were sufficient to cause alarm for the safety of the hands among which they sometimes occurred].

L. and M. distinctly and simultaneously saw a small bright light rapidly moving in front of them above the table, like a spark or a firefly. The small table rose high into the air in fair light, and remained there barely touched by E. on the top, while eleven was counted.

An arm chair in the window, four feet of clear space intervening between it and the back of Eusapia, now began to move. It was very visible to Lodge and to all; the shutters being open and sky-light glinting on the back of the chair. It was seen to approach and otherwise move a few inches several

times, it also made intelligent visible tilts in reply to
questions. Eusapia was well held, and all conditions perfect.
No one was near the chair. . . .

Noise as of key being fumbled in the door, and Ochorowicz
from outside asked who was unlocking the door. Eusapia's
hands were well held and no one was near the door. The clear
space of several feet near door was plainly enough visible.
Blows occurred on the door. The key then arrived on the
table, [and was felt there by L.]. It disappeared again, and
was heard to be replacing itself in the door with a sound as of
the door being locked (or unlocked); then the key came
again on to the table into Richet's hand and stayed there. (At
the beginning of the séance the door had been locked, and
at the end it was still locked; judging by the sound, it had
probably been unlocked and locked again during this
episode. The door certainly remained shut all the time.) Richet
saw an indistinct black square-looking object which seemed
to prolong the key when it was brought towards his head.

There was light enough to see the position of everybody's
normal hands all the time on this occasion, and we were
sitting some four or five feet distant from the door. [It was a
perfectly distinct phenomenon.]. . .

M. was seized from behind while standing, and vigorously
pulled and shaken about; while all four were standing holding
hands round the table. . . . A loaf and other objects from the
buffet hard by arrived on the table, and a pile of five plates.
Our small table was in front of the buffet. . . .

Medium now conducted the standing group to near the
writing desk in the corner, and made three little movements
with her held hand. They seemed to take effect and tilt the
desk backwards, after a very short but appreciable interval.
Then she moved further away and repeated the action; the
same movement of the bureau occurred, but with more delay.
Then once more, this time two metres from the desk; and the
interval elapsing before the response was now greater,
perhaps as much as two seconds. (Lodge, 1894, pp. 355–7)

Although the sessions at the Ile Roubaud are eclipsed in most
respects by the 1908 Naples sittings, they must be treated as
substantial pieces of evidence. Myers and Lodge were so

impressed that they urged the Sidgwicks to come and observe Eusapia's phenomena for themselves. The two S.P.R. colleagues agreed, but as veterans of many séances with fraudulent mediums, they were less than enthusiastic. Eusapia already had a reputation for dishonesty, and the Sidgwicks, who had been rather vocal in their opposition to investigating mediums detected in fraud, were eager to protect the Society's reputation. Moreover, like many leading members of the S.P.R., they simply had a distaste for and distrust of physical phenomena.

The Sidgwicks participated in eight sittings, and although the conditions of light were generally less satisfactory than in the earlier series, phenomena occurred which at the time they regarded as genuine. In most cases, Mrs Sidgwick controlled Eusapia's left hand, while Prof. Sidgwick held her right hand. Ochorowicz lay beneath the table holding Eusapia's feet. Despite these controls, the Sidgwicks felt touches and pushes, and saw object movements they could not account for. Also, a piano behind Eusapia and apparently beyond her reach sounded notes. Mrs Sidgwick wrote in her unpublished notes (now in the S.P.R. archives),

> The final sounding of notes occurred at the end of séance and when the light had been partially turned up so that the keyboard of piano could be seen. R. had both E.'s hands – her arms stretched across the table to him. I had my left foot without shoe on her right foot and my right foot more or less in contact with her left foot, but the foot moved a good deal and I could not answer for contact all the time. If E. did the piano at all it must have been with her *right* foot and it would almost certainly have been seen. (Gauld, 1968, p. 231)

At the last sitting, on September 4, Mrs Sidgwick witnessed a melon and small wicker table move from behind Eusapia to the sitters' table. Visibility was apparently adequate. Mrs Sidgwick said 'it was never completely dark, and sometimes the light was very fair' (Gauld, 1968, p. 231). Later, at a meeting of the S.P.R., she said,

> As far as they go, my experiences with Eusapia Paladino entirely confirm Professor Lodge, though they did not go so far – for the phenomena I witnessed were never, I think, such

124

as could not have been produced by normal means had her hands alone been free, whereas for some of his experiences it seems necessary to assume her body also free. Still, my experiences were the most impressive of the kind I have ever had, though I have sat with a good many mediums.

Although the evidence, so far as my own experiences go, entirely depends on whether her hands were efficiently held, yet, if they were so held, I see no means of avoiding the supposition that a supernormal agency was at work. . . . [T]he phenomena which impressed me most could not have been produced by means of her mouth or her feet; for instance, a grasp resembling that of a hand on the head cannot be produced by a foot, nor can a billiard ball or a large heavy melon without a stalk be conveyed from the table behind the medium to the table in front by her teeth. . . . [D]uring the most important parts of the séances. . . , the feet were almost always held by the hands of one or other of the investigators who placed himself under the table.

. . . I felt sure that I held the hand for which I was responsible, that it was Eusapia's hand, that it had the texture of her skin, that it was continuous with her arm and sleeve, and that it was her left hand, as could be verified by the position of the thumb. (Lodge, 1894, pp. 339–40)

Hodgson (1895) quickly attacked the conclusions of his S.P.R. colleagues. He maintained that the phenomena could all have been produced by a free limb, or by devices like concealed straps and hooks (for table levitations) and concealed rods and dummy hands (for touches and object movements). Myers, Lodge, and Ochorowicz each wrote a reply (appended to Hodgson, 1895). Myers observed that he was a veteran of nearly 400 séances before the S.P.R. was even founded, and knew how to control a hand. All the investigators, he noted, knew the means by which mediums might try to free a hand, and were careful to hold each of Eusapia's hands across the palms and fingers (and sometimes thumbs), so that there was no room for another sitter to hold the hand as well. Myers added, wryly, that he could hardly have mistaken Lodge's 'massive, steady, round-nailed hand' for Eusapia's 'small, perspiring, quivering, sharp-nailed' hand, or to mistake a stuffed glove for 'that very living extremity which fingered the palm of my own hand, or spasmodically squeezed it, for so many hours' (Hodgson, 1895, p. 58). As to the possibility of dummy feet, Myers quipped,

> whereas in the notes of the first séance I am described as wearing soft slippers, in the later séances . . . I discarded even these, and exercised, with the intervention only of silk socks, the faculties which I inherit from a prehensile and quadrumanous ancestry. I feel as sure about the feet guaranteed by me as about the hands – even supposing that, if not held, a foot could manage to press one between the shoulders or on the head with a sensation as of five large separate fingers, and wind up with a series of smart and sounding slaps on the back. [Myers adds in a footnote that during most of the second series of séances each foot was held separately by the hand of an observer under the table.]
> (Hodgson, 1895, pp. 58–9)

The tone of Myers's reply betrays a certain annoyance with Hodgson. And no wonder. Hodgson's criticisms were exasperatingly superficial and inadequate. Concerning the episode of the key in the first series' fourth sitting, he suggested that Eusapia could have managed it all 'quite easily' with a free foot (Hodgson, 1895, p. 53). But Hodgson never tells us the *precise* means by which the phenomena could have been produced. One frequently encounters such lacunae in skeptical responses to reports of good phenomena, even today. The reason, I suspect, is that, despite his conviction that the phenomena must be fraudulent, the skeptic simply has no idea how to produce the phenomena normally under the conditions in which they actually occurred. In the fourth sitting, the light was good enough for the proposed movement of the foot to have been seen. And besides, Eusapia could not have moved the key more than four feet away from her position at the table without the rest of her body leaving the chair.

Concerning the subsequent episode with the writing desk, Hodgson proposed that Eusapia might have 'fixed' the desk with threads or cords, either before or during the sitting. This suggestion strikes me as preposterous and desperate. First of all, Hodgson never explained *exactly how* Eusapia might have prepared the desk to tilt backwards when she waved her hands, nor why there should have been an appreciable interval between the wave and the object movement, much less an interval that noticeably increased as Eusapia moved away from the desk. He merely mentions how his skeptical S.P.R. colleague Davey moved pieces of chalk with thread. Hodgson never explained, however, why a procedure for surreptitiously moving chalk with thread could be deployed to move a massive piece of furniture *backwards*. Two issues must be addressed here: (1) the *weight* of the object allegedly moved, and (2) the *direction* of the object's movement. A piece of chalk might be moved by a cord or thread attached on one end directly to the chalk and on the other to the conjuror. Suppose, then, that Eusapia had managed to attach a cord directly between her hand or arm and the desk. Clearly, that would not explain how she could have made the desk tilt backwards. Any object connected merely between Eusapia and the desk, yet rigid and strong enough to tilt the desk backwards, would presumably have been visible or otherwise detectable to the sitters, especially to those holding Eusapia's hands. A cord might have been sufficient to *pull* the desk *towards* Eusapia. But neither a cord nor a thread could have directly tilted it backwards. Perhaps, then, Eusapia had planted a pulley of some sort in the room, by means of which a wave of the hand could have tilted the desk backwards. This suggestion likewise has little plausibility. Since the room and its contents had been arranged, guarded, and locked by Lodge, the suggestion that Eusapia had prepared the trick and planted the apparatus beforehand seems unlikely. And no device, such as a pulley or a supply of sufficiently strong cords, was discovered later, or (for that matter) in any other successful sitting with Eusapia in which large objects moved (including sittings where the movements occurred in bright light).

In any case, as far as Hodgson and some others were concerned, it was still an open question whether Eusapia ever produced genuine phenomena. So in July of 1895, the medium was invited to Myers's house in Cambridge for further testing. The whole affair seems to have been a fiasco (for a critical summary, see Gauld, 1968 and Inglis, 1977; also, Nicol, 1972, pp. 360–2, for comments). Despite some good phenomena early in her visit (before Hodgson's arrival), and despite the precaution of having Mrs Myers help Eusapia undress and then check her clothing for concealed devices (none were discovered), the Sidgwicks and Hodgson maintained that all Eusapia's phenomena in Cambridge had been due to trickery (see H. Sidgwick, 1895, 1896; S.P.R., 1895). Therefore, they claimed, no justification remained for regarding any of her phenomena as genuine. (See also Richet, 1895.)

Consequently, the S.P.R. dismissed Eusapia Palladino as if she were merely another fraud, unworthy of further investigation. But Richet and other researchers on the Continent refused to accept the Society's blanket condemnation, and continued to report good results from their sessions with Eusapia. They were convinced that she had been unhappy at Cambridge, and that she disliked not only her hosts, but also the English climate and food. Moreover, they objected to Hodgson's intentional relaxation of controls (and hasty inferences therefrom), as well as his insensitivity to and ignorance of Eusapia's usual modes of operation. The modern skeptic Dingwall also claimed that the atmosphere in Cambridge could not have been conducive to good phenomena, and that Eusapia and her hosts were almost certainly not comfortable with one another (Dingwall, 1962b, pp. 189ff.). He writes,

> it was inevitable that [Eusapia's] hosts and their intimates must have felt an antipathy towards her, however veiled it might have been by an icy politeness and attempts at friendliness. . . .
>
> According to Mr Myers and Mrs Sidgwick, Eusapia seemed quite happy and at ease at Cambridge, although it seems to me that such is so unlikely to have been the case that any assertion to the contrary should be regarded with some suspicion. (p. 190)

Eventually, the S.P.R. felt bound to respond to the pressure from abroad. They proposed, however, that Eusapia should be tested by persons especially well-trained in the ways of fraudulent mediums, rather than well-meaning but possibly gullible scientists. So the Society dispatched three confirmed skeptics to Naples in 1908. Apparently, everyone concerned – including the investigators – expected to find nothing but fraud. The S.P.R.'s 'Fraud Squad' (as Inglis called it) consisted of the Hon. Everard Feilding, Hereward Carrington, and W. W. Baggally. Feilding claimed to be a complete skeptic, and had already detected numerous frauds. Carrington, an amateur conjuror, had just published *The Physical Phenomena of Spiritualism* (Carrington, 1907) the year before, three-fourths of which was devoted to an analysis of fraudulent mediumship. And Baggally was a skilled conjuror, who 'claimed to have investigated almost every medium in Britain since Home without finding one who was genuine' (Inglis, 1977, p. 426). Dingwall knew the trio well. Considering his skepticism regarding physical phenomena, and the outcome of the 1908 sittings, his description is particularly interesting.

I was intimately acquainted with all three investigators. Mr Carrington was one of the keenest investigators in the United States. He had unrivalled opportunities to examine the host of frauds and fakers who flourished there, and his results had led him to suppose that of the alleged physical phenomena the vast bulk was certainly produced by fraudulent means and devices, as he himself asserts in his book. . . . Mr Feilding was also a man of vast experience and one of the keenest and most acute critics that this country has ever produced. He possessed a unique charm, and his sense of humour invariably saved him from the excesses into which others fell when they had become convinced. He was totally unmoved by that peculiar form of moral uplift and infallibility which characterized certain senior members of the Society, and it is noteworthy that he never occupied the Presidential Chair. He would go anywhere and see anything, treating everyone alike from the most humble workman to the dukes and duchesses among whom he moved. Moreover, his scepticism was extreme, although it was modified by an attitude of open-mindedness and an unwillingness to accept critical comments when these were unaccompanied by properly adduced evidence. Mr Baggally almost equalled Mr Feilding in his scepticism and desire for investigation. He knew more about trick methods than his illustrious colleague and thus he was better able to concentrate upon essentials. For over thirty years he had attended séances, but had come to the conclusion that rarely if ever had he encountered one genuine physical medium. (Dingwall, 1962b, pp. 201–2)

d. The 1908 Naples sittings

Feilding and Carrington arrived in Naples in November. They were joined later by Baggally, by which time four séances had already been conducted. Baggally's late arrival is somewhat fortunate, from the reader's point of view. The report of the eleven sittings with Eusapia is valuable, not only as a document about physical mediumship, but also as a fascinating record of a major psychological odyssey. The investigators' notes made after each séance reveal the steps by which they were gradually and grudgingly converted to a belief in the reality of PK. By the time Baggally arrived, Feilding and Carrington had already been shaken deeply by their experiences with Eusapia, and were disturbed that they could find no plausible normal explanation for her phenomena. Baggally's appearance at the fifth séance marked the beginning of a similar process for him. Indeed, his comments after each of the final seven séances chronicles an evolution in his attitudes and beliefs strikingly like that already described by Feilding and Carrington. As a result, the reader has the opportunity to study, not only a third and delayed version of the psychological drama begun earlier, but also the reactions to it of Feilding and Carrington. The description of Baggally's conversion, then, as well as the response to it of his predecessors, helps clarify the psychodynamics of a profound conceptual change. No doubt many will find this aspect of the report at least as interesting as the account of Eusapia's phenomena.

Feilding and Carrington took three adjoining rooms on the fifth floor of the Hotel Victoria. Séances were held in the middle (Feilding's) room (see Fig. 5), illuminated by a group of electric lights hanging from the ceiling, whose intensity could be varied among four pre-set positions. Eusapia supplied the curtain and small table for her 'cabinet'. These were carefully inspected by Feilding and Carrington and 'concealed no mystery' (Feilding. 1963, p. 31; Feilding, Baggally, and Carrington, p. 321). [*N.b.* Hereafter, I shall only give page references for both sources, in the same order.] The objects placed inside the cabinet were procured by the investigators. Anticipating the objection that they made too many concessions regarding séance conditions, Feilding observed that

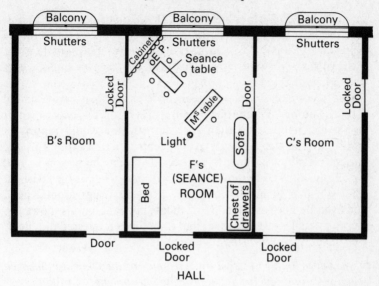

Fig. 5

our time in Naples was limited, and . . . after due
consideration we preferred to adopt conditions to which the
medium was used and in which therefore it was probable that
effects would be produced, rather than impose others which
might possibly impede the production of what we had gone to
study. . . .

Rightly or wrongly, we believed, and still believe, that the
simplest plan would be to allow matters to take their
accustomed course, while adopting every precaution that
occurred to us as necessary to the end we had in view. We
felt that if, in a reasonable number of experiments, persons
specially versed in conjuring tricks and already forewarned
concerning, and familiar with, the particular tricks to be
expected, were unable to discover them, it would not be
presumptuous to claim as a probable consequence that some
other agency must be involved. (pp. 32–3; pp. 322–3)

Before each séance, the room would be examined and the
cabinet prepared. Then one experimenter would go downstairs
and escort Eusapia up to the room alone. The room would then
be locked, and Eusapia would straightaway go to her place at the

séance table. The experimenters would take positions next to her, and the stenographer, Mr Albert Meeson (an employee of the American Express Co., and a stranger to Eusapia), would go to his own table to write down whatever the experimenters called out to him.

The record of the eleven séances is as cinematic as a verbal report can be. When phenomena occurred, an experimenter would call it out, and then each investigator would report his control at that time. The degree of control permitted by Eusapia varied, usually according to her mood. When she was in a good mood, she allowed her investigators to control her as they wished. They could hold her entire hand, wrap their legs around hers, and even tie her hands and feet. In less buoyant moods, however, Eusapia was less cooperative, and sometimes requested dim light. But to the surprise of the investigators,

> *We never found . . . that the adequacy of the control influenced unfavourably the production of the phenomena.* On the contrary, it was on the nights when she was in the best humour, and consequently when our precautions were most complete and the light the strongest, that the phenomena were the most numerous. . . . [When Eusapia was in bad health or bad humour] the phenomena . . . were rarer and of small account, *and we did not find that the reduction of light, and the consequent increased facility for fraud had any effect in stimulating them.* (pp. 33–4; pp. 323–4)
>
> . . . [On good nights] she never objected to our moving our free hands about as we wished, placing them on her knees, head or shoulders, or feeling about behind her, or passing them up and down the whole length of her arms and legs.
>
> On certain occasions. . . , she permitted us, and on others, invited us, to tie her hands to our own and to one another, and her feet to her chair or to ours. But as already stated, the occurrence of the phenomena appeared to depend entirely upon her own condition, to the 'psychic trim' in which she happened to be, and not at all upon the severity or laxity of the control or the degree of light permitted at the time, or upon the closeness of our attention. (p. 37; p. 327)

Despite the rigid controls and bright light, numerous good phenomena occurred. In fact, the table levitated completely so

many times that the experimenters eventually tired of the phenomenon and urged Eusapia to produce something else. While the
observers virtually draped themselves all over Eusapia, objects
moved about, a guitar in the cabinet behind Eusapia was
strummed, a table 'walked' from the cabinet into the room, hands
and other objects appeared in and out of the cabinet, and the
experimenters experienced various touches and other tactile
phenomena. Eusapia's behavior and performance, then, was not
at all what Hodgson, the Sidgwicks, and even the Fraud Squad,
had expected. In fact, not only did the best phenomena occur
under the best conditions, and not only did Eusapia not insist on
conditions conducive to trickery, she often behaved so as to make
conjuring *easier* to detect. Baggally observed,

> . . . I have made a study of [conjuring] from my boyhood.
> Just before the occurrence of a manifestation Eusapia often
> observed that it was about to take place, and she frequently
> described the nature of the anticipated phenomenon, and
> asked the sitters to be sure that they had, at the same time,
> proper control of her hands and feet. This procedure on her
> part is contrary to one of the fundamental rules of the
> conjuring art, which enjoins that the attention of the
> audience should not be directed to (nor their vigilance
> increased at) the actual moment that the necessary steps for
> the production of a trick are being carried out. (p. 170;
> p. 460)

Furthermore, Feilding recognized that on those occasions when
Eusapia was in a bad mood, 'the conditions were precisely those
that seem to have chiefly prevailed at the Cambridge sittings' (p.
36; p. 326). Light was dim, and Eusapia's hands moved restlessly
on top of those of her controllers. Apparently (and plausibly), the
overall success of the Naples sittings was due, in large measure, to
the rapport established between Eusapia and her investigators.
Feilding and his colleagues were more approachable as human
beings than the Cambridge investigators. And although the Naples
trio was flexible in its concessions to Eusapia's preferences for
séance conditions, they never insulted her as Hodgson had, by
playing the fool and encouraging her to cheat. In fact, the Naples
investigators did not commit certain errors of which the majority
of their Cambridge colleagues seem to have been guilty. Not only

were they not condescending toward Eusapia, but they did not underestimate her practical intelligence and discernment. Eusapia may have been uneducated and unsophisticated; but she was neither stupid nor imperceptive.

It is difficult to convey the flavor of the sittings by excerpting the blow-by-blow report. The minuteness of detail – valuable though it may be as evidence – robs the account of dramatic continuity. But for the benefit of the curious reader (who may in any case find the text difficult to obtain), I present the following short passage from the report of the ninth séance, held on December 13, 1908.

Medium's feet tied to rungs of chairs of controllers on each side of her, length of rope on left being 20 ins., on right 21½ ins. Hands tied to one another – distance apart 22 ins., also left hand tied to B.'s right, distance being 16½ ins.; medium's right hand tied to C.'s left, distance 18 ins.

10.12 p.m. Séance begins.
Light I [brightest light].

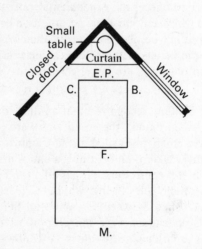

Tilts begin almost immediately.
F. Table tilts on the legs away from her.
10.13 p.m. Complete levitation of the table.
    C. Her right hand resting on the table touching mine, my wrist

being between hers and the edge of the table. Her right foot in contact with my right foot. I saw a clear space of about eight inches between her dress and the leg of the table.

B. Complete levitation of the table for a second time [during dictation of B.'s control. Dec. 14/08].

B. My right hand on both her knees. Her left foot touching my right foot.

10.14 p.m. Complete levitation for a third time.

B. Another complete levitation.

F. Both medium's hands completely on the top of the table touching C.'s and B.'s.

C. I can see a clear space of about 8 inches between her dress and the table leg all the way down.

B. My right hand on her two knees. My right foot against her left foot, and I can see between her left leg and the table leg.

10.16 p.m. Another complete levitation.

F. Her right hand off the table altogether, left hand on B's, pulling it upward and the table appeared to stick to it.

10.17 p.m. Another complete levitation of the table.

F. First of all a partial levitation, which lasted about ten seconds, then a complete levitation, off all four legs.

F. Her right hand touching the table, left hand on B.'s – She raised her right hand from the table and the table slid sideways in the air under B.'s hand.

B. My right hand across both her knees. My right knee against her left knee and my right foot against her left foot, and I see a clear space between her leg and the table leg.

C. Her right hand clenched (at first) on the table within three inches of my eyes. My left hand across both her knees. Her right foot on my left foot. I can clearly see a space of at least six inches between her dress and the table leg, all the way down.

[*The light was sufficient to read small print by with comfort, at the further end of the room, the hands were always plainly visible and always situated so that it was clear that the table was not lifted by them. The extreme rapidity of the levitations made complete descriptions almost impossible, and it was decided to confine the description of the control to the feet, the control of the hands being obvious to all and description rendered unnecessary . . . F., Dec. 14/08]* (pp. 217–19; pp. 507–9)

For present purposes, I believe that the comments made by the investigators *after* the sittings are at least as valuable as the running account of the phenomena and controls. The following lengthy remarks by Feilding are particularly noteworthy, but not simply for what they reveal about the phenomena and the conditions under which they occurred. They also stand as a monument to Feilding's intellectual integrity, and afford a candid glimpse into the profound psychological conflict he was experiencing.

It is singular that the impression made upon our minds by any particular séance seems to vary inversely with the effectiveness of the shorthand notes. Certain it is that the report of the sixth séance, which we went through last night, while doubtless accurately recording what took place, gives a most inadequate account of the emotional effect of it all. We were all three completely bowled over. Eusapia had arrived very late owing to the non-arrival of her cab. When she did come she was in a very talkative mood, and buttonholed me at every landing of the five flights of stairs to our rooms to give a fresh instalment in Neapolitan dialect (I do not understand Neapolitan dialect) of a burglary which she had once endured. Our journey upstairs occupied 25 minutes; but it was not enough for the dimensions of her story, which continued long after we sat down at the table. Every device failed to distract her, and it was very late before the first symptoms of the oncoming mediumistic condition, stertorous yawns and amazing hiccoughs, gladdened our eyes and ears. Silence at last prevailed: but nothing happened. We waited patiently. The table occasionally tilted feebly; sparse raps, or rather bangs, were heard on the table; – nothing else. 'The phenomena lag much,' said Eusapia. We were almost disposed to abandon the attempt for the night, when suddenly things began.

I shall not, in this note, go through the séance in detail, but wish to record the fact that it has certainly had a very profound effect on our mental attitude. My own frame of mind, when starting on this investigation, was that, in view of the concurrent opinion of practically all the eminent men of science who have investigated Eusapia's phenomena, it

was inconceivable that they could, in turn, have been deceived
by the few petty tricks that have, from time to time, been
detected, and that it was therefore probable that the
phenomena were real. At the same time I could not believe
in them. All my own experiments in physical mediumship had
resulted in the discovery of the most childish frauds. Failure
had followed upon failure. While, therefore, I tended to accept
the general hypothesis that the facts of so-called spiritualistic
physical manifestations must, on the evidence, be regarded as
probably existent, my mental habit had become so
profoundly sceptical, when it came to considering any given
alleged instance of them, that I had ceased to have any
expectation of finding it able to bear examination. The first
séance with Eusapia, accordingly, provoked chiefly a feeling of
surprise; the second, of irritation – irritation at finding oneself
confronted with a foolish but apparently insoluble problem. The
third séance, at which a trumpery trick was detected, came as
a sort of relief. At the fourth, where the control of the
medium was withdrawn from ourselves [due to the presence
of 'guest' sitters – S.B.], my baffled intelligence sought to
evade the responsibility of meeting facts by harbouring
grotesque doubts as to the competency of the eminent
professors, who took our places, to observe things properly;
while at the fifth, where this course was no longer possible,
as I was constantly controlling the medium myself, the mental
gymnastics involved in seriously facing the necessity of
concluding in favour of what was manifestly absurd, produced
a kind of intellectual fatigue.

After the sixth, for the first time I find that my mind, from
which the stream of events had hitherto run off like rain from
a macintosh, is at last beginning to be capable of absorbing
them. For the first time I have the absolute conviction that
our observation is not mistaken. I realise, as an appreciable
fact in life, that from an empty cabinet I have seen hands
and heads come forth, that from behind the curtain of that
empty cabinet I have been seized by living fingers, the
existence and position of the very nails of which could be felt.
I have seen this extraordinary woman sitting visible outside
the curtain, held hand and foot by my colleagues, immobile,
except for the occasional straining of a limb, while some

entity within the curtain has over and over again pressed my hand in a position clearly beyond her reach. . . .

Since writing the above I have read the notes of C. and B. The former has apparently submitted with the same completeness as myself to the evidence of facts. B., who is evidently passing through the same stages as I did in my earlier séances, toys with the suggestion of an apparatus, by way of easing his mind. It would be an interesting problem to set before a manufacturer of conjuring machines to devise an apparatus capable of producing alternatively a black flat profile face, a square face on a long neck, and a 'cello like face on a warty nobbly body two feet long; also, a white hand with moveable fingers having nails, capable of reaching high above the medium's head, or patting, pinching and pulling hair, and of so vigorously grasping B. by the coat as almost to upset him into the cabinet. Our manufacturer must so construct the apparatus that it can be actuated unseen by a somewhat stout and elderly lady clad in a tight plain gown, who sits outside the curtain held visibly by hand and foot, in such a way as to escape the observation of two practical conjurers clinging about her and on the look-out for its operation. It must further be of such dimensions as to be concealed about the lady while parading herself for inspection upon a chair, clad in her stays and a short flannel petticoat. (pp. 171–3; pp. 461–3)

Carrington's remarks after the sixth séance are also worth quoting.

That human hands – having all the peculiarities of hands, even to the presence of finger nails, should become visible and tangible during a séance – these hands not being Eusapia's nor any of the sitters' – this is so utterly at variance with common sense that one finds it next to impossible to believe it. And yet these hands are real, and by no possible means could they have been Eusapia's. During almost the whole time when the touches were taking place she was resting her head against mine, my right hand being around her shoulders, her body resting against my body. Her left hand, passive, was lying in my left hand, firmly grasped by me, while I frequently pressed the whole of her left arm against my body, lifted the hand to the light to make sure that it was really her hand, and traced its connection with her body. The hand was certainly hers, and could not possibly have been any dummy left in my care. I frequently verified that fact. This left hand rested the greater part of the time on Eusapia's left knee, and was at least two feet away from her right hand, which B. was firmly holding *upon* the table. At no time did she attempt even to approximate the hands, far less to effect any substitution. That was out of the question.

Both B. and I are absolutely certain that we continuously held one hand of the medium (which we constantly verified was hers), and during the actual moment of the touch, we frequently disregarded the phenomenon and turned our attention to the control of the hands. Her feet were meanwhile held securely by ours under the table. But there is no doubt whatever that the touches were made by a hand and not by a foot, nor by a non-living thing. I frequently felt the separate fingers and the thumb during the touch, and F. on one occasion distinctly felt the finger nails, which pressed into the upper side of his outstretched finger. Whatever may be the nature and origin of these hands, I am absolutely positive that they are not produced by her head, her feet or any part of her body. The theory of dummy hands, manipulated somehow by the medium during the trance state, is the only possible normal hypothesis, but I consider that also quite excluded for the following reasons:

(1) A careful search of the medium, after the séance, failed to reveal the presence of any such hands.

(2) The sensation of the touch was distinctly human, and quite unlike the sensation that would result from a touch by a dummy hand.

(3) Some part of the medium's body must be free in order to work such an apparatus. No part of her body, however, was free, and no suspicious movements of the kind necessary to manipulate such an instrument were ever perceived by us.

(4) It is almost impossible to conceive the elaborate apparatus that would be necessary to produce all the effects observed by us. . . .

At the conclusion of the sixth séance, we asked to medium if we might search her. She at once consented, and proceeded to take off her bodice and skirt, and hand them to us for examination. There was certainly no slit or other contrivance in the skirt or in the bodice, and we also examined her petticoats and other under garments, and felt over her body with our hands, through the remaining clothes. So far as we could discover, nothing was concealed about her person or her clothes. (pp. 166–8; pp. 456–68).

By the time the series of sittings was completed, Baggally felt compelled to admit,

Taking into consideration the manner of the control, that no mechanism was found on the medium's person, that no accomplice was present, and also that the three S.P.R. investigators were men who had been accustomed for years to the investigation of so-called physical phenomena of every variety, and who had detected fraud after fraud, I find it impossible to believe that Eusapia could have been able to practice trickery constantly during the many hours that the séances lasted and remain undetected. (pp. 268–9; pp. 448–9)

Baggally actually took the time to itemize and count all the phenomena reported during the sittings, and concluded, 'Eusapia was not detected in fraud in any one of the 470 phenomena that took place at the eleven séances' (p. 276; p. 566).

Contrary to their original expectations, all three investigators had come to believe that Eusapia's phenomena were genuine. The conversion had been painful. Feilding and his colleagues had reached their verdict 'with great intellectual reluctance, though without much personal doubt as to its justice' (p. 54; p. 344). In his final comments on the Naples sittings, Feilding made the following penetrating observation:

It has constantly, and in my opinion most absurdly, been said that no one is so easy to deceive as a man of science. I think it would be nearer the mark to say that if in fact there be such a thing as a supernormal physical force, no one is so easily converted to a belief in it as a conjuror. The *savant*, steeped in his experience of the normal forces of nature, is constitutionally averse from the conception of an apparently *bizarre* departure from them. Aware of his own lack of knowledge of the possibilities of *legerdemain*, he naturally prefers to suspect himself of having been the sport of some undiscovered form of deception rather than to remodel his philosophy. The conjuror, on the other hand, has the experience, not only of the possibilities, but also of the limitations of his own art, and having no particular philosophy beyond that of an ordinary layman regarding the forces of nature, has no special difficulty in remodeling it, if necessary, when confronted with a series of events which he knows his art is incapable of explaining. (pp. 277–8; pp. 567–8)

I am quite aware that the reader's response to the 1908 Naples report cannot be as profound as that of the investigators to the phenomena themselves. But we must concede, I think, that the report is a remarkable document of the reality of large-scale PK, and that it simply cannot be dismissed. The skeptical hypotheses surveyed in the previous chapter are totally inadequate as counter-explanations. It would be preposterous, I submit, to propose that Eusapia cheated throughout, or that the investigators did not observe what they claimed (by reason of biased misperception, outright malobservation, or collective hypnosis). And while this may be a viscerally unsatisfying road to a belief in PK, it seems to me that to an intellectually honest and open-minded person, no other option remains.

2.4 MISCELLANEOUS MEDIUMS

a. Introduction

Although I have chosen to focus on the cases of Home and Palladino, that is simply because those cases are unusually strong or well-documented, and because they display a great variety of phenomena observed under decent conditions. But other cases are also both instructive and capable of standing on their own. Indeed, familiarity with them is essential for a well-rounded picture of PK generally and mediumship in particular. But since physical mediumship is only one of the topics covered in this book, I cannot survey comprehensively all the other cases that warrant detailed examination. Still, a few remarks about some of the best cases will show that those of Home and Palladino are far from isolated (even if uncommonly good), and guide the reader wishing to examine the evidence in greater depth.

b. *Rudi Schneider (1909–1957)*

In the next section I shall backtrack historically to turn-of-the century material. But the case of Rudi Schneider is an appropriate place to begin this quick survey, for it occupies an intermediate position between old-fashioned and modern experiments in psychokinesis (for accounts of the latter, see Braude, 1979). Although ingenious mechanical devices had been used before to study the phenomena of mediumship, Rudi's case is the first in which state-of-the-art electrical equipment plays a central role. The phenomena studied by means of this equipment were much less dramatic than those of previous physical mediums. But because the experiments seem exceptionally clean methodologically, many regard them as especially important.

Rudi was born in Braunau, the youngest of nine children. His brothers Karl and Willy were also mediums, and it was Willy who first attracted the attention of scientists. In fact, Willy's case alone merits some attention, since experiments with him frequently produced good results (see, e.g., Dingwall, 1922, 1926a; Inglis, 1984; Schrenck Notzing, 1923a). Both Willy and Rudi produced their phenomena while in trance, ostensibly through the control of a discarnate personality. And although their repertoire of phenomena initially included materializations, the only phenomenon persisting to the end of their careers was the movement of remote objects. In fact, the Schneider brothers exhibited the eventual decline in mediumistic ability that characterized the careers of Eusapia and most other mediums.

On the whole, Rudi's career was probably more successful than that of his brother; but it was also more controversial. After years of successful work with various researchers, Rudi became involved in an apparently spurious scandal invented by parapsychologist Harry Price. The story of Price's behind-the-scenes machinations is fascinating, but too complex to be surveyed here (see Gregory, 1977, 1979, 1982, 1985; Gauld, 1978, 1979; and Inglis, 1984). But the scent of scandal seems to have passed by the very interesting results obtained in the experiments of Eugene Osty at the *Institut*

Métapsychique International in Paris (see Osty, 1933, and Osty and Osty, 1931/32; also, Besterman, 1932b), later replicated in England (Hope, *et al.*, 1933; also Hope, 1934).

Rudi (like Willy) produced his phenomena in darkness or in low light; and Osty devised an innovative technique for experimenting under those conditions. His method was to use a variant of the photoelectric cell to detect surreptitious movement of the medium. An infrared beam directed over the séance table guarded the object to be displaced (e.g., a handkerchief or flower). At first, Osty connected the infrared apparatus to four cameras, so that when the beam was interrupted, photos were taken. But although the cameras were triggered during the initial tests, the photos showed nothing unusual; Rudi had not been caught in the act of manually moving the test objects. Osty then replaced the cameras with a bell. If the medium escaped from the controller and tried normally to move the object, the beam would be intercepted and the alarm would ring.

It so happened that the bell did ring, even though the medium seemed to be entranced and controlled. In fact, sometimes the bell rang for intervals of between 30 to 100 seconds. During these extended periods of bell ringing, flashlight photos were taken; but once again they failed to reveal Rudi cheating. The photos showed him hunched over as usual, with his head sunk forward, his hands held, and his knees between those of the controllers. Nothing was photographed as being in the path of the infrared beam. And when the beam was illuminated to see more clearly what, if anything, triggered the alarm, the bell stopped, as if normal light inhibited the phenomena.

The experimenters were also interested to note that on many of the occasions when the alarm had been triggered, the test object had not been moved. So they decided to concentrate simply on the phenomenon of the interception of the infrared beam. In place of the bell they hooked up a galvanometer with a photographic recording drum designed to produce a continuous graph of the intensity and duration of the beam's deflection. To their surprise, they found that the interference was never as complete as it would have been had a solid object deflected the beam. Absorption of the beam ranged from 1 per cent to 75 per cent, with the majority between 5 per cent and 35 per cent. Moreover, some of the largest deflections occurred while the area occupied by the beam was illuminated in red light, visible to the sitters. (See Rayleigh, 1938, pp. 13ff. for a discussion of the flaws in skeptical counter-explanations of the results.)

Eventually, the experimenters decided they wanted finer-grained evidence of the nature of the deflections. So they replaced the galvanometer with a newer, faster-acting model. With this device, the experimenters observed that the infrared absorptions corresponded to Rudi's loud and rapid breathing. During trance, Rudi's rate and volume of respiration increased dramatically; and it turned out that each inhalation and exhalation corresponded to a deflection. The experimenters described the phenomenon in terms of the deflection of the beam by an 'invisible substance,' whose rate of vibration was double that of Rudi's respiration (e.g., at 5 vibrations per second, Rudi breathed 2.5 times). This result seemed to show that Rudi was not using a confederate; the absorptions were somehow produced by him, and were correlated with his breathing. Once the experimenters realized the correlation obtained, they arranged to record the movements of Rudi's chest and the infrared absorptions together on the same chart. The results verified their earlier observations.

It seemed clear that the number of absorptions/breaths varied in such a way as rule out the hypothesis that Rudi was producing them mechanically, and by stealth (see Rayleigh, 1938, pp. 14–15). Rayleigh also points out the implausibility of supposing that Rudi cunningly prepared a trick to produce the phenomena. For one thing, the correlations between absorptions and breaths was not discovered until the experiment was well under way, and only after Osty introduced the use of the fast-acting galvanometer, an instrument unfamiliar to most physicists of the time. It is highly unlikely that Rudi knew about it either, much less that he planned his performance in anticipation that the experimenters would eventually have recourse to that device.

c. Materializers

As the career of Rudi Schneider drew to a close, so did the golden age of physical phenomena. In fact, the history of physical mediumship exhibited a decline similar to that found in the individual careers of most mediums. In both cases, the variety and magnitude of phenomena diminished as time went on. But although that period may have ended with a whimper, its earlier stages were marked by a flurry of activity, as researchers examined a steady stream of apparently gifted European subjects. Perhaps none of these additional cases is as strong individually as those of Home and Palladino. But some are quite impressive nevertheless.

Undoubtedly, some consider certain of the cases particularly suspicious because the mediums specialized in producing material-izations. The problem is not simply that many find materialization even harder to swallow than 'mere' object movements, although that surely has something to do with it. A further difficulty is that those who produced full-form (or full-figure) materializations shunned light, claiming it inhibited or interfered with the phenomena. And the partial materializations produced under better illumination seemed equally suspicious, since they often took forms that looked like props or items that could be concealed on the medium's person. But as with the other skeptical positions examined in Chapter 1, the easy dismissal of materialization is abetted by an unfamiliarity with the source material, along with some general misconceptions about the evidence. Hence, before looking briefly at some of the principal materializers, we had better examine some background issues.

Many of the most interesting cases of physical mediumship concern phenomena apparently produced in darkness or in dim light. These ranged from the relatively modest productions of the Schneider brothers to the full-form materializations of Florence Cook and Eva C. In view of the fact that so many frauds were perpetrated under cover of darkness, a medium's preference for or reliance on darkness or low light naturally arouses suspicion. But just as Eusapia's preference for a cabinet seems to have been either an idiosyncrasy of her view of mediumship or a condition genuinely conducive to phenomena (perhaps given her idiosyn-cratic beliefs – recall Feilding's comments in section 3.d), the same may be true of a medium's preference for darkness. Besides, in many of these cases, phenomena were also produced under good light, or at least in light sufficient for visual control. But once we know that a medium is able to produce phenomena under decent conditions, preference for low light is not inherently suspicious. Naturally, researchers ought to be especially vigilant under low light, and should tighten conditions as much as possible in order to prevent cheating. But it would be a mistake to assume that a medium's preference for darkness can *only* be grounds for suspicion. Indeed, if we adopt that attitude, we might overlook vital clues concerning the nature of the phenomena.

Richet's remarks on the subject are worth quoting.

> many phenomena of telekinesis . . . do not take place in full light. Everything happens as though darkness were one of the necessary conditions for the manifestation of the power. This is not absurd; there are many physical phenomena that do not take place in the light, as there are others that do not take place in the dark. If a sceptic on photography were to object to the feeble red light by which plates are developed, the photographer could reply that light interferes with the development. So likewise the experimentalist has the right to reply that light interferes with telekinesis. (Richet, 1923/1975, p. 405)

Moreover, there is no reason to think that a full-form materialization is inherently less plausible than a partial materialization – or, for that matter, less plausible than any other form of PK. We have already considered good evidence for some remarkable phenomena, from object movements to musical performances on untouched instruments. But as we saw in chapter 1.3, we are in no position to say what the limits of PK might be, or that certain phenomena are inherently more incredible than others. Besides, there is an abundance of good evidence for partial materializations, including evidence from the cases of Home and Palladino. But once we entertain that evidence seriously, I see no additional conceptual obstacle posed by the evidence for full-form materializations. The evidence may not be as clean as some evidence for partial materializations, but as Richet noted,

> it is as difficult to understand the materialization of a living hand, warm, articulated, and mobile, or even of a single finger, as to understand the materialization of an entire personality which comes and goes, speaks, and moves the veil that covers him. (Richet, 1923/1975, p. 491)

One of the first major materialization mediums was Florence Cook (1856–1904). Those sympathetic to the case consider her the first English medium to produce full-form materializations in good light. Others dismiss the entire case as fraudulent. The actual story, as one might imagine, is quite complex; and I will not even attempt to do it justice. One of Florence's champions was Crookes, who claimed to see both Florence and her usual materialized companion, 'Katie King', side by side (see Medhurst *et al.*, 1972, pp. 130–41). Consider the following account, taken from notes dictated at the time to a friend who was adept at shorthand.

I went cautiously into the room, it being dark, and felt about for Miss Cook. I found her crouching on the floor. Kneeling down, I let air into the lamp, and by its light I saw the young lady dressed in black velvet, as she had been in the early part of the evening, and to all appearance perfectly senseless; she did not move when I took her hand and held the light quite close to her face, but continued quietly breathing. Raising the lamp, I looked around and saw Katie standing close behind Miss Cook. She was robed in flowing white drapery as we had seen her previously during the *séance*. Holding one of Miss Cook's hands in mine, and still kneeling, I passed the lamp up and down so as to illuminate Katie's whole figure, and satisfy myself thoroughly that I was really looking at the veritable Katie whom I had clasped in my arms a few minutes before, and not at the phantasm of a disordered brain. She did not speak, but moved her head and smiled in recognition. Three separate times did I carefully examine Miss Cook crouching before me, to be sure that the hand I held was that of a living woman, and three separate times did I turn the lamp to Katie and examine her with steadfast scrutiny until I had no doubt whatever of her objective reality. (p. 135)

Crookes noted that Katie and Florence differed in some relevant respects. Although Katie's height varied, she was always taller than Miss Cook. During the session recorded above, Crookes observed that Katie's neck was bare and that her skin was smooth both to touch and sight. But on Florence's neck there was a large blister, which under the same conditions was visible and rough to the touch. Moreover, although Miss Cook wore earrings, Katie's ears were unpierced.

In 1874, Cromwell Varley devised an interesting test for Florence. He made her part of an electric circuit, comprised of a battery, resistance coil, and a galvanometer, the latter being outside her cabinet and visible to the sitters throughout the séance. The purpose of the experiment was to see if the appearances of Katie outside the cabinet were really just appearances of Florence. If the medium moved, the galvanometer would exhibit distinct fluctuations; and if she broke the circuit, even for a moment, the galvanometer reading would fall to zero. Nevertheless, Katie appeared, waved her arms, and shook hands with the sitters, although the galvanometer readings showed nothing untoward.

Trevor Hall has charged that Crookes's evidence cannot be trusted, and that the physicist was either deceived by the teenage medium, or else that he was covering up a secret affair in which the two were engaged. He also has alleged that the Varley experiments are not evidential, and that Varley's reasoning was simply confused (see Hall, 1962). While I cannot examine the arguments here, let me record my opinion that Hall's case is characteristically unimpressive. As in his subsequent book on Home (see Braude, 1985), Hall relies on innuendo, irrelevant detail, avoidance of relevant detail, and transparently fallacious arguments. Although there are reasons for thinking that Florence may have cheated on occasion, her case (like Eusapia's) is complex and her apparent interests and motivations likewise far from simple. Readers interested in more sober and clear-headed appraisals of the Varley experiments are directed to Broad, 1964, and Stephenson, 1966. For an interesting and detailed rebuttal to Hall's overall assessment of the case, see Medhurst and Goldney, 1964. See also Zorab, 1964, 1980; the latter is a full-scale sympathetic account of the case.

Another very interesting case is that of 'Eva C.' (Marthe Béraud). Relatively little is known about her early life. Apparently, she began her career as a medium in 1903, at about the age of 17. During the next 15 years, she produced dramatic phenomena for several researchers (including Richet, Schrenck Notzing, and Geley); but by 1922 her powers had apparently fizzled out completely. As with Florence Cook, and physical mediums generally, Eva was accused of fraud. Her first serious scandal concerned the apparent full-form materializations provided for Richet in Algiers in 1905. An Arab coachman named Areski, who had been accused of theft and dismissed by the family at whose home the séances were held, claimed that the materialized figures were none other than himself. But it turned out, first, that there were full materializations for which he was the wrong size, and second, that he simply had not been present at the sittings. A lawyer named Marsault, who had also not attended the séances, claimed that Eva had confessed to him that it was all a trick, done by means of a trap door at the Villa Carmen, where the sessions were held. Richet replied that nothing could be easier to discover than the existence of a trap door. Submitting a supporting affadavit from an architect who examined the premises, he denied that there was a trap door. (For an example of how the story can be told without mentioning relevant information repudiating the charges, see Brandon, 1983, and Verrall, 1914. Inglis, 1984, pp. 27–34, 95–105, provides a some-what sketchy but more balanced account, of that case and of Eva's mediumship generally. And for an account of the phenomena at the Villa Carmen, see Richet, 1905, and 1923/1975, pp. 504–9; also, Maxwell, 1906.)

In any event, the Villa Carmen affair has been blown out of proportion. The studies of Eva C., like those of Home and Palladino, provide evidence that seems to resist any plausible normal explanation. And it is precisely that evidence which most skeptics fail to discuss, choosing instead to focus only on questionable incidents. For example, just as Trevor Hall resolutely ignores all the good evidence for Home's phenomena in his alleged expose of the medium, Brandon and Miss Verrall fail to note the irrelevance of Eva's alleged confession of fraud to Marsault, in view of the excellent eyewitness accounts of materializations *in the process of formation*. In fact, what makes the case of Eva C. particularly important is that several researchers were able to make extended and repeated observations, near at hand and in adequate light, of mobile and developing materialized forms (Richet coined the term 'ectoplasm' to refer to the stuff of which the forms were composed).

Before considering some of the better eyewitness accounts, I should mention that the other standard charge against Eva was that her materialized forms were often two-dimensional images, some looking like formerly crumpled paper cut-outs, and others made of a material more like chiffon. And some of her alleged materialized faces or other images bore striking similarities to published pictures (in one case, the masthead to the journal *Le Miroir*). Not surprisingly, many found this suspicious; they assumed (unjustifiably) that if materializations occur at all, they must be lifelike and three-dimensional, and not resemble conceal-able props or mere copies of other two-dimensional images. But the defense of Eva's less dramatic phenomena does not rest solely on the abstract point that in principle, materializations can assume any form. When one considers certain features of the phenomena, as well as the conditions under which they were produced, there are several good reasons for taking them seriously.

First, if the flat images were indeed props or copies of images smuggled into the séance room, then the folds in them would suggest extreme stupidity on Eva's part. Not only did Eva know in advance that photographs would be taken of her manifestations; she must also have known that the phenomena would appear suspicious. In fact, if Eva had wanted to encourage suspicion, few things would have been quite as effective. Besides, since many of her manifestations seemed to be three-dimensional living forms, it was simply unnecessary to produce folded flat images. Those additional manifestations actually did more harm than good, and the harm done was easy to anticipate.

Second, if the images or apparent drawings had been concealed props, then Eva would have needed to hide them initially and later make them disappear. But several considerations suggest that this did not occur, and could not have occurred. For one thing, the flat images appeared when Eva's hands were in sight. For another, she was minutely examined before and after the séances. Indeed, Eva's cooperation often bordered on the heroic. According to Richet,

> At each séance the cabinet was closely searched, Eva was completely undressed and in presence of the experimenters clothed in a close-fitting garmet covering her from head to foot. Her head was covered by a veil of tulle sewn to the other garment. Her hair, armpits, nose, mouth, and knees were examined; in some cases even examination *per rectum et vaginum* was resorted to. As the materialized substance frequently comes from her mouth, syrup of bilberries was administered, whose deep colouring powers are well known, but notwithstanding this the extruded forms were absolutely

white. Experimental rigour was even pushed to the point of giving her an emetic before a séance. (Richet, 1923/1975, p. 510)

Moreover, the flat figures appeared *outside* the veil of tulle covering her. And sometimes, like the manifestations of Home and Palladino, they would also disappear suddenly (rather than be dragged away). But perhaps most important, the forms often exhibited movement and seemed to be living, *growing* things.

Compare Richet's comments above with Schrenck Notzing's account of a sitting conducted in Paris on November 26, 1913.

The initial and final examination of the medium (mouth, nose, and hair, as well as a gynaecological examination), of the séance costume and the cabinet, conducted by the Paris physician, Dr Bourbon, and the author, were negative. . . . Eva dined at seven o'clock. The sitting commenced at 8.45 P.M. in a feeble white light. Hands and knees were visibly inactive during the whole sitting. The medium did not leave her chair in the cabinet for a moment. The curtains were open while the phenomena took place.

Between 9 P.M. and 9.10 P.M., without the help of the hands or knees, a flowing white substance emerged from the medium's mouth, which was inclined towards the left. It was about 20 inches long and 8 inches broad. It lay on the breast of the dress, spread out, and formed a white head-like disk, with a face profile turned to the right, and of life size. Even after the flash-light was ignited the curtain remained wide open. At the same moment the author illuminated the structure with an electric torch, and found that it formed a folded strip, which receded slowly into the medium's mouth, and remained visible until the sitting closed at 9.20 P.M.

While in the state of hypnosis, the medium rose from her chair and took an emetic tendered to her by the author (1 gramme ipecacuanha and ½ gramme tartar emetic), was completely undressed while standing half in and half out of the cabinet, and examined in detail by the author and Dr Bourbon, who took charge of the séance costume, and also examined it carefully. The final examination of the cabinet and chair gave no result. Dressed in a dressing-gown, Eva

C. was then laid on a couch in the room, and was not left unobserved for a moment.

After two further doses of the same strength, vomiting set in at 9.30 P.M., which brought up the contents of the stomach. The quantity was about a pint, and was taken charge of by the author, who did not give it out of his hands until he handed it over to the Masselin Laboratory in Paris for analysis. The vomit was brown in colour, and besides the wafers taken with the powders there was no trace of any white substance such as observed by us. The detailed report of the Laboratory in question, dated 29th November 1913, closes with the words: 'The final result of the examination shows that the vomit consisted exclusively of food products and the emetics, and contained fragments of meat, fruit, and vegetables, probably mushrooms, which were found in pieces of considerable size. The rest of the contents consisted of food in an advanced state of digestion. There was not the slightest trace of a body whose appearance or histological structure gave the impression of a foreign body, or of a substance not used for nutrition, and, in particular, there was no trace of paper or chiffon.' (Schrenck Notzing 1923a, p. 289)

Despite the precautions of having Eva swallow an emetic or drink syrup of bilberries, some continued to insist that Eva regurgitated the materializations. Of course, that hypothesis fails to explain the many phenomena that did not issue from Eva's mouth. And it also does not explain those that did, especially the ones that moved and grew under the close inspection of witnesses. Even in the 1920 S.P.R. experiments, when the aforementioned precautions were not taken, the phenomena exhibited features that seemed, at best, very difficult to explain by recourse to the regurgitation hypothesis. Richet, who had been irritated by the S.P.R. leaders' close-mindedness ever since his work with Eusapia, scoffed at their allegiance to that and other absurd counter-hypotheses. (See, e.g., Dingwall's preposterous attempt to explain how a pointed waxy object could appear first inside, and then outside the veil covering Eva's face – S.P.R., 1922, pp. 320ff. He admitted, in fact, that the only alternative to his suggestion was hallucination, which he considered even more implausible.)

Concerning their refusal to acknowledge any of the phenomena as definitely genuine, he wrote,

> The members of the S.P.R., when they fail to understand, say 'It is difficult to understand how this is produced.' Mr Dingwall, who is an expert in legerdemain, having seen the ectoplasm emerge as a miniature hand, making signs before disappearing, says, 'I attach no importance to this.' We may be permitted to remark that very great importance attaches to Mr Dingwall's testimony. (Richet, 1923/1975, p. 544)

For additional criticisms of the S.P.R. investigations, made at the time, see Geley, 1922.

Consider, now, the following descriptions of Eva's materializations in the process of formation. According to Richet, they generally began as

> a whitish steam, perhaps luminous, taking the shape of gauze or muslin, in which there develops a hand or an arm that gradually gains consistency. This ectoplasm makes *personal* movements. It creeps, rises from the ground, and puts forth tentacles like an amoeba. It is not always connected with the body of the medium but usually emanates from her, and is connected with her.
>
> Two phases can be distinguished: a rudimentary phase, a sort of rough draft, and a phase of building up. With other mediums the organized form may probably appear immediately without being preceded by the indistinct cloudy phase. (Richet, 1923/1975, pp. 523–4)

The following notes from a sitting on October 20, 1906, in daylight sufficient to read the title of a book, provide a specific example.

> On the floor is a small white tract that grows into an ovoid, puts out an extension, and mounts on the arm of the chair. At this moment there are two horns like snail's horns that seem to direct the movement of a part, B, that climbs over the arm of the chair, united to a mass, X, that lies on the floor. I can look at this very closely: the stem is a greyish white, less white than the trimming of Marthe's bodice and softer in outline. There are swellings in it like an empty snake-skin

153

whilst the two masses, B and X, seem to swell and get fuller. Slowly the mass X mounts up and the mass B descends, so that X is on Marthe's knees and B below it, the latter becoming the base on which the whole formation rests, for it spreads out like an amoeba on the floor, and takes the form of a split base (two feet?). While these two parts continued to flatten out on the floor I had plenty of time to look very closely into the greyish, gelatinous, and barely visible mass X. I was not permitted to touch it. It was then on Marthe's knees. It then slowly divided into clefts at its extremity, resembling a hand, in embryo, but sufficiently clear for me to say that it is a left hand seen from the back.

Another change sets in: the little finger separates from the rest, and in the grey, cloudy mass a hand can be clearly seen from the back, the fingers closed, the little finger extended, and a swelling resembling the carpal bones appeared, like a Röntgen-ray radiograph of these bones. Soon the cloudy mass disappears and I see an ill-formed hand like a cast in plaster. I think I see the folds and creases in the skin slowly form. I am holding both Marthe's hands, and can see them. (Richet, 1923/1975, pp. 516ff.)

Compare this description to the notes of Gustave Geley, made in 1910 without knowledge of Richet's results.

From Eva's mouth a band of white substance about two fingers' breadth slowly descends to her knees. This ribbon takes varied form under our eyes: it spreads as a large, perforated, membranous tissue, with local swellings and vacant spaces; gathers itself together and retracts repeatedly. Here and there from the mass appear prolongations, a kind of pseudo-pods, and these take for a few seconds the form of fingers and rudimentary hands, returning into the general mass. Finally the cord turns on itself, lengthens on Eva's knees, and, raising its end, moves towards me. I then see its end thicken, and this kind of bud expands into a perfectly modelled hand. I touch it, and it gives me the feeling of a normal hand; I feel the bones and the fingernails. Then it retreats, diminishes in size, and disappears in the end of a cord. . . . (Geley, 1927/1975, pp. 186–7; cf. the translation of this passage in Richet, 1923/1975, p. 524)

Schrenck Notzing reported results similar to these with the Polish medium, Stanislawa P. (Schrenck Notzing, 1923a).

Somewhat more rudimentary materialized forms were examined and photographed by W. J. Crawford, an Irish mechanical engineer who experimented from 1914 to 1920 with a young Belfast medium, Kathleen Goligher. Miss Goligher's forms issued usually from her navel or vagina, and often raised upward like a cantilever to lift the table in front of her.

In earlier experiments, Crawford had not been able to see any materialized forms in the red light of the sittings. But he nevertheless got results suggesting that an invisible cantilever was producing the effects (Crawford, 1918, 1919). Among the more interesting findings were those concerning weight changes in the medium and sitters (and some of these results were obtained with mediums other than Miss Goligher). Crawford discovered that during object levitations the medium's weight increased by approximately the weight of the levitated object (see, e.g., 1919, pp. 28ff.). And when the invisible cantilever lifted the table according to Crawford's request by resting itself on the floor, thereby putting most of the reaction on the floor rather than on the medium, Miss Goligher's weight *decreased* slightly (1919, pp. 36ff.). Crawford also found that when what he called the 'invisible operators' increased the table's weight, Miss Goligher's weight decreased by approximately the same amount (1919, pp. 52ff., esp. 54–6; also 69–70). Equally interesting, he discovered that sitters suffered slight but permanent weight loss after the séances (see, 1918, pp. 146–50; 1919, pp. 132ff., 181, 185–6, 190, 196; also Courtier, 1908, p. 441 and Perovsky-Petrovo-Solovovo, 1909c, p. 572, regarding similar results with Eusapia Palladino).[10]

Not surprisingly, Crawford's work stimulated its share of controversy (see Inglis, 1984, for a good summary), and was dismissed rather contemptuously and superficially by members of the S.P.R. (see esp. E. Sidgwick, 1917a, 1917b; also Dingwall, 1921; Fournier d'Albe, 1922). Inglis is correct in maintaining that many of the criticisms were unjust and facile, and probably due in part to the prevailing aversion to physical phenomena. (See also Rayleigh, 1938, for a criticism of Fournier d'Albe's careless charges.)

In any event, Crawford was not the only person to report good phenomena with Miss Goligher (see also Barrett, 1919; Smith, 1919; Stevenson, 1920); and the medium left a legacy of interesting manifestations which her S.P.R. critics were never able to discredit. These included: (a) extremely loud raps, some, resembling blows of a 'sledge hammer on an anvil' (Barrett, 1919, p. 335), loud enough to shake the room or floor; (b) levitated objects (including tables) that could not be moved or wrestled to the ground; (c) phonograph recordings made while the medium was several feet from the horn, but which exhibited the 'blasting' distortion that ordinarily required the voice being very close to the horn; (d) some remarkable observations and photographs of materialized cantilevers in their various stages of development. Later in her career, after Crawford's death in 1920, Kathleen may have resorted to cheating; but many of her earlier phenomena are exceedingly difficult to explain away.

Consider the following first-hand accounts. According to Sir William Barrett, who attended a séance around Christmas, 1915, in red light sufficient to see the objects and sitters in the room, a tin trumpet

below the table . . . began to move about, and the smaller end poked itself from under the top of the table towards Dr W. and myself. We were allowed to try and catch it, but in spite of all our endeavours it eluded us, darting in and out and changing its position as we tried to seize it. The medium was on the opposite side of the table to us and *all the circle* held up their hands – so that we could see each linked hand clearly – as the trumpet played hide and seek with us.

Then the table began to rise from the floor, until it reached a height of some twelve or eighteen inches, and remained thus suspended and quite level. We were allowed, first myself and then Dr W., to go beneath the clasped hands of the sitters into the circle and try to force the table down. This both of us found it impossible to do; though we laid hold of the sides of the table it resisted our strongest efforts to push it down. I then sat on the table when it was about a foot off the floor and it swayed me about, finally tipping me off.

We then returned outside the circle, when the table turned itself upside down and moved up and down with the legs uppermost. Again we entered the circle and tried to lift the table top from the floor, but it appeared riveted, and we were unable to stir it. When we resumed our place outside the circle, the table floated up and turned itself over again with its right side uppermost. During these experiments, and whilst the table was levitated, all the sitters repeatedly held up their clasped hands, so that we could see no one had any contact with the table, they were in fact so far from it that we could walk between them and the table. (Barrett, 1919, pp. 335–6)

W. Whately Smith reported similar experiences, both with a large metal trumpet that separated into two parts, and a table. The séance took place on December 9, 1916, in red light 'a good deal stronger than I should care to use in a photographic darkroom', sufficient to 'clearly see every object in the room unless it happened to be in deep shadow' (Smith, 1919, p. 313). Concerning the levitated table,

> I grasped the table firmly with both hands and did my utmost to prevent it moving, but I was quite unsuccessful. By dint of great exertion I could prevent it from moving in any one direction and could keep it steady for a second or so, but it instantly moved in some other direction, the force changing with great rapidity. . . . At one time the table was made so heavy that I could not lift it. (pp. 315–16)
>
> During the whole of this time I was standing within three feet of the medium and, most of the time, facing her. I could see distinctly the whole of her body down to the knees, and the light from the lamp fell directly on to her lap. Her feet were in shadow and I could not make them out distinctly. This is natural as she always sits with them tucked under her chair and her heels against its crossbar.
>
> I could infallibly have detected any movement of the medium, and I can certify that she sat absolutely motionless during the whole time that the table was performing these violent evolutions. . . .
>
> Finally, [the table] pushed me to the extreme edge of the circle, moving to a distance of fully four feet from the medium in the process. In this position I tried my hardest to push it back. Again it felt like pushing against a solid strut. By

putting out all my strength I was only able to move it an inch or so. (p. 316)

Crawford also conducted an extended series of experiments in producing impressions of the materialized forms in clay. In some, the medium's legs were tied to her chair, and the sitters' legs were all bound together as well as to their respective chairs. No one's legs could get within 18 ins. of the clay, which was placed in a box tightly fitted inside the table legs. In other tests Miss Goligher's feet were locked inside a box; and in still others, her feet were placed on an electrical device such that if she lifted them, an alarm would ring. The results suggested that material issued from the medium's feet, passed through her clothing, made an impression in the clay, and then withdrew inside her body, taking some of the clay back with it. Although controls seem to have good, clay was discovered around her feet, the ropes (which took five minutes to untie), box, and even inside both her tightly laced high boots and the stockings beneath them. The boots and stockings were marked with clay in a way that seemed to trace the material's path into the boot and along the foot, and the stockings were also stretched or torn on occasion. Once, the fabric of a stocking was 'badly ruffled and distended as though it had been severely mauled by the transit of the psychic matter' (Crawford, 1921, p. 112). Crawford also showed that the 'plasma' (as he called it) carried material (e.g., chalk, crayon, powder, paint, and carmine dye) *out* from and around the stocking and over the boot (e.g., 1921, pp. 113ff., 138ff., 144ff.). Later tests suggested that the plasma originated in the trunk (not the feet) and travelled down to the stocking, entering between the boot and stocking (1921, pp. 158ff.). Overall, Crawford's experiments and analyses are complex, ingenious, subtle, and very interesting.

Another case in which the medium apparently produced mobile ectoplasmic forms is that of 'Margery' (Mina Crandon). But this case is enormously complex; and while some phenomena seem hard to dismiss, it is very difficult to determine how many of the accusations of fraud are justified. An up-to-date attempt to sort out the controversy can be found in Inglis, 1984. (See also, Crandon, 1928; Dingwall, 1926b; Fielding, 1926; S.P.R., 1926; Tietze, 1973; Woolley and Brackenbury, 1931.)

Still another controversial case is that of the late nineteenth-century medium Henry Slade. Although occasional materializations occurred in his presence, those were not the most remarkable of his manifestations. Witnesses reported that Slade produced a variety of physical phenomena, some as good as any produced by Home.

The case of Slade, like many others, has received very bad press, and has been seriously distorted by skeptics. As a result, Slade is now remembered primarily for a farcical trial, an alleged exposure by the Seybert Commission, and for the phenomenon of slate-writing. The last, admittedly, is easy to fake, though not clearly so under some of the conditions imposed on Slade. Besides, Slade produced much more impressive phenomena. The second is suspicious itself for reasons similar to those in the case of Eusapia's American investigations. And the first is typically reported as a case in which Slade was convicted of fraud. But as a matter of fact, the testimony was weak in the extreme, and the judge's verdict was based largely on the intuition that Slade's phenomena could not possibly have been genuine, since they conflicted with established natural laws. (See Inglis, 1977, and Randall, 1982, for details.)

To be sure, Slade's case is not as carefully or extensively documented as some others. But it is much stronger than skeptics allege, especially when the better and large-scale phenomena are considered. Slade's principal investigator was J. C. F. Zöllner, who (like Slade) has been unjustly (and sometimes absurdly) maligned. Zöllner's work was far from incompetent; indeed, it is often quite ingenious (see Zöllner, 1888/1975). Slade was also studied by professional magicians, who admitted their inability to account for his phenomena. Perhaps the most important such testimony came from the famous conjuror, Samuel Bellachini, who provided Slade with a witnessed affidavit, claiming that the phenomena were 'impossible' to produce by prestidigitation.

As with other cases of mediumship, the best way to evaluate Slade's case is to focus on the most recalcitrant pieces of evidence. (Skeptics often shun this procedure.) Granted, slate-writing was perhaps the most popular of Slade's phenomena. But I suspect that is partly because the phenomena produced ostensible spirit communications, and because the majority of those interested in Slade were concerned with the possibility of survival. Slade's other phenomena, however, are not so easy to dismiss. They were frequently large-scale, and produced in daylight or strong artificial light. In fact, many of the phenomena matched those of Home, both in style and in magnitude. They included: materialized hands (see Zöllner, pp. 58, 86–89), occasionally violent large object movements (e.g., a filled bookcase) at a distance (p. 56), accordion phenomena (pp. 57–8), apports (including the disappearance and reappearance of objects) (pp. 91–3, 102–10, 135–47), and the tying of knots in untouched endless cords (pp. 41–3, 82–6, 102–10).

One also finds interesting connections with other bodies of data. For example, after a sea-shell apparently passed through the top of a table (p. 102), Zöllner and his friend Oscar von Hoffman found it to be very hot to the touch – almost too hot to hold. This is particularly interesting in light of numerous reports from poltergeist cases of the heat of apported objects. Moreover, as Randall recognizes (p. 105), the object's high temperature blocks the skeptic's move of supposing that Slade had merely distracted Zöllner and Hoffman, and palmed the shell, making it appear to have passed through the table. That gambit does not explain how the shell could have been heated to a high temperature.

Among the threads running through the mediumistic literature are reports of materialized forms dissolving or disappearing. I have already mentioned this phenomenon in connection with Home and Eva C. But additional reports can also be found in accounts of experiments with Eusapia Palladino (see, e.g., Richet, 1923/1975, pp. 473ff., p. 500), and in the mind-boggling accounts of the Brazilian medium Carlos Mirabelli (1889–1951). Mirabelli reportedly produced full-form materializations in bright daylight. Sitters would watch them form; attending physicians would carefully examine them for up to 30 minutes and report ordinary bodily functions; photographs of the figures would be taken; and then they would slowly dissolve or fade before everyone's eyes. The case of Mirabelli, unfortunately, never received the full scrutiny and documentation accorded Home, Palladino, and some others. Hence, it cannot be considered as one of the most strongly evidential. Nevertheless, there are many eyewitness accounts of his phenomena; and the good conditions of observation force us to take the case seriously, especially in view of the totality of evidence for materialization. After all, the phenomena reported are not particularly outlandish when compared to lesser materialization phenomena for which there exists good evidence. They are simply more virtuosic. Indeed, if the accounts of Mirabelli can be trusted, he would seem to have been the most spectacular physical medium of all time. (See, e.g., Besterman, 1930, 1936; Bruck, 1936; Dingwall, 1930, 1936, 1961; Driesch, 1930; Inglis, 1984; Medeiras, 1935; Playfair, 1975; Walker, 1935.)

Before concluding this section, one interesting feature of materialization phenomena deserves special mention. In many cases human figures are apparently materialized along with clothing; and some find it particularly vexing or suspicious that inanimate objects might be materialized. With regard to apparitions, for example, that attitude manifests itself in the rhetorical skeptical question 'How can ghosts have clothes?' (See Chapter 3 for a discussion of apparitions, and their connection with the phenomena of materialization.) But I cannot see why the materialization of 'dead' matter is any more problematical than the materialization of 'living' matter. Richet is correct in maintaining that 'the materialization of a hand is no easier to understand than of the glove that covers it' (Richet, 1923/1975, p. 475). In fact, descriptions of materializations in the process of formation suggest that animate and inanimate matter often differentiate from what begins as a uniform mass or vapor. In many cases it seems as if a cloudy or gelatinous undifferentiated substance gradually takes shape and becomes organized and specialized. The process often seems to be the reverse of the dissolving or melting phenomena mentioned above.

2.5 JOSEPH OF COPERTINO (1603–1663)

a. Introduction

The case of St Joseph provides the earliest outstanding evidence for human levitation, and quite possibly the best from any era. But from a certain conventional viewpoint, the case has several strikes against it from the start. In many people it triggers deep-seated prejudices, either about historical evidence generally, or the evidence for alleged religious miracles in particular. Even those willing to be open-minded with regard to nineteenth-century evidence for paranormality may balk at taking seventeenth-century evidence equally seriously. And even those willing to be open-minded with regard to seventeenth-century evidence may draw the line at evidence for religious miracles. Here, they would urge, the problems of biased observation and reporting are especially acute.

But the reason the case of Joseph is important is that it tends to be strong just where one would expect it to be weak. There is a great deal of impressive testimony; independent accounts tend to converge on striking and unexpected details; depositions were often provided by laypersons with no motive for lending support to the Church; and perhaps most important, the Church itself subjected the evidence to very detailed scrutiny, partly as a general procedure to avoid subsequent embarrassment over endorsing hoaxes, but also because there were good reasons for thinking that the canonization of Joseph might have been contrary to its interests.

Before examining the case in detail, I should say that it is clearly unreasonable to discount seventeenth-century evidence for paranormality, once we have allowed more recent historical evidence to be admissible. As Ducasse recognized,

> the age of a piece of circumstantially stated, intelligent, and
> sincere testimony has no logical bearing on its force unless
> the testimony was biased by beliefs commonly held in the days
> of the witness but since proved to be groundless or false; or
> unless some normal explanation of the events judged by him
> to have been paranormal has since been discovered.
> (Ducasse, 1954b, p. 823)

The testimony in Joseph's case has many of the virtues characteristic of the best spontaneous cases. For example, depositions tend to display unexpected patterns of detail, witnesses were often apparently unbiased, or at least had nothing to gain (and perhaps something to lose) from offering testimony, and the observations frequently occurred under favorable conditions.

b. Biographical remarks

Giuseppe (Joseph) Desa's family was poor; according to one account he was born in a stable while his parents were fleeing from creditors. His religious proclivities manifested themselves while he was quite young, and he was only eight years old when he experienced his first state of rapture. Joseph also displayed, from the start, modes of behavior that were to become even more extreme with time. In school he used to sit motionless, with mouth open and eyes raised heavenward, thereby earning him the nickname 'boca-aperta' (open-mouth). And since young Joseph's religious ecstacies were complemented by an extreme – not to mention precocious – asceticism, many soon came to regard him as either crazy or retarded. Even as a child he inflicted miseries on himself, of a sort usually reserved for more mature zealots. He would fast for days at a time, and when he ate he would cover his food with an awful powder of his devising. Others who sampled even small amounts of the substance experienced severe nausea. Joseph also wore a hair shirt, and later in life wore underneath – and also around his loins – sharp pieces of metal which dug into his skin. Since by that time he had also begun to flagellate himself, his body was eventually covered with lacerations and festering sores.

At the age of seventeen he decided to devote his life to religion. But his peculiar and absent-minded behavior, as well as his frequent ecstatic states, led him to be dismissed from a Capuchin monastery. Eventually he was received into the Order of St Francis, and became a priest on March 28, 1628. Apparently, Joseph passed his examination only through a procedural fluke. The examiner, Battista Deti, Bishop of Castro, was so impressed with the first few students he questioned, that he assumed the others were of equal calibre, and admitted all the rest (including good Joseph) without examination.

Joseph's asceticism now reached a peak. He attached pins and star-shaped pieces of metal to his whip, and the continued scourgings (inflicted now both by himself and others) caused blood to spurt out and stain his cell walls. Eventually, his Superior banned the use of some of these devices. In fact, even Joseph's ecstasies were becoming a nuisance, and he was eventually forbidden from services, choir practice, as well as dining with the others in the refectory.

Joseph's levitations apparently began soon after entering the priesthood. It is not surprising, then, that between the occasional report of a miracle and continual episodes of eccentric behavior, news of Joseph began to spread. Eventually, he was called to the Holy Office in Naples, and although he was brought before the Inquisition three times, the charges against him were finally dropped, and Joseph was allowed to say Mass. After Mass, he went into a corner of the church to pray. Dingwall recounts what then occurred.

> Suddenly he rose up into the air, and with a cry flew in the upright position to the altar with his hands outstretched as on a cross, and alighted upon it in the middle of the flowers and candles which were burning in profusion. The nuns of St Ligorio, who were observing each one of his acts and movements, and saw him first in the air and later among the burning candles, cried out loudly: 'He will catch fire! He will catch fire!' But Fr Lodovico, his companion, who was present and who made a statement in the Process [the ecclesiastical record], and who was accustomed to such sights, told the nuns not to lack faith as he would not burn himself. Then, with another cry, Joseph flew back into the church in a kneeling position and, alighting upon his knees, began to whirl round upon them, dancing and singing, being filled as he was with joy and exultation and exclaiming: 'Oh! most Blessed Virgin, most Blessed Virgin!' (Dingwall, 1962a, pp. 12–13).

Compare the foregoing description with the following eyewitness account, also from the Process. Joseph had been dancing ecstatically, when

> suddenly he gave a sob, then a great cry, and at the same time he was raised into the air, flying from the middle of the church, like a bird, to a high altar, where he embraced the tabernacle (a distance of about forty feet). A most wonderful thing is that the altar being covered with lighted candles, Brother Joseph flew and alighted among these candles and threw down neither a candle nor a candlestick. He remained thus about a quarter of an hour on the altar, kneeling and embracing the tabernacle, and then came down without being helped by anybody and did not disturb anything. (Leroy, 1928, p. 90)

These incidents appear to be typical of Joseph's levitations. His flights would often be preceded by a cry, sob, or shriek, and when levitating inside a church, he would not disturb the objects crowded around him on the altar. In fact, many reported, from many different cases, that Joseph would not extinguish candles as he flew among them.

But not all Joseph's flights occurred indoors. Often they took place outdoors, in broad daylight, where Joseph allegedly soared as much as thirty yards over the heads of onlookers to the branches of trees. Witnesses frequently comment that the branches would not ordinarily have been able to sustain his weight, and that Joseph accordingly seemed to weigh no more than a bird. One curious and recurring observation is that during his flights outdoors, Joseph's clothing would not be disturbed by wind or by his movement through the air. His robes were also reported to have remained dry in the rain. These accounts would appear to connect with reports that Joseph's flights indoors failed to extinguish nearby candles.

Evidently, all that was needed to provoke one of Joseph's levitations was something to arouse his religious awe, such as an image of the Virgin or an inspiring remark. On one occasion, while walking in the garden, another priest said to him, 'What a beautiful heaven God has made!', in response to which Joseph shrieked and flew to the top of an olive tree where he remained in a kneeling position for thirty minutes. When he regained his senses, he had to be helped out of the tree with a ladder.

From time to time, Joseph took others on his flights with him, sometimes taking them by the hand, and sometimes grasping them by the hair. This latter procedure was no doubt frightening and uncomfortable; on one occasion it allegedly cured a man of lunacy. Moreover, Joseph's repertoire of miracles was not limited to levitation, although the levitations are by far his best attested phenomena. He was also credited with healings, clairvoyance, multiplying food, and reading the thoughts of those for whom he was serving as confessor.

Toward the end of his life, Joseph's religiously-inspired self-abuses had taken their toll, and in 1663 his health declined rapidly. This turns out to have been a boon for the quality of evidence, since the physicians attending him were often able to study his raptures and levitations very closely. During Joseph's last illness, the surgeon Francesco Pierpaoli was cauterizing his right leg when he noticed that Joseph was entranced and senseless. When the cauterization began, Joseph was seated with his right leg lying across the doctor's knees; his arms were spread wide, his eyes and mouth were open, and his face was turned heavenward. Then Pierpaoli noted that Joseph was hovering in that position several inches above his chair. He tried to lower Joseph's leg, but was unable to do so. He also observed that a fly had settled on the pupil of one of Joseph's eyes, and remained there despite his efforts to drive it away. Then Pierpaoli and a second physician knelt down to confirm that Joseph was indeed raised above his chair. Joseph remained in this state for about fifteen minutes, and when he returned to his senses he had no awareness that the cauterization had been performed.

c. *The quality of the evidence*

No doubt many will be tempted to dismiss the evidence for Joseph's levitations as nothing more than the ravings of religious fanatics. But this would be an inexcusably glib response to a remarkable body of material. For one thing, many accounts were volunteered by laypersons (such as Joseph's physicians). Some, in fact, were converted to Catholicism after witnessing Joseph's feats. Perhaps the most interesting case of this sort is that of Leibniz's patron, the Duke of Brunswick, whose observations on two separate occasions persuaded him to abandon his faith as a Lutheran. (Although Leibniz knew why Johann Friedrich converted, he offered no theoretical speculations about the phenomena.) Others had rather more difficulty integrating the phenomena into an agreeable conceptual system. The Duke's friend, Heinrich Blume, who accompanied him on the trip to see Joseph, found that experience a source of profound irritation, while not questioning the reality of the levitations.

Naturally, the Church record also contains depositions from the many monks who observed Joseph's flights fairly regularly, as well as testimony from numerous high Church officials. Even Pope Urban VIII witnessed a levitation. The Father-General of Joseph's Order had arranged for him to kiss the Pope's feet, and upon seeing the Pontiff, Joseph became enraptured and rose into the air, where he remained until called back to his senses.

Nevertheless, when we evaluate the testimony from Church

members, and assess the decision to canonize Joseph, it would be a serious mistake to assume that all biases would have been in Joseph's favor. Indeed, there are good reasons for thinking that many witnesses would have had biases against Joseph, and that many (if not most) Church officials would have preferred to deflect attention away from him. Canonization is, among other things, an act of endorsement by the Church. But in many respects Joseph was a public relations nightmare – hardly an appealing standard bearer or advertisement for Catholicism. Apart from his levitations and other alleged paranormal feats, Joseph was generally an embarrassment to the Church – certainly a far cry from what the Church would have liked to select as a model of saintliness. No one questioned Joseph's sincerity; but his life-style and demeanor led many to doubt his sanity. His behavior was unimpressive at best, and usually odd; and his physical condition was repulsive. In fact, as Eisenbud quips, because of Joseph's festering sores, his odor of sanctity must have been oppressive (1979, p. 146). Even his raptures were more theatrical than inspiring; they made Joseph appear crazy or fanatical rather than noble or godlike.

It is no wonder, then, that the Church took its time in deliberating over the merits of Joseph's case. In the absence of very strong evidence for the miraculous nature of his phenomena, the Church probably would have preferred to withold its most treasured seal of approval. In any case, it is Church policy that the process of conferring sainthood be protracted and circumspect. Rash decisions might only lead to humiliation later, should the allegedly miraculous phenomena turn out to have been fraudulent. For this reason, the Church carefully collects the evidence, and then appoints a *Postulator* to argue the case in behalf of canonization. The evidence is presented before a body known as the Congregation of Rites, and another official, the *Promotor Fidei*, acts as devil's advocate and attempts to find flaws in the testimony. He acts, in other words, as a sort of prosecuting attorney. In Joseph's case the *Promotor Fidei* happens to have been Prosper Lambertini, who later became Pope Benedict XIV, and whose treatise, *De Canonizatione*, became a standard Church guide on the evaluation of evidence. Lambertini was initially opposed to Joseph's canonization, since he disapproved of Joseph's brand of asceticism. Eventually, though, he yielded to the evidence, despite the affront to his religious aesthetics.

I should emphasize that Joseph was regularly observed *in flight*, or sometimes just suspended in air. He was not simply observed *at* the locations to which he had been ostensibly transported. Furthermore, on those occasions when he was merely hovering above the ground, witnesses frequently confirmed the fact by passing their hands beneath him.

Although Joseph's case deserves to be taken seriously on its own merits, it appears even stronger when viewed in the light of the evidence for levitation generally (see Leroy, 1928; and Thurston, 1952). And it appears stronger still when we consider it alongside the best evidence for large-scale PK generally. However exceptional Joseph's flights may be, they seem no more remarkable than the many well-documented phenomena of Home and Palladino.

Finally, a recent source of evidence is the Sidhis program of the Transcendental Meditation movement. Those who practice the 'sutras' or techniques taught in the program reportedly develop various powers or siddhis, among them 'flying' or 'hopping' – kinds of minor-league levitation. Although for various reasons the TM movement has been reluctant to cater to demands for demonstrations by members of the scientific establishment, first-hand accounts of flying or hopping have been offered recently by philosophers taking the TM-Sidhis program (see Franklin, 1980; and Haight, 1984). Their descriptions, of both their own flights and those of others, are most interesting.

Franklin also mentions that hopping is enhanced in a group setting. Although he refrains from discussing the TM-theoretical reasons for this, it is quite possible that the group phenomenon is related to the success of group-PK. Various researchers have found that group settings can be especially conducive to table tilting and other moderate-scale PK effects, if for no other reason than that the personal responsibility for the phenomena is deflected or shared. (See, e.g., Batcheldor, 1966, 1984; Brookes-Smith, 1973; Brookes-Smith and Hunt, 1970; Isaacs, 1984; Owen, 1975; Owen and Sparrow, 1974, 1977.)

2.6 CONCLUSION

It should be clear by now that the evidence for large-scale PK is respectable. Observers often ranged from the competent to the skillful; they were not blinded by credulity; in the best cases, conditions of observation ranged from good to excellent and did not allow for fraud of the sort necessary to produce the best phenomena; and phenomena were often of a kind or magnitude that cannot be explained away by fraud (especially sleight-of-hand) or malobservation.

Of course, physical mediumship is only one source of evidence for large-scale PK. It is simply the best, as far as the quality and amount of documentation is concerned. Naturally, it is regrettable that the evidence is not more current. But once one dispels the myths and prejudices (discussed in Chapter 1.4) about eyewitness testimony in these cases, that problem seems quite minimal.

Apart from mediumistic phenomena, only poltergeist phenomena are represented by a substantial literature. And unlike cases of physical mediumship, many poltergeist cases are relatively recent. But these cases are evidentially inferior, on the whole, to the best cases of mediumship, despite the fact that the standard skeptical dismissals of the poltergeist evidence are defective (see Chapter 1.4). Hence, since the mediumistic evidence was gathered under superior conditions of repeated observation, I thought it best to focus only on those. Nevertheless, the literature on poltergeists is fascinating and repays careful study, especially for those seeking interesting theoretical connections with the mediumistic evidence, or patterns in the PK data as a whole. (See especially Gauld and Cornell, 1979; also Roll, 1972.)

I want to examine next a body of evidence that is seldom associated with the evidence for PK – namely, cases of apparitions. That discussion will pave the way for the theoretical issues raised in Chapters 4 and 5.

3

APPARITIONS

3.1 INTRODUCTION

The topic of apparitions was among the very first to be examined in depth by the founders of the British S.P.R. Their Census of Hallucinations and monumental studies of apparitions of the living (see Gurney, Myers, and Podmore, 1886, E. Sidgwick, 1922, and S.P.R., 1894) laid the groundwork for systematic study and contain a wealth of valuable material. These days, however, in what I consider a zealously wrongheaded campaign to keep the field of parapsychology scientific – but only in a rigidly inappropriate sense of the term 'scientific' – the study of apparitions, like that of poltergeists and physical mediumship, has taken a back seat to the accumulation of laboratory evidence.

When the S.P.R. was founded, interest in apparitions was due largely to the widespread interest in survival. Parapsychologists and laymen alike considered apparitions to be a form of paranormal mental phenomena, and believed that mental phenomena pointed to a realm of the spirit not only free from familiar constraints on physical systems, but also neither describable nor explicable in terms of the materialistic theories then in vogue. Furthermore, in those days the prevailing philosophical approach to dualism was Cartesian. Most understood dualism to be a theory positing the existence of two different *substance*-kinds, rather than two different *event*-kinds or *levels of description*. (To some extent, the tendency persists even today, at least in the sciences. See Braude, 1983.) Therefore, since most conceived a 'spirit realm' along ontological (rather than merely explanatory) lines, even ordinary telepathy and apparitions of the living seemed to strengthen the case for survival.

Of course the interest in survival permeated the investigation of physical mediumship as well. Although some did suggest that physical phenomena might be paranormal productions of the medium, that explanation was the minority view, and hardly the live option it would be today. Now I have no wish to discount evidence of any sort for survival. That is simply a subject whose careful analysis I shall have to postpone for another occasion. (I will, however, offer some brief comments at the end of this chapter.) Since this is a book about psychokinesis and apparent paranormal ante-mortem agency, my present concern is to consider the extent to which the evidence for apparitions might be evidence for PK. This aspect of the the topic of apparitions has (I believe) been unjustly neglected and inadequately explored.

In fact, I suspect that one reason early parapsychologists lavished so much attention on apparitions and regarded their study as thoroughly respectable, despite the contemporaneous rocky career of research into physical mediumship, is that hardly anyone took seriously or even raised the possibility of an ante-mortem PK interpretation of apparitions. A. R. Wallace believed apparitions to be ordinarily perceivable entities; but he considered them to be produced by post-mortem individuals (see Wallace, 1896/ 1975 esp. pp. 231–78). F. W. H. Myers felt that collective apparitions are objective entities produced by both the living and the dead; but he considered them to be non-physical (see, e.g., Myers, 1903, vol. I, pp. 215–16, 263–5, vol. II, p. 75). To my knowledge, only Richet seriously considered the possibility that both apparitions and the materializations witnessed in the séance room are physical psychokinetic products of living agents (see Richet, 1923/ 1975, p. 544, pp. 591ff.). One reason, no doubt, is that materialization phenomena had typically been produced under conditions quite unlike those in which apparitions occurred. But poltergeist phenomena likewise occurred in conditions different from those found in experimental or semi-experimental cases; and that did not obscure their possible connection to the physical phenomena of mediumship. So perhaps another reason is that many considered materializations to be antecedently more suspicious than other physical phenomena. And in Great Britain that attitude might have been nourished by the prevailing S.P.R. prejudice against physical phenomena generally. In fact, the distaste many felt for the 'lower' phenomena of spiritualism may have blinded even those who (like Myers and Podmore) considered some apparitions to be objective entities. In their view, the entities were localized but *non-physical*. More on these matters shortly.

Before proceeding with a sketch of the evidence and a survey of theories, some further introductory remarks are in order. The first point concerns methodology. The purpose of this chapter is to consider whether the evidence for apparitions – particularly collective cases – becomes more intelligible or manageable in light of the evidence for large-scale PK. One may be tempted to suppose at the outset that all apparitional phenomena are nomologically continuous – that is, that they may all be explained as instances of some general paranormal process (e.g., telepathy). But as we will see, different sorts of cases pose different sorts of theoretical problems, and explanations that work neatly for one sort may be cumbersome or implausible when extended to another. In my opinion, then, it is a mistake to assume that apparitional phenomena must be united by anything deeper than a name. The evidence consists of cases occurring both while awake and during sleep, perceived both individually and collectively, most of them visual but others not, some suggesting the persistence of consciousness after death, others suggesting only interaction with the living, some strongly suggesting the presence of localized objective apparitional entities, and others suggesting nothing more than telepathic interaction. Like the various somatic phenomena we designate generally as *pains*, different sorts of apparitional phenomena may require quite different sorts of explanations. In fact, even phenomenologically similar cases may demand different explanations, just as phenomenologically similar headaches may proceed from different causes.

Nevertheless, it seems reasonable to expect some unity to underlie the diversity of phenomena, and no doubt some superficially distinct phenomena require similar explanations. In fact, one would expect many cases of individual and collective apparitions to result from similar processes; the number of potential percipients may be an accidental feature of the cases. But it may well be that only in accounts of collective apparitions are we likely to discern the theoretically relevant features of a certain kind of apparitional phenomenon, which cases of individual apparitions simply tend to obscure. This is one reason why I regard the collective cases as important. Explanations which seem plausible for individual apparitions frequently seem implausible for collective apparitions, although the converse is rarely the case.

Moreover, a striking feature of the evidence is that apparitions tend to be collectively perceived when there is more than one potential percipient present. Tyrrell (1942/1961, p. 23) claimed that in about one-third of the cases where there is more than one potential percipient, the apparition is experienced collectively. And Hart's figures (in Hart *et al.*, 1956) are even more impressive and revealing. Whereas Tyrrell considered cases in which there was more than one potential observer 'present', Hart considered cases that 'reported other persons *so situated* that they would have perceived the apparition if it had been a normal person' (p. 204, emphasis added). Therefore, Hart's case selection excludes those in which potential observers were present but asleep, or facing away from the apparition, or with viewpoint obstructed by walls or other objects. Hart found that 46 out of 167 cases (28 per cent) had two or more properly situated potential observers, and that 26 of those (56 per cent) were reported as collective. Perhaps, then, the processes at work in the collective cases are more pervasive than the small proportion of collective cases would suggest.

But let us not yet immerse ourselves in matters of theory. Since many readers, I would imagine, are not at all familiar with the data, let us first examine some cases of apparitions. This should help us later to sort through the tangled snarl of issues.

3.2   SAMPLE CASES

Discussions of apparitions tend to observe the customary distinction between apparitions of the living and apparitions of the dead. Although I shall present a few marginal cases in which the identity of the apparitional figure is unknown, or in which it is not clear whether the ostensible agent was dead or alive at the time of initiating the apparitional process, the following selection is drawn primarily from the former group. In so doing I do not mean to discount the importance of the evidence for apparitions of the dead. I simply wish to avoid, for now, the topic of survival. As the reader will see more clearly in section 3.4, my main interest here is to determine the extent to which apparitions may be considered perceptible changes in the material world, and not merely direct influences on the subjective experiences or inner episodes of percipients. Whether or not consciousness may survive bodily death and thereafter continue to influence the physical world is an issue that must be postponed for another occasion.

It is also not my aim here to mount a conclusive defense or survey of apparitional case material. Rather, I am interested merely in presenting a sample of the cases many have found to be theoretically interesting. Those wishing to pursue the topic further may examine the sources cited in this chapter. One unfortunate feature of the case material is that little of it is recent. Investigations of apparitions have decreased drastically since the initial flurry of interest around the turn of the century; hence, many of the best cases remain those investigated by the founders of the S.P.R. I would find it gratifying if this chapter should stimulate some enterprising psychical researcher to conduct a new census of hallucinations.

In any case, my principal goal in selecting cases was to choose those in which theoretically relevant features stand out clearly. And although collective cases are more theoretically puzzling than cases of individual apparitions, for the sake of completeness I shall present examples of both sorts. Moreover, whenever possible, I have chosen cases in which the evidence is relatively strong and well-documented. For example, in cases where the apparition is veridical, I have favored those in which testimony was presented or records made *before* the percipient learned of the confirming events. I have also favored cases in which accounts were written or conveyed relatively soon after the apparition was experienced, and in which a competent and independent researcher investigated the case. Fortunately, there are many good cases to choose from. In most instances, I shall be content to summarize the often complex web of events, leaving the reader free to consult the primary material for the full accounts and supporting documents. I have also tried to avoid presenting cases that are discussed in easily available forms elsewhere, particularly in Broad, 1962a. Some overlap was inevitable, however, since certain cases are either too fascinating or too important to be ignored. In any case, I suggest that interested readers consult Broad's traversal of the evidence for valuable supplementary material and for penetrating remarks about the cases.

Let us begin our survey with one example each of so-called *crisis* and *experimental* cases. These are of particular interest because the individual whose apparition is perceived seems to have some obvious intention or motive for 'appearing' to or communicating with a remote person. Cases lacking this feature we might call *inadvertent*, although (of course) equally potent needs or intentions might be operating under the surface, unrevealed by the evidence.

(1) *Miss Hervey* (S.P.R., 1894, pp. 282–4). In April, 1892, Miss Hervey recounted the experience she had four years earlier of her cousin's apparition. The case was subsequently investigated by Frank Podmore in July, 1892.

In April, 1888, Miss Hervey was in Tasmania, while her cousin was working in Dublin as a nurse. The two women had been close friends, but had not seen one another since Miss Hervey moved to Tasmania in 1887. The cousin's apparition was seen coming upstairs, dressed in grey, between 6 and 7 p.m. on April 21. The experience was so vivid that Miss Hervey ran to Lady H., in whose home she was staying. Lady H. laughed at her, but suggested she write a note about the matter in her diary. Podmore later saw the entry, which read, 'Saturday, April 21, 1888, 6 p.m. Vision of [nickname given] on landing in grey dress'. Miss Hervey wrote a letter that night to her cousin, telling her about the vision. The letter arrived after she had died, and was returned to Miss Hervey, who then destroyed it.

At the time, Miss Hervey was unaware of the fact that her cousin had been stricken by a sudden and quickly fatal attack of typhus fever, lasting only five days. Death came on April 22, 1888, at 4.30 p.m., about 32 hours after the apparition occurred. News of the event did not arrive until June. Miss Hervey retained a letter, written April 22, 1888, giving an account of her cousin's death. Podmore examined the letter, and reported that it speaks of the cousin being 'so heavy with fever all through'. Podmore also examined the material used for the nurses' dresses at the hospital where the cousin was employed. In his opinion, Miss Hervey's apparent perception of a grey dress was not especially significant, although the pattern of white, dark navy blue, and red in the nurses' dresses had 'a greyish tone at a little distance'.

(2) *Mr Kirk and Miss G.* (E. Sidgwick, 1922, pp. 270–3). Mr Kirk was employed as an administrator at Woolwich Arsenal. In a letter to the S.P.R. dated July 7, 1890, he described a series of experiments conducted between June 10 and June 20, 1890, in which he tried to produce a visual apparition of himself for his friend, Miss G. During the previous four years, the two friends had collaborated on some slightly different experiments, in which Mr Kirk tried simply to produce a *general* impression of his presence, not specifically a visual impression. In the present series, however, Miss G. had no normal knowledge that Mr Kirk was conducting experiments once more, much less that he was trying to produce a visual apparition of himself.

All but one of the new experiments were conducted at Mr Kirk's house, between the hours of 11 p.m. and 1 a.m. The one exception was the second experiment of the series, which took place in Kirk's office on Wednesday June 11, between 3.30 and 4 p.m. Mr Kirk and Miss G. met occasionally during the 10-day period of experimentation, and although Kirk made no mention of his activities, Miss G. complained each time of sleeplessness and restlessness from an uneasy feeling she was unable to describe or explain. One night, she said, the feeling was so strong that she had to get out of bed, dress, and do some needlework until 2 a.m., when the uneasiness finally disappeared. Mr Kirk offered no comments and dropped no hints, although he naturally suspected that his efforts were causing the unpleasant feelings in his friend. Since he felt that he had failed to produce a visual apparition, and had succeeded only in depriving Miss G. of rest, he soon discontinued the experiments.

But on June 23rd, during a conversation with Miss G., Kirk learned that he had apparently succeeded after all, during the one experiment conducted from his office. His decision to conduct the trial had been made on the spur of the moment, in the midst of doing some tiring auditing work. He had laid down his pencil, and while stretching himself had an impulse to try to appear to Miss G. He did not know where she was at the time, but (either by luck or by ESP) thought of her as in her bedroom, and accordingly tried to appear to her there. By another apparent stroke of luck, Miss G. was in her bedroom at the time, dozing in her chair, a condition which (if telepathy is the explanation of the phenomenon) perhaps made her particularly receptive.

176

Miss G. described what happened in a letter written on Saturday, June 28. On the morning of June 11 she had taken a long walk, and by mid-afternoon was tired, and fell asleep in the easy-chair near her bedroom window. Suddenly she woke, and apparently saw Mr Kirk standing nearby, dressed in a dark brown suit she had seen before. He stood with his back to the window, and passed across the room to the door, which was closed, approximately 15 ft. away. When the figure got to about 4 ft. from the door, it disappeared.

It occurred to Miss G. that perhaps Kirk was trying to affect her telepathically, since he had tried to do so in the past. But she had no idea that he was presently so engaged, and dismissed the thought anyway, since she knew that at that time on a weekday he would have been working in his office. She concluded, then, that her experience had been purely imaginary, and resolved not to mention it to Kirk. Her resolve lasted until their conversation on the 23rd, when she told him all about it 'almost involuntarily'. Kirk was very pleased to learn of his success, and asked Miss G. to write an account of her experience. He mentioned that he had purposely avoided the subject of telepathy in her presence lately, and had hoped she would introduce it herself. Miss G. also insisted that she was awake at the time of the experience, and had neither been dreaming of Kirk immediately beforehand nor thinking of him that afternoon.

According to Kirk's account, when Miss G. related her experience to him, he had asked her to describe how he was dressed. This was certainly not a leading question, and Miss G. replied that he had been wearing his dark suit, and that she had clearly seen a *small check* pattern on it. Kirk states that he had in fact been wearing his dark suit on that occasion, and, moreover, that it was unusual for him to do so. As a rule he wore a light suit in his office; but on the day of the experiment it was at the tailor's shop for repairs.

(3) *Rider Haggard and the dog Bob* (E. Sidgwick, 1922, pp. 219–31). On July 16, 1904, novelist Rider Haggard wrote a letter to *The Times*, along with various supporting documents, all of which were published in the issue of July 21. This case owes much of its interest to the fact that the apparent agent and victim of a crisis was a black retriever named Bob, belonging to Haggard's eldest daughter, and of whom the author was quite

fond. Haggard described him as 'a most amiable and intelligent beast'.

On the night of Saturday, July 9, Haggard retired to bed around 12.30, and then had a nightmare. He was awakened from it by his wife, who slept in a bed on the other side of the room. In a letter written by her on July 15, Mrs Haggard confirms the fact, and adds that the sounds emitted by her husband were very disturbing.

Haggard's dream was 'long and vivid', but faded quickly after he was awakened. Still, he remembered the overall quality of the dream, which was dominated by 'a sense of awful oppression and of desperate and terrified struggling for life'. And between the time when he heard his wife's voice and responded to it, he had a second dream, which he remembered clearly. He dreamed that Bob was lying on his side in the rough undergrowth near water. He felt as if he were somehow arising or issuing from the dog's body; he felt his head against the dog's head, which was lifted up at an unnatural angle. The dog appeared to be trying to speak to him, and when that failed, to communicate nonverbally that he was dying. Then Haggard awoke and heard his wife ask why he had been making such strange and horrible noises. Haggard replied that he had suffered a nightmare in which he seemed to be engaged in a fearful struggle, and that Bob was trying to communicate to him that he was in trouble. Mrs Haggard confirmed this reply in her letter, and guessed that the episode took place around 2 a.m. on July 10. Both Haggards noted that it was dark at the time.

The next morning at breakfast both Mr and Mrs Haggard told the story to a group including their daughter Angela, a relative named Miss Hildyard, and Mr Haggard's secretary. The first two wrote confirmatory letters dated July 14, and the third wrote one dated the 15th. Angela remarked that they had all laughed at the story, since they had no reason to believe that anything had happened to Bob. Angela herself had seen the dog the previous evening, around 8 p.m.

On the evening of the 10th, Haggard was told by the young daughter who usually fed Bob that their dog was missing. The next day Haggard set out to look for him; but it was not until the 14th that he and his servant, Charles Bedingfield, found Bob floating in the river Waveney against a weir at Falcon Bridge,

Bungay. Bedingfield signed a confirmatory statement dated July 14.

Haggard took Bob's remains to a veterinary surgeon, Mr Mullane, who described the dog's conditions in a letter dated July 14, and speculated therein on the cause of death. He observed that Bob's skull had been smashed almost to a pulp by a heavy blunt instrument, and from the condition of the body judged that Bob had been in the water for more than three days, and that probably he had been killed on the night of July 9. He further surmised that Bob's injury had been caused by a large trap.

Mullane's conjecture, however, was incorrect, as Haggard discovered on July 15, when he went to Bungay to offer a reward for the discovery of the persons whom he assumed to have killed Bob in the manner suggested by Mullane. En route, he was hailed by two plate-layers, George Arterton and Harry Alger, who told him that Bob had been killed by a train. They took Haggard on a trolley down to an open-work bridge crossing the water between Bungay and Ditchingham, and showed him the evidence.

Alger's account was given orally, and then written down and signed by him. He had been working on the line between Bungay and Ditchingham at 7 a.m. on July 11, and found the broken collar of a dog lying there. He had to scrape off dried blood and bits of flesh from the line. From the way the flesh had been carried, he concluded that the dog must have been hit by a train going towards Bungay. Alger also found marks of blood on the piles where the dog had fallen from the bridge into the reeds below. The dog was first spotted by Arterton, who saw it later in the day on July 11, after it had risen to the surface.

Haggard recognized the collar as Bob's, and found further portions of black hair on the line. The evidence suggests strongly that Bob was killed on *July 9* by a train which departed from Ditchingham at 10.25 p.m. in the direction of Bungay. No trains ran the next day, which was Sunday. One train did travel the line on Monday the 11th, at 6.30 a.m. But its driver denied hitting a dog, and when Alger questioned two men who had been working near the bridge at the time, they likewise denied seeing or hearing a dog. Besides, the condition of Bob's body indicated that it had been dead for a longer period. Therefore, it seems quite certain that Bob was hit by a train sometime after 10.25 p.m. on the night of July 9, and that (dead or dying) it fell from the bridge into the river, later rising to the surface and floating down to the weir where Haggard and his servant found it on July 14. And judging by the condition of the dog's skull, it is likely that death was instantaneous. It appears, then, that Bob's accident and death occurred several hours *before* Haggard's two dreams.

The reader should keep in mind that this case does not necessarily provide evidence of survival. One might argue, instead, that Haggard and Bob interacted telepathically at the time of the dog's accident, but that the effect of the interaction was delayed until Haggard was asleep. Therefore, the case of Haggard and Bob may well provide evidence, not only of ordinary telepathic interaction, but also of what Gurney called *telepathic deferment*, in which the effect remains latent for awhile before emerging into consciousness.

Turning now to collective cases, we find reports of phenomena which appear to be more intractable than those surveyed above.

(4) *Mr and Mrs Barber* (*Jour. S.P.R.* 6, 1893, pp. 22–5; E. Sidgwick, 1922, pp. 372–6). Shortly before sunset on April 19, 1890, in light still bright enough for reading outdoors, Mr and Mrs Barber were returning home from a walk. When they were about 6 yards from their gate, Mr Barber saw a woman pass through the open gate and walk toward the house. Mrs Barber's eyes had been fixed on the ground, making sure she would not trip over the loose stones on the road. When she looked up, a moment later, she saw the figure about a yard inside the gate. Nevertheless, Mrs Barber saw the apparition before her husband had spoken. In fact, the two exclaimed, nearly simultaneously, 'Who is that?' (Mrs Barber asserts that her remark slightly preceded that of her husband.) The figure appeared 'thoroughly commonplace and substantial', and walked quietly up the path, and then up the two steps to the door, at which point it disappeared. Mr Barber then ran toward the house with his latchkey, expecting to find the woman inside. After unlocking the door, he and Mrs Barber carefully searched the house (the daylight was still sufficient), but found nothing. According to Mrs Barber, the woman was dressed in grey; Mr Barber observed a plaid shawl and a grey-black bonnet 'with a bit of colour in it'.

Mr and Mrs Barber submitted accounts in January, 1891, and were interviewed by F. W. H. Myers in August of that year.

(5) *Canon Bourne* (*Jour. S.P.R.* 6, 1893, pp. 129–30). Bourne

and his two daughters were out hunting on February 5, 1887. In a statement written jointly, the daughters assert that at about midday they decided to return home with the coachman, leaving the father to continue on his own. They were delayed for a few moments when somebody came to speak to them, during which time Bourne presumably went on his way. Then, when they turned to go home, all three saw the father waving his hat and beckoning to them with his usual gesture. Mrs Sidgwick noted, after interviewing the Bournes, that this gesture was 'peculiar', apparently unlikely to have been that of anyone else. Mr Bourne appeared to be on the side of a hill, standing near his horse. 'The horse looked so dirty and shaken,' the sisters wrote, 'that the coachman remarked he thought there had been a nasty accident.' Mrs Sidgwick later determined that the sisters were familiar with the horses in the neighborhood, and that no other horse would have been mistaken for that of the father. His was the only white horse in the area, and since Mr Bourne was a heavy man, the horse eventually 'adapted to carry [his] weight, [and] was quite unlike any other horse in the neighborhood'. The sisters also distinctly 'saw the Lincoln and Bennett mark inside [their father's hat], though from the distance we were apart it ought to have been utterly impossible . . . to have seen it'. The strangeness of seeing the mark did not register until later.

The daughters and the coachman feared that Bourne had suffered an accident, and hurried down the dip in the field toward the hill where he had been seen. The terrain forced them to lose sight of the figure en route; but although the trip to the hill took only 'very few seconds', when they reached the spot Bourne was nowhere to be seen. They 'rode about for some time looking for him, but could not see or hear anything of him'. When they later met at home, Bourne told his daughters that he had not even been near the field where they apparently saw him, that he had never waved to them, and that he had not met with an accident.

The following month, one of the daughters saw an apparition of their father when she was out walking alone. He was again seen with his horse Paddy. This time he appeared to stop at a plantation of his to examine a wall that needed repair. But Bourne claimed to have been nowhere near the plantation that day, having ridden home another way. The sister then realized that from where she stood it was impossible to see either the plantation or the wall.

(6) *The Scott sisters* (*Jour. S.P.R.* 6, 1893, pp. 146–50). This is a case of a collective and reiterative apparition. The first incident occurred on May 7, 1892, at about a quarter to six in the afternoon. Miss M. W. Scott was returning home from a walk near St Boswells, England. She had reached the top of an incline from which the whole road ahead could be seen, with a hedge and a bank on each side. She had just begun to hurry home down the road when she saw a tall man dressed in black walking ahead of her at a moderate pace. She felt uncomfortable at the idea of a stranger watching her run, and so she stopped to let him proceed further. She watched him turn the corner, and although he was still distinctly visible between the two hedges, he vanished instantly. As she approached the spot where the man had disappeared, she saw her sister, Miss Louisa Scott, looking around 'in a bewildered manner'. She asked her sister where the man was, and then found that Louisa had also seen a similar figure.

But apparently the two experiences were successive rather than simultaneous. Louisa had seen the figure approaching her, and took his black clothing to be that of a clergyman. She looked away momentarily, and when she looked up again was surprised to discover that the man had disappeared. She was certain that had he attempted to scale one of the high hedges on either side of the road she would have seen it. In any case, she looked around into the fields, but could find no trace of him. As she continued further down the road, she saw her sister starting to run down from the incline, stop suddenly, and then look around her much as she herself had done about 5 minutes earlier. Neither sister had expected to find the other on the road that afternoon.

Toward the end of July, at about the same time, Miss M. W. Scott and another sister were walking down the same spot in the road when the former saw a dark figure approaching, and exclaimed, 'Oh, I do believe *that* is *our* man. I won't remove my eyes from him!' Both sisters kept their gaze fixed on the figure, although Miss M. W. Scott once again saw the entire figure, while her sister saw only the head to below the shoulders. 'The man was dressed entirely in black, consisting of a long coat, gaiters, and knee-breeches, and his legs were very thin. Round his throat was a wide white cravat, such as I have seen in old pictures. On

his head was a low-crowned hat. . . . His face, of which I saw
only the profile, was exceedingly thin and deadly pale'. While the
sisters looked at the figure, it seemed to fade away toward the
bank on the right side of the road. Both women rushed forward,
but discovered no trace of the man. They questioned some boys
who were on the top of a hay-cart nearby, and to whom the entire
road was visible. But they claimed that no one had passed that
way.

Miss M. W. Scott reported that during this period, two girls
from the village had had similar experiences as they stopped by
the road to pick berries. They had heard a thud or thump on the
ground, and since when they looked up they saw nothing, they
resumed their task. But the sound occurred again, and this time
they saw a figure matching the description given above (the principal difference being that his garments were enveloped in a white
filmy vapor or sheet). The apparition gazed intently at the girls,
who were so frightened by its countenance that they fled down
the road. When they turned to look back, they saw the figure still
standing; and while they watched he gradually faded away. Two
years earlier two boys reportedly had similar experiences; and
for nearly a fortnight many people followed moving blue lights
occurring near the spot on the road after dark. According to
legend, a child had been murdered close by.

Separate statements were submitted by Louisa and Miss M. W.
Scott, within a year of the incidents. The third sister approved
the account of the second incident, but felt that an additional
statement from her would be of little value.

On June 12, 1893, at about 10 a.m., Miss M. W. Scott saw the
figure again, but this time she was alone. At first, she thought she
had spotted a woman she wanted to see, and hurried after it.
When she found that it was the same apparitional figure, she
followed it boldly, feeling no fear this time. Although she ran
after the man in close pursuit, and although the figure was apparently walking slowly, she was unable to get closer than within a
few yards, since he seemed to float or skim away. Eventually he
stopped, and feeling afraid once again Miss Scott stopped as well.
The figure turned, and gazed at her with a vacant expression and
the same pallid features. He was dressed as before, although this
time Miss Scott noticed black silk stockings and shoe-buckles.
Finally, the figure moved on and faded from view at the usual

spot near the right hedge. Miss Scott related this incident in a letter two days after it occurred, and in a second letter, on June 28, mentions that the figure's costume was that of a clergyman of the previous century.

(7) *The Revd H. Hasted* (*Jour. S.P.R.* 6, 1893, pp. 131–3). Revd Hasted, of Pitsea Rectory, Essex, seems to have been unusually prone to apparitional appearances. The two young Williams sisters reportedly saw him coming along the road toward the Rectory from behind some nearby bushes in their garden. At the time of the experience, however, Hasted claimed to have been at least a mile from that location. On another occasion, a lady friend reportedly saw him on the beach at Bournemouth, when he was not in Bournemouth at all. And on still another occasion, a woman reportedly saw Hasted ride up to the gate of a neighboring rectory, raise the latch with the loop of his whip, and stoop down to push open the gate. She also thought she recognized his horse, which was unlike any other in the neighborhood.

But the most impressive and best documented case is the following. On March 16, 1892, at 11.30 a.m., two of Hasted's servants, Eliza Smallbone and Jane Watts, were standing outside the Rectory talking with the rat catcher, N., who had come to tell Hasted about a dog. The servants noted the time, because they looked at the clock when telling N. that their master would return by 12.15 for lunch. Mrs Watts was watching N. drive away with two dogs in his cart, when she said 'Here comes the master!' Eliza saw him also, accompanied by his dog. They watched N. approach Hasted, expecting them to meet; but instead of stopping to talk, N. drove on.

At about that time they lost sight of Hasted, even though the lane was straight and open to full view. They thought he might have gone to Mr Wilson's house, since Wilson was seen to be standing in front of his house by the road. Mr Wilson confirmed he was standing where the servants saw him, but claimed that no person other than N. was on the lane. When the servants mentioned the event to Hasted, he told them he had been at the home of Mr Williams at the time. Hasted's location was confirmed by a statement of Mrs Shield, written later that day. It was Mrs Shield who submitted the case to the S.P.R. The servants gave a joint account the next day.

Mrs Sidgwick investigated the case a month later, and queried

Hasted, Wilson, and the two servants. She added that the servants struck her as good witnesses, and that they had noticed Mr Hasted's peculiar way of walking and his swinging his stick. Furthermore, the only other dog in the neighborhood like Mr Hasted's brown and white spaniel was kept tied up. Mrs Sidgwick also records that both Mrs Shield and Miss F. Williams noted the time when Mr Hasted was at the Williams' home. Hasted had been hurrying to finish some work, and they had wondered whether he would be done in time to go for lunch at 12.15.

The last case is contemporary, and is an example of the sort of 'reciprocal' case occasionally reported in connection with 'travelling' clairvoyance, or out-of-body experiences (OBEs). It is also one of the few cases where the apparition is reported to have left behind physical traces. Hence, some might prefer to consider the case a possible instance of bilocation or teleportation. But of course, if we allow apparitions to be materialized entities, that may be unnecessary.

(8) *Dadaji* (Osis and Haraldsson, 1976). Dadaji (Mr Chowdhury) is a former celebrated radio singer. After leaving radio for the life of a businessman, he trained at a Himalayan ashram and returned to India as 'elder brother' – Dadaji. Apparently, he practices OBEs as an integral part of the guru-devotee relationship.

Early in 1970 Dadaji was touring in Allahabad, about 400 miles north-west of Calcutta. While his devotees were singing religious songs in one room of a house, Dadaji was alone in the prayer room. After emerging from the prayer room, Dadaji asked one of the ladies present to contact her sister-in-law in Calcutta to see if he had been seen at a certain address there at the time. The sister-in-law complied, and found that the Mukherjee family, who lived at that address, had indeed seen Dadaji's apparition. Osis and Haraldsson interviewed Dadaji's hosts in Allabahad, the sister-in-law in Calcutta, and the Mukherjee family.

The Mukherjee's story is the following. Roma, the daughter, was lying on her bed studying for an English examination, when she heard a noise. She looked up, and through an open door saw Dadaji in the study. At first, he seemed semi-transparent and she could see objects in the study through his figure. But eventually the figure became opaque. Roma then screamed, alerting her brother (a physician) and mother. The apparition did not speak, but through sign language told Roma to be silent and to bring him a cup of tea. Roma then went to the kitchen, leaving the door to the study ajar. Her brother and mother followed her when she returned to the study with the tea. Roma reached through the partially open door and handed the figure the tea and a biscuit. Her mother, through the crack in the door, saw the apparition. The brother's vantage point was not so good; he saw only Roma's hand reach in through the opening and come back without the tea. But there was no place for Roma to set the cup without entering the room.

At that point, the father, a bank director, returned home from doing the morning shopping. When the family told him about the apparition, he was incredulous. But when he peeked through the crack in the door, he saw a man's figure sitting on a chair. The family remained in the living room, within full view of the study door, until they heard a noise. Thinking Dadaji had left, they then entered the study. All four observed that the other door leading from the study was locked from the inside, by an iron bar across it, and also a bolt from above. The apparition was indeed, gone, as was half of the tea and part of the biscuit. Moreover, a cigarette was still burning on the table, and it was Dadaji's favorite brand.

Osis and Haraldsson describe the daughter as a 'long-term devotee' of Dadaji. The brother and father apparently visit him infrequently, and the mother does not visit him at all.

3.3 DEFINITIONS

Let us now consider matters of terminology, and attempt to define 'apparition'. Although in my opinion definitions are of less utility than many philosophers suppose, and are certainly never as crisp or exact as some pretend, nevertheless it should be possible to arrive at a useful working definition. I propose that we begin by examining Price's (1960) suggested definition, since it is clearly – but instructively – inadequate (Price himself admits that it is rough). According to Price,

(D1) 'Apparition' = df 'A visible but non-physical phenomenon closely resembling a particular human being (either dead or alive)'

(D1) has several outstanding drawbacks. The first is that it begs the question on the nature of apparitions by taking them to be non-physical. Even though Price considered apparitions to be objective entities of a sort, he apparently believed (as have many others) that they are so different from ordinary material objects that they cannot be physical. I will discuss this error in the next section.

Another difficulty with (D1) is that it takes apparitions to be essentially *visible* phenomena.[1] But many apparitions are also heard or felt, and some are *only* sensed non-visually. Sometimes the apparition speaks, and even more often percipients hear noises accompanying the movements of apparitional figures. In still other cases subjects experience touches (e.g., pinches, strokes, or kisses) or breezes and changes of temperature. Most damaging, however, are cases in which apparitions are sensed but not seen at all. Witnesses often report feeling the presence of the apparition *before* the figure is seen (see Tyrrell, 1942/1961, pp. 74–5). Tyrrell even cites a case in which the witness feels not only the (unseen) apparition's presence, but also its pressure on her bed (1942/1961, p. 75). In other cases, apparitions are heard – sometimes collectively – but not seen (e.g., the Morton ghost – see Tyrrell, 1942/1961, pp. 55–6; also the cases in E. Sidgwick, 1922, pp. 393ff.). Of course, theoretical considerations might later compel us to regard certain phenomenological aspects of apparitions as significantly different from others. For example, it could turn out that tactile impressions are all subjective constructs while the other sensory properties of apparitions tend to result from ordinary perceptual causal chains. But these insights must come later, if they come at all. All we want now is a working definition of 'apparition', one designed merely to help delineate the topic under consideration, and (therefore) one with as few theoretical commitments as possible.

Another questionable feature of (D1) is that it takes apparitions to be *only* of human beings. But since the classical studies of apparitions contain reports of apparent perceptions of animals, elements of scenery, and clothing or other appurtenances of human figures, this maneuver leads to classificatory chaos. To begin with, it makes the status of apparitions of inanimate objects unclear. For example, Price considers Tyrrell's 'Pillow Case' 'not quite realistic enough' (Price, 1960, p. 119) to be counted an apparition. In that case,

A lady woke early one morning and saw what appeared to be half a sheet of note-paper lying on her pillow with the words written on it: 'Elsie (pseudonym) was dying last night.' There was only one person to which the message could refer and it turned out that she had, in fact, died during that night. (Tyrrell, 1938/1961, pp. 24)

Now I see no reason, especially in the absence of a detailed justificatory theory, to refuse to classify the image of the paper as an apparition. Price's decision strikes me as arbitrarily restrictive. He claims it is 'not exactly an apparition' (1960, p. 119) because it is less realistic than other cases. But Price never states on what grounds the case counts as insufficiently realistic. Besides, if hallucinations of lower animals are not to count as apparitions, it would presumably be for some other reason. Nothing in the case material suggests that apparent perceptions of non-humans are less vivid or realistic than those of humans. Moreover, by making the status of animate and inanimate apparitions separate issues, Price's approach makes the question 'Why do ghosts wear clothes?' much more problematical than it need be.

C. D. Broad (1962a) adopted an approach rather different from that of Price. And curiously, he eschewed the use of the term 'apparition', preferring instead 'hallucination', even when discussing the cases Tyrrell, Price, and others label 'apparitions'. Actually, Broad's discussion extended well beyond the phenomena of parapsychology, and his overall approach was ambitious and quite impressive. He treated the term 'hallucination' as synonymous with 'hallucinatory quasi-perception', and offered a characteristically detailed taxonomy of hallucinatory phenomena. But he made no attempt to define a separate class of apparitions. Apparently, he regarded experiences of apparitions as nothing more than a motley subset of the set of hallucinations. The definition he offered (in a condensed form) was as follows (see Broad, 1962a, pp. 190–1).

(D2) '*S* hallucinates *x*' = df '(a) It seems to *S* as if he perceives *x* through one or more of the recognized sense modalities, and (b) neither *x* nor any physical

reproduction of *x* was present or occurring in such a
way as to be perceptible to *S*'.[2]

On this account, hallucinations need not be pathological or
totally delusory; in fact, even ordinary dreams count as hallucinations. Therefore, hallucinations may occur both while awake
and while asleep. Although some might find this use of 'hallucination' surprising, it conforms to the reigning use of the term in
parapsychology, and reflects the S.P.R.'s early interest in telepathically-induced dreams. (D2) also allows for both externalized
(extra-somatic) and internalized (intra-somatic) hallucinations.
Instances of the former are the most common. Instances of the
latter would be, for example, experiences of demons in one's
stomach or moving about under one's skin. Here, the relevant
sense modalities are (of course) intra-somatic. So far, so good.
But (D2) has some conspicuous apparent weaknesses, both on
general philosophical grounds and in relation to the topic of
apparitions.

One curious feature of (D2) – though not clearly a defect – is
that it permits hallucinations to be *veridical*. We can say that *S*
has a veridical hallucination of *x* when, in addition to the satisfaction of conditions (a) and (b) above, the following two conditions
are also satisfied.

(c) there exists a certain object or event *y*, closely correlated
    in content and detail with *S*'s ostensible perception, and
(d) it is unlikely that this closeness between *x* and *y* is
    fortuitous, or attributable to normal information,
    expectation, or inference on the part of *S*.

(The reader should note that this interpretation of veridicality
does not insist on closeness in *time* between *S*'s experience and
the object or event *y*, thereby allowing for precognitive and retro-
cognitive veridical hallucinations.) The reason one might quibble
with all this is that, as the term 'hallucination' is commonly used
(at least outside parapsychology), hallucinations are non-veridical
by definition. But we must remind ourselves, again, that Broad's
use of 'hallucination' falls squarely within the parapsychological
tradition (such as it is), and that this tradition (of course)
developed in response to the peculiar needs of an unorthodox
subject matter. In any event, Broad would nevertheless have been

entitled to propose an unconventional technical use of the term, especially if it had considerable utility.[3]

More troublesome, perhaps, is the fact that (D2) blurs the venerable philosophical distinction between *illusions* and hallucinations, the thrust of which has been to mark a contrast between two kinds of causal chains. Traditionally, philosophers have considered illusions (e.g., mirages, a bent stick in water) to be experiences caused by extra-somatic states of affairs, while taking hallucinations to be experiences produced intrasomatically – for example, by drugs or auto-suggestion. (In fact, this was the sense of 'hallucination' used earlier in Chapter 1.4, in connection with the skeptical hypotheses of collective hallucination and hypnosis.) But at least some illusions – mirages, for example, but not the bent stick – satisfy (D2), since they are not physical *reproductions* of the objects apparently perceived. Of course, the illusion/ hallucination distinction is not sacred; and needless to say, we are not now on the specialized philosophical terrain for which it was intended. On the contrary, we are now concerned with a subject matter according to whose literature a *paradigm* case of a hallucination is one that appears to have an extra-somatic cause. Hence, (D2)'s incompatibility with the distinction may be more of a virtue than a defect. In any case, had Broad's approach been satisfactory in other respects, we could have tentatively and conscientiously abandoned the distinction between illusions and hallucinations, agreeing thereby to speak of externally-induced hallucinations.[4] That would have been an appropriate concession to the domain under consideration.

It turns out, however, that (D2) is seriously flawed, at least as far as the topic of apparitions is concerned. Interestingly, the problem stems precisely from Broad's attempt to treat apparitions as a subset of the set of hallucinations. As a result, (D2) is incompatible with the explanation of apparitions most relevant to this book, according to which apparitions are materializations. A materialization of an object or person x would presumably be a physical reproduction of x, and would be perceivable by ordinary sensory means. Therefore, if apparitions are materializations, clause (b) is not satisfied. So (D2) has the unfortunate feature of blocking a major theoretical approach to apparitions, one that Broad himself acknowledged in his criticism of Myers and Tyrrell (see sect. 4).

Yet another general approach was suggested to me (in correspondence) by Alan Gauld. Gauld maintains that according to the primary meaning of 'apparition', and the related terms 'ghost', 'phantasm', and 'spectre', something is objectively present, perceived in more or less the usual way. He also maintains that it was not until the middle of the nineteenth century that most people came to regard apparitions as hallucinatory. But, Gauld claims, to say that apparitions are hallucinations is really to say that there are no such things as apparitions. He recommends treating apparitions as a class of perceivable objective things, and suggests that we regard telepathic explanations of apparitions as attempts to explain them *away*.

Although Gauld's approach has much to recommend it, it seems to break too severely with the prevailing parapsychological tradition, represented by Broad, and most of the writing on apparitions since the very first (telepathic) theory proposed in the *Proceedings of the Society for Psychical Research* (S.P.R., 1884). It may be, as Gauld says, that this now well-entrenched tradition is relatively recent. But it is now too pervasive to be brushed aside, and it has influenced over 100 years of case selection. Indeed, even if Gauld has history on his side, the fact remains that many of the classic examples of apparitions in the literature since 1882 are dream cases or others for which telepathic interaction is a plausible explanation. Even if apparitions were originally considered non-hallucinatory, times have changed, the meaning of 'apparition' has evolved, and as a result the recent literature on apparitions is dominated by cases widely considered to be explained (*not* explained away) as telepathically-induced hallucinations. Hence, Gauld's proposal seems, in its own way, as theoretically and taxonomically one-sided as Broad's.

What we need, I suggest, is a theory-neutral definition of 'apparition' that encompasses the different sorts of cases found in the literature. Perhaps such a definition would be as uninformative as the definitions of 'telepathy' and 'clairvoyance' (see Braude, 1979), which are mere categorizations of different kinds of phenomena-we-know-not-what. But all we need is a rough and ready way of demarcating the class of phenomena under discussion; and there is no need to demand more than that from the definition.

With that modest goal in mind, then, we can state a minimal,

191

but useful, definition of 'apparition'. We need only to articulate two underlying prevailing intuitions. The first is that an apparition of *x* appears, but fails, to be a genuine perception of *x* by means of the familiar senses. But not every merely apparent perception of *x* is an apparition. Some, of course, we know or assume to be ordinary dreams, or drug- or stress-induced, or the result of suggestion, tricks, or optical illusion. Apparitional experiences, I suggest, are the remainder, believed to lack any such familiar causal history. The second intuition, then, is that apparitions are apparent perceptions that do not result from well-recognized causal chains – either the kinds producing genuine perceptions by means of the familiar senses, or else the kinds that produce dreams or common hallucinations and illusions.

At one time I had thought that the second intuition was rather stronger – namely, that apparitional experiences were products of *paranormal* causal chains. But Gauld has persuaded me that this is wrong. The cases collected in the literature are not cases whose causes are known; they are cases awaiting satisfactory explanation. Hence, although apparitions *may* have paranormal causes, we needn't know what the cause is of an experience properly classified as an apparition. It simply needs to be mysterious in the general way outlined above. We need only suppose that certain familiar kinds of causal stories will not explain it.

Consider, then, the following definition.

> (D3) '*S* experiences an apparition of *x*' = df '(a) it seems to *S* as if he perceives *x* through one or more of the recognized sense modalities, (b) *S* does not perceive *x* through any of the recognized sense modalities, (c) *S*'s apparent perception is not produced by such familiar causes as drugs, stress, suggestion, optical illusion, etc.'

(D3) still allows certain dream experiences to count as apparitional, provided they do not result from the sorts of conditions ordinarily producing dreams. And objectively perceivable entities will also count as apparitional, provided they are not such things as mirages, optical illusions, or tricks with mirrors. Hopefully, then, (D3) will countenance the full range of cases classified as apparitions, even if it is less than enlightening.

In any event, I think we have gone far enough with terminological considerations. It should be more interesting and profitable to consider the nagging question: How do we explain the evidence for apparitions (messy or disorganized though it may be)? I suggest, then, that we allow our concerns over the concept of an apparition to recede gracelessly into the background, and turn our attention to the leading theories.

3.4 THEORETICAL REMARKS

a. General issues

Traditionally, theories of apparitions have divided into two main groups: *telepathic* (or subjectivist) and *objectivist*. The former treat apparitions as constructs of inner experience, while the latter take them to be localized external entities of some sort. Naturally, each of these general theoretical approaches assumes a variety of forms, particularly with regard to cases of collective apparitions. But before considering these – in fact, before examining specifically the conceptual issues posed by collective apparitions, let us survey some outstanding general features of these two main theoretical approaches, as well as the issues they address.

In rough outline, the telepathic theory proposes that a mental state in agent *A* produces a mental state in apparition-percipient *B*, and that the telepathically induced mental state of *B* manifests itself in the form of an hallucination. What is initially plausible about this theory (as Price, 1960, observes) is that telepathy is usually and reasonably considered to be a two-stage process. First, the agent telepathically affects the percipient; then the effect manifests itself somehow in the percipient. And, of course, this second part of the process can presumably take different forms. For example, the telepathic effect could emerge in a dream or in a waking mental state. And if the latter, it could manifest either as an image, a vague change of mood or feeling, a more precise and sudden disruption of the mental flow, an impulse to do something (e.g., 'I should telephone so-and-so'), or perhaps even as automatic or semi-automatic bodily behavior (as in automatic writing and speech). As far as the topic of apparitions is concerned, a more relevant option is that the telepathic effect manifests itself as an hallucination of an external object. On the telepathic theory, then, apparitions would simply be one of the many possible kinds of effects of telepathic interaction.

Furthermore, Price suggests that if the telepathic theory is correct, then we would expect apparitions to be a particularly realistic or vivid subset of the set of telepathically-induced hallucinations. He suggests, in other words, that telepathic hallucinations would naturally fall on a continuum of vividness or realism, and that apparitions belong at one extreme. I am inclined to agree that telepathic experiences will exhibit different shades of vividness or verisimiltude; but it is not clear to me why we should *expect* apparitions generally to be vivid or realistic. Quite possibly, Price's intuition is that apparitions, unlike drug- or stress-induced hallucinations, tend to be readily mistaken for real objects and persons, and lack the fantastic qualities characterizing hallucinations of other sorts. On the other hand, according to the parapsychological literature, apparitions sometimes occur during sleep; and it is not clear why dream-like experiences should be placed toward the realistic end of the continuum. Perhaps, then, Price meant only to consider waking apparitions. But in that case he would have been ignoring a substantial portion of the case material widely considered to fall within the purview of his topic.

Be that as it may, the objectivist theory raises different issues; some might consider it to be far more radical than the telepathic theory. In outline, it proposes that an apparition is a real, localized externalized entity, and not simply a subjective construct of the percipient. Early proponents of the theory maintained that the entity was non-physical, although it bore certain similarities to ordinary material objects. To some extent (as we will see), this claim rests on confusions over what physical objects are. In any case, it is not essential to the objectivist theory that the apparition be of a particular ontological kind. Initially, all it must claim is that the apparition has certain properties not belonging to the material object it resembles. For example, apparitions – but not persons – are able to pass through walls and closed doors.

Myers and Tyrrell were among those who argued that if apparitions are objective localized entities, they are nevertheless sufficiently unlike physical objects to be classed as non-physical (Wallace, 1896/1975, was non-committal on this issue). The principal points of dissimilarity, as itemized by Tyrrell (1942/1961, p. 59), are: (i) apparitions appear and disappear in locked rooms,

(ii) they vanish while being watched, (iii) sometimes they become transparent and fade away, (iv) they are often seen or heard only by some of those present and in a position to perceive any physical object genuinely at that location (v) they disappear into walls and closed doors and pass through physical objects apparently in their path, (vi) hands may go through them, or people may walk through them without encountering resistance, and (vii) they leave behind no physical traces.

But as Broad (1962a, pp. 234ff.) correctly noted, various familiar spatial *physical* objects display these and related peculiar properties. Hence, the properties are not signs of an object's immateriality. For example, a *mirror image* is a physical phenomenon located in the region of space occupied by the mirror. But (a) it is visible only to those properly situated, (b) tactual impressions of the image fail to correspond to its visual impressions, and (c) although the image appears *behind* the mirror, the mirror has no depth. Furthermore, the mirror image is *caused* to exist by an ordinary physical object, which resembles it in appearance, and which occupies a region of physical space distinct from that occupied by the image. Therefore, if apparitions are objective entities, they might be akin to mirror images, not only with regard to their perceptible properties, but also with regard to their causal dependency on ordinary physical objects. Moreover, some physical objects, such as gases, electromagnetic fields, and rainbows, are present in or spread out in a region of space, but are more intensely localized in and perceivable from certain specific locations. Indeed, they exhibit the anomalous properties of apparitions precisely because of the manner in which they are extended in space. The moral here, of course, is that not all physical objects occupy space as a *solid body* does. Gases and rainbows have Tyrrell's properties (ii), (iii), (iv), (vi) and (vii), and electromagnetic fields have properties (i), (iv), (v), (vi), (vii).

The initial advantage of the objectivist theory is that it seems to account for collective apparitions more easily than the telepathic theory. If apparitions are hallucinations or subjective constructs, it is not clear, first, why more than one person should simultaneously suffer a spontaneous exceptional experience of that sort, and second, why the content of the various experiences should correspond at all, much less in the manner of ordinary impressions of physical objects. Partisans of telepathic theory have dealt with these problems in various ways. For example, Tyrrell claimed that collective percipience could be accounted for in terms of requirements for *dramatic appropriateness*. The apparitional drama, he suggested, is something an agent manipulates unconsciously, trying to make it as realistic as possible by having the apparition fit (or appear to fit) smoothly into the physical environment of the percipient. But of course in some cases others are present in this environment, and accordingly they get *drawn into* the drama. How this might be accomplished is a matter I shall consider below, in surveying the various forms of the telepathic theory. In any case, some have felt that a telepathic account of collective apparitions is artificial and needlessly complex, and that by contrast the positing of externalized entities seems more parsimonious.

But however attractive the objectivist's theory's apparent simplicity may be, it seems to me that we are not clearly entitled to oppose the telepathic account on the grounds of complexity or artificiality. That maneuver appears to rely on the tacit assumption that telepathic interaction has limits to its range or efficacy, which we can specify in advance of empirical investigation (presumably on grounds of antecedent reasonableness or plausibility), and which the production of collective apparitions exceeds. But that assumption seems no more justifiable than its analogue in the case of PK (see my remarks in Chapter 1.2 and 1.3, and Chapter 4.2). Just as we have no grounds at present for assuming that PK has any limits at all, the same is no doubt true with regard to the forms of ESP. If ESP can occur at all, then for all we know, it is possible to paranormally induce a collective hallucination.

Naturally, the unjustifiability of imposing antecedent limits on psi phenomena also undermines a standard objection to the objectivist theory – namely, that the production of the appropriate entities exceeds plausible limits on the range of PK. In fact, I consider it a sound general policy to be wary of ruling out any explanation of apparitions on the grounds that it posits a psi performance of implausible magnitude. Disheartening as it may be, we simply have no decent idea what (if any) magnitude of phenomenon is implausible or unlikely, once we have allowed psi to occur at all.

Nevertheless, the telepathic theory faces substantial obstacles. One is posed by so-called *reciprocal* cases, in which the prototypical situation is as follows. Agent *A* experiences an OBE in which he ostensibly 'travels' to percipient *B*'s location, and is subsequently able to describe features of the state of affairs there that he could not have known by normal means. *B*, in the meantime, experiences an apparition of *A* at that location. (In a few instances, others on the scene also experience *A*'s apparition.) Moreover, the details *A* describes are those that would have been visible *from the position* at which his apparition was ostensibly seen. Usually the apparition is visible only, but sometimes it is also sensed aurally and tactually.

The difficulty presented for the telepathic theory concerns the status of *A*'s apparition. That apparition seems to be where *A*'s consciousness is, since from that position one would normally see the things *A* reports seeing while ostensibly out of his body. And of course *B* is not located at that position, although he is in the general vicinity. The problem, then, is that according to the telepathic theory, the apparition of *A* is *B*'s hallucination. It is supposed to be something *B* creates in response to a telepathic stimulus from *A*. Therefore, it is unclear why *B* should create an apparition where *A*'s consciousness seems to *A* to be, and also why *A* seems to be sensorially aware of information from a position not occupied by *B*, but ostensibly occupied by *A*'s consciousness (or so-called secondary or astral body). The difficulties may be further compounded in collective cases, in which more than one percipient experiences *A*'s apparition. I shall return to this topic shortly, in our survey of theories of collective apparitions.

One last difficulty for telepathic theories generally concerns what Broad terms 'reiterative' cases, in which the apparition appears on more than one occasion in a single location occupied by a series of different individuals. Cases of this sort are frequently considered examples of 'hauntings'.

From what has already been discussed, readers might be able to anticipate how proponents of the telepathic theory attempt to handle reciprocal and reiterative cases. But we have now reached the point where it would be most profitable to pass directly to the explanations of collective apparitions. After all, these are the cases against which the telepathic and objectivist theories must ultimately be tested, and in which the problems examined above arise in their most potent forms.

b. *Collective apparitions*

Telepathic explanations of collective apparitions have taken various forms. One of the earliest was proposed by Gurney; Broad dubbed it the theory of 'Multiply Directed Telepathic Initiation'. I prefer to descend into the vernacular for a more compact label, and propose that we call it the *Shotgun Theory*. According to this theory, agent A telepathically influences percipients $B_1 \ldots B_n$, *each independently*, and each B_i thereafter responds to the telepathic stimulus by creating an apparition.

Gurney was quick to recognize certain outstanding problems with the Shotgun Theory (although he seemed surprisingly oblivious to their persistance in his own alternative theories). He noted that *every* hallucination – whether telepathically initiated or not – is partially a construct of the individual experiencing it. When a person hallucinates, he presumably employs material from his own supply of past experiences and repertoire of images and symbols. But then it seems unlikely that people simultaneously stimulated by a telepathic agent would have very similar or concordant hallucinations. In fact, even if we ignore the cognitive contribution or elaboration of the percipient, and consider a more passive and mechanistic analogy from radio transmission, a similar problem remains. Although I consider mechanistic analogies dangerously misleading in this area, one might compare the Shotgun Theory's scenario to one in which different receivers pick up a signal from a certain transmitter. In such a case, the state of each receiver will be partly a function of the idiosyncracies of its circuitry (e.g., sensitivity, frequency response, spurious signal rejection, etc.), and can therefore be expected to differ in various details.

Furthermore, cases of crisis apparitions and recent experiments in dream telepathy suggest that there may be a period of latency between the sending of a telepathic message and the subsequent telepathic experience of the percipient (i.e., telepathic deferment). In fact, the evidence suggests that the emergence into consciousness of, or the behavioral response to, a telepathic stimulus frequently awaits moments in the subject's life when that event is convenient or otherwise appropriate relative to the ongoing flow of events or the subject's state of mind. For example, the subject's response might be delayed until a time of repose or relaxation, or at least to a time when surrounding events are not particularly distracting. But in that case it seems unlikely that different people, affected by the same telepathic stimulus, would hallucinate at the same time.

Broad (1962a, pp. 225–6) noted, in addition, that the Shotgun Theory seems unable to explain why the collective experiences of an apparition should be correlated in the way different perceptions of an object are correlated from different points of view. He cautioned, however, that the evidence for these detailed correspondences may be greatly overrated. And Broad is quite right; no one has conducted a careful study of collective apparitions while they are occurring. Commentators have simply *inferred* the existence of perspectival correspondences between the various experiences from the testimony, and it is possible that non-perspectival differences between the individual experiences may have been overlooked or inadvertently suppressed in the course of discussion among the percipients. Still, we are entitled to ask whether the Shotgun Theory can explain why perspectival correlations would *ever* occur – i.e., whether it could explain such correlations should the evidence turn out to be reliable. And in fact, it seems as if the theory would have difficulty. Indeed, Broad's objection may even be superfluous; it seems merely to be a corrollary of Gurney's first criticism. If the Shotgun Theory cannot satisfactorily explain why telepathically induced hallucinations should be similar *at all*, or share any but the grossest similarities, *a fortiori* it will have difficulty in accounting for one sort of fine-grained similarity in particular.

Still another possible difficulty with the Shotgun Theory, discussed by both Gurney and Broad, is this. There is good reason to believe, they argued, that *A* and *B* will interact telepathically only if there already exists a *rapport* of some sort between the two – e.g., blood relationship, friendship, love, etc. At very least one might think that such rapport *facilitates* telepathic interaction, even if it is not a necessary condition for it. But in that case, we would not expect *A* to telepathically produce an apparition in *B* when – as it sometimes happens, both in collective and individual cases – *A* and *B* are strangers. Moreover, we would expect to find more instances than the literature contains of what Broad called *disseminated co-referential hallucinations* – that is, apparitions of *A* reported by widely separated individuals each of whom is in close rapport with *A*. Now there are some reasonably well-documented cases of disseminated hallucinations, but they are much less common than cases of collective apparitions. In any event, Broad was inclined to minimize this objection on the grounds that cases of disseminated hallucinations would very likely be overlooked, even if they occurred frequently (1962a, p. 201).

It seems to me, however, that both Broad and Gurney were needlessly concerned with the issue of pre-existing rapport. Of course, their concern was by no means unprecedented. Since the early days of the S.P.R., researchers have tended to assume that rapport between agent and percipient was at least highly conducive to telepathic interaction, even if it wasn't necessary for it. But I would like to suggest that this assumption seems forceful only from a presently unjustified viewpoint concerning the scope or power of telepathy. If (as I have been urging) we must be open to the possibility that telepathic interactions (or psi interactions generally) are potentially unlimited in magnitude or refinement – e.g., if as far as we know they may occur between any two people, or any number of people, with no inherent limits on the degree of control exhibited or amount of information conveyed or received, then we are not entitled to assume that *A* and *B* must be in rapport for telepathic interaction to occur.

Granted, the evidence for telepathy consists largely of cases of apparent telepathic interaction between individuals who *are* in rapport with each other. But even if telepathy turned out to have no inherent limitations, I think one would expect the evidence to take just this form. Strangers would be very unlikely to discover that they have interacted telepathically, even if such interactions occur all the time. So although the evidence for telepathy is strongly weighted in favor of evidence for pre-existing rapport between agent and percipient, that fact does not support so much as the innocuous assumption that rapport is merely *conducive* to telepathic interaction. Indeed, the assumption that rapport is psi-conducive may simply be a vestige of the widespread and deeply entrenched tendency (among parapsychologists, at any rate) to underestimate or downplay the potential magnitude or power of psi.

Moreover, even if pre-existing rapport is conducive to telepathic interaction, it would probably be only one of a complex network of factors determining the likelihood, success, or extent of any given interaction. And if so, one would expect the importance of rapport to vary from case to case. For example, if an agent's underlying need or motivation to produce apparitional experiences telepathically is sufficiently urgent or intense, the relative lack of rapport between the agent and certain potential percipients might easily be sidestepped or surmounted. In fact, in some cases it might even be in the agent's interest that the apparition appear to a stranger (see my comments below with regard to *dramatic appropriateness*). But in the absence of such countervailing factors, the degree of rapport may be more relevant.

As a matter of fact, certain recent experiments in dream telepathy suggest that rapport between agent and percipient was indeed favorable to the experimental outcome. But since the underlying psychodynamics of these experiments were undoubtedly quite different from those of most spontaneous cases of telepathy, their relevance to the topic of apparitions is unclear. For one thing, the experimenters (and perhaps the subjects) presumably expected or hoped that rapport would be conducive to success, either because that result would confirm a familiar view of telepathy (one that would lead to certain obvious lines of experimentation), or because telepathy seems far less intimidating when it can work only between properly 'tuned' subjects. Hence, it would not be surprising if the participants got precisely the result they expected. And for another, the situations in which telepathy apparently occurred were experimental, if not downright clinical. The needs and motivations of the participants were bound to be different in those cases (and perhaps less intense or personally meaningful) than they would be in crisis situations, and even in informal experiments done at home, where the prevailing level of tension or concern over success would be relatively low.

It seems to me, then, that we may safely bypass the issue of pre-existing rapport when evaluating theories of apparitions. We know too little about the full psychodynamics of most cases to be able to judge the actual importance of rapport on a case-by-case basis. And we certainly are in no position to assume that telepathy has any limitations at all – much less that it would be inhibited generally by lack of rapport between subjects.

Notice, however, that even if we grant the possibility that telepathy has no inherent limitations, the problems raised above concerning the simultaneity and similarity of percipients' experiences continue to have some force. As I see it, the difference between these problems and that posed by the apparent lack of rapport between some agent/percipient pairs, is this. A concern about pre-existing rapport is a concern about conditions necessary for or simply conducive to telepathic interaction. But even if we assume that conditions for telepathic interaction are *optimal*, we must still wonder why several percipients would have similar or simultaneous experiences. The obstacles here do not seem to concern any limitations on telepathy; rather, they have to do with factors that might limit or affect the *manifestation* of the interaction once that interaction has occurred.

As long as we accept the apparently plausible assumption that telepathy is at least a two-stage process, with an *interaction* (stimulus) stage followed by a *manifestation* (response) stage, the problems posed for the Shotgun Theory by simultaneous and similar experiences seem quite serious. One would think that the experience of or response to any stimulus (telepathic or ordinary) permits the operation and interference of causal processes *independent of* those producing the stimulus – in particular, processes *idiosyncratic to* the subject. In cases of apparitions the relevant processes would concern such matters as a person's cognitive or behavioral style and psychological history (i.e., *dispositional* matters that partly determine or influence a person's repertoire and choice of symbols, images, and responses), as well as more immediate contextual matters concerning the subject's state of mind at the time of interaction (e.g., whether the subject is distracted or in some other state conducive to the temporary repression of a reaction to the stimulus). Therefore, even if nothing either in principle or in fact stood in the way of unimpeded telepathic interaction, one might still expect to find the manifestation of or response to the telepathic stimulus affected by a variety of factors.

Gurney's original alternative to the Shotgun Theory is usually called the *Infection Theory*. He suggested that agent A telepathically influences primary percipient B_1 (in whom he is particularly interested), and while B_1 (in response to the telepathic stimulus) creates his own apparent sensory image to himself, he in turn acts as a telepathic agent, causing others in his vicinity to have similar experiences. The principal difference, then, between the Shotgun and Infection Theories is that in the latter the secondary percipients $B_2 \ldots B_n$ are affected telepathically by a person at the same location, rather than by a remote agent.

But as Broad correctly observed, the spatial proximity of B_1 to $B_2 \ldots B_n$ makes it no easier to understand why the experiences of all the percipients should be simultaneous with or similar to each other. Gurney's points about the cognitive elaboration or contribution of the percipient, and about telepathic deferment, apply with equal force to the Infection Theory. In fact, if the telepathic infection spreads from B_1 to B_2, and then from B_2 to B_3, etc., the scenario envisioned in the Infection Theory may perhaps be compared to the familiar situation in which a person tells a story or phrase to another, who then repeats it to yet another, and so on. In such cases, of course, it often happens that the story or phrase gets considerably transformed in the process.

Myers raised a further objection to the Infection Theory. If the theory were true, he suggested, we would expect to find cases of *non*-telepathic hallucinations (e.g., arising from purely intra-subjective causes) spreading by telepathic infection to others in the vicinity. But, according to Myers, there are no clear cases of this. After some hedging, Gurney conceded that ordinary halluci-nations do not seem to spread by infection. I wonder, however, whether Gurney should have yielded so easily to that criticism. After all, ordinary hallucinations are not collective. Hence, he might have replied to Myers that both collectivity and infection are peculiarities of telepathically-induced hallucinations. (Tyrrell later argued that at least collective percipience seemed to be a peculiarity of telepathic apparitions.) Of course, the Infection Theory would in any case still be plagued by its apparent inability to account for the simultaneity and similarity of subjects' experiences.

As it turned out, Gurney was dissatisfied with the Infection Theory anyway. He felt it could not adequately account for inter-actions between individuals who were apparently not in rapport with one another. Accordingly, he developed some complicated hybrid theories, borrowing elements from the Shotgun and Infec-tion Theories. These were designed to explain how percipients might be telepathically sensitized or brought into temporary rapport with the telepathic agent. But I see little reason to survey those theories here. For one thing, they are no better able than the pure Shotgun and Infection Theories to account for the simultaneity and similarity of percipients' experiences. And for another, their concern with the issue of rapport seems excessive, for the reasons mentioned above. I therefore refer the interested reader to Broad (1962a, pp. 227ff.) for a discussion of Gurney's hybrid theories.

The only other major telepathic theory is the one proposed by Tyrrell, which I suggest we call the *Extravaganza Theory*. As I noted earlier, Tyrrell appealed to *dramatic appropriateness* as a way of explaining why apparitions are experienced collectively. More specifically, he suggested that agent *A* telepathically affects primary percipient *B*, and then *B*, in creating his apparitional experience, does whatever is necessary to render it dramatically appropriate. And since *B* is sometimes in the company of other people, it would be appropriate for at least properly situated members of that group also to experience the apparition. So *B* accordingly creates in them the appropriate apparitional experience.

Although Tyrrell is unclear about the nature of the telepathic interaction between the primary and secondary percipients, that portion of the Extravaganza Theory resembles the Shotgun Theory (at least on the surface), and is similar in certain respects to one of Gurney's hybrid theories. In fact, since primary percipient *B* is 'passing along' a motif communicated from agent *A*, the Extravaganza Theory seems to combine elements of both the Infection and Shotgun theories. According to perhaps the most straightforward reading of Tyrrell, the primary percipient (after telepathic interaction with *A*) telepathically affects each of the other percipients *individually*, but in such a way that their experiences conform to his own. The major difference between Tyrrell's approach and Gurney's is that while Gurney took pains to explain how certain of the percipients could be properly sensitized or brought into temporary rapport with *A*, Tyrrell seems willing to grant telepathy a greater degree of control or efficacy. On Tyrrell's view, it is of little relevance that agent and percipient may not be in rapport; telepathic influence is constrained primarily by considerations of dramatic appropriateness.

Price was uncomfortable with Tyrrell's reliance on the concept of dramatic appropriateness, for both individual and collective cases. In fact, he offered an apparent counter-example (see Price 1960, pp. 123–4). He cited a case in which the *wrong* person evidently saw an apparition and the right person did not – specifically, a case in which the apparition of a resistance fighter during the second World War was seen on his parents' doorstep by a neighbor. But the young man's parents were not home at the time, and only later learned of the apparition from the neighbor, who had never seen their son in the flesh. Price argued that if this were a case of telepathy, as Tyrrell's theory demanded, then presumably

> one or other of the parents would have received the telepathic impression and would have seen the apparition: and if a complete stranger saw it too, he ought to have been someone who was with the parents at the time. The fact that the parents were away from home at the moment should have made no difference. Telepathy, so far as we know, is a purely mind-to-mind relation, and the spatial location of the agent and the percipient makes no difference to it. If so, one would think that the parents would have received the telepathic impression wherever they were. (1960, p. 124)

Price's argument has some plausibility; but it is not fully convincing. Too little is known about the underlying psychodynamics of the situation to be able to say how inappropriate the apparition might have been. At about the time the apparition appeared, the son was a prisoner of the Gestapo; and no one knows whether or why it might have been paramount to him to have the apparition appear on his parents' doorstep. One could argue, in fact, that the apparition's appearance to the neighbor was *maximally* impressive and effective. The parents would naturally have had their son's fate on their minds anyway, and an apparition or ostensible telepathic communication from him could easily have been dismissed as an artifact of their concern.

If one wishes to attack a theory's reliance on dramatic appropriateness, it might be more effective to challenge the appropriateness of certain standard features of apparitions – for example, their tendency to fade away or pass through solid objects. These apparitional characteristics don't seem, on the surface at least, to contribute at all to a smooth blending of the apparition into the percipient's environment.

But however interesting these matters may be, I suggest we set them aside. Attacking a theory's reliance on dramatic appropriateness is as futile as objecting to explanations in terms of unconscious motivations. For one thing, not only are we unable to specify antecedent limits on psi in general or on any agent's ability in particular, but we cannot determine the *specific* constraints that any particular situation might impose on an agent's performance. Just as athletes and musicians sometimes exceed or perform below their standard level of ability, for quite situation-specific reasons, the same might be true of a psi-agent. But in the case of psi, the specific constraints might not only be psychological (which are already difficult enough to pin down), but paranormal – having to do with a large nexus of under-the-surface psi interactions. Moreover, what seems dramatically inappropriate on the surface may be totally appropriate relative to underlying needs or concerns of which we can have no certain knowledge. Finally, there is no reason to think there could be general specifiable requirements on dramatic appropriateness that apply across all cases. What is appropriate in one case may be quite different from what is appropriate in another. I doubt, therefore, that we could ever confidently point to any feature of a case and argue that it would have been different had the agent wanted to render the apparition dramatically appropriate.

Nevertheless, there is good reason to think that the Extravaganza Theory is as impotent as the Shotgun and Infection theories to explain the simultaneity and similarity of the percipients' experiences. It seems to depend on what Tyrrell meant by saying that the secondary percipients are 'drawn into' the apparitional drama. Tyrrell argued that an apparition 'cannot be merely a direct expression of the agent's *idea*; it must be a drama worked out with that idea as its *motif*' (1942/1961, p. 100). And later he says. 'The work of constructing the drama is done in certain regions of the personality which lie below the conscious level' (p. 101). Finally, and perhaps most crucially, he concedes (quite plausibly), 'The apparitional drama is . . . in most cases a joint effort in which . . . both agent and percipient take part' (p. 101).

But if in collective cases the primary percipient affects his colleagues *individually*, then Tyrrell's theory posits several different agent/percipient pairs: the initial interaction between *A* and the primary percipient, and the individual interactions between the primary percipient and each secondary percipient. But since each secondary percipient helps construct the apparitional drama of which he is a spectator, one would expect the idiosyncratic contributions of the various participants to lead to a diversity of results. Analogously, if a drama teacher instructed one student to improvise on a given theme with each of the other students in the class *individually*, one would naturally expect the results to differ from one case to the next. And since the other students may have radically divergent personalities, psychological histories, and immediate concerns and interests, one would expect the individual improvisations to differ considerably.

Furthermore, Tyrrell is sympathetic to Gurney's notion of telepathic deferment; but then it is unclear how his theory accounts for the simultaneity of percipients' experiences. Even if it is dramatically appropriate for primary percipient *B* to have the secondary percipients experience an apparition along with him, the other potential percipients will have their own immediate concerns and interests, some of which may be incompatible with those of *B*. Therefore, it may be highly inappropriate or inconvenient for one or more of them to experience an apparition at that time, and very much in their interest to defer their response to telepathic interaction with *B*.

There is, however, another way of understanding Tyrrell's claim that the primary percipient draws the other percipients into the apparitional drama. I question whether this interpretation is actually justified by the text; but we are free to employ the principle of charity. Tyrrell might have been maintaining that the primary percipient interacts with the other percipients in the way the drama student would have led *all the other students together* in a group improvisation on the teacher's theme. At very least this suggestion would seem to explain the similarity of percipients' experiences, since the resulting drama would be a cooperative effort of the group members. And on the surface, at least, it seems to explain the simultaneity of experiences, since the primary percipient may be supposed to have captured the attention of his colleagues (i.e., the rest of the class).

But I wonder whether the advantages of this interpretation are more than superficial. We have been supposing (plausibly) that telepathy is at least a two-stage process, with an interaction (stimulus) stages preceding a manifestation (response) stage. Moreover, Tyrrell likewise accepted this view; and he conceded that the initial stage might be subconscious. But in that case, the problems originally plaguing the Shotgun and Infection theories remain. Even if the primary percipient interacts simultaneously and jointly with all the secondary percipients, one would still expect their individual responses to be idiosyncratically timed and tailored to their needs and interests. It would not be surprising, then, if the apparitional experiences of the secondary percipients differed considerably or occured at different times. Hence, the group improvisation example is disanalogous in an important respect from the second interpretation of Tyrrell. A real group dramatic improvisation requires conscious participation right from the start, whereas Tyrrell and others concede that telepathic inter-action need not be conscious.

It would seem, therefore, that telepathic theories cannot account very neatly for some cases of apparitions. In particular, they cannot successfully bridge the gap between interaction and manifestation (stimulus and response) in collective cases, and thereby explain the similarity and simultaneity of percipients' experiences. By contrast, objectivist theories seem, on the surface at least, to have certain clear advantages over telepathic theories – not only with regard to collective cases, but also with regard to reiterative cases. (As we will see below, when it comes to reciprocal cases, the situation is more of a toss-up.) Reiterative cases are easily explained in terms of the persisting presence at a location of some kind of entity. Of course it is no easy matter to say what that entity is; and accounts may have to vary between apparent post-mortem cases (i.e., ghosts) and ante-mortem cases. But if it seems unparsimonious to posit an enormously complex and *successful* web of telepathic interactions and responses to explain why different percipients on different occasions – often independently – have similar apparitional experiences at a given location, then we may have no choice but to swallow the bitter pill and posit the existence of an appropriate entity at that location. I suppose we might find some solace in the reflection that the positing of novel entities is a familiar and thoroughly respectable move in scientific theorizing. The existence of micro-organisms and carriers of hereditary organic traits were posited before they were actually detected; and needless to say, theoretical physics virtually lives by the readiness to enlarge the directory of entities.

But as I mentioned earlier, one cannot conclusively – much less antecedently – rule out a telepathic explanation of reiterative cases on the grounds that the magnitude of telepathy required is implausible. We have no reason at present for supposing that telepathy is subject to any inherent limitations whatever. Still, this does not mean that we can never have a reason for deciding between the telepathic and objectivist theories. Even if telepathy and PK are subject to no inherent limitations, presumably not all conditions will be equally conducive to their occurrence, much less their more virtuosic manifestations. Psi abilities would be similar in that respect to many other human abilities or functions, whose scope or refinement are not always permitted full expression. A great basketball player, for example, is not always able to achieve what he or she *could* achieve in the absence of certain hinderances (e.g., injury, poor health, loss of confidence, skillful opponents). Hence, no matter how extensive or refined psi interactions *can* be, one would expect them to be subject to actual case-by-case limitations. For example, telepathic interactions would presumably occur as part of a complex network of interactions, psi and non-psi, overt and covert, and would be susceptible to various constraints or checks and balances within the network as a whole. Certain sets of conditions will be favorable, and others unfavorable, to the occurrence of telepathy. Regrettably, one will never know for certain whether the total nexus of underlying conditions is psi-conducive or not, or whether they favor one form of psi more than another. Nevertheless, if we assume that conditions are not psi-prohibitive, and if we allow ourselves modest speculations about underlying psychodynamics, then we can make some (albeit small) headway in deciding which forms of psi are most likely to have occurred in certain cases.

Suppose, for instance, that a telepathic explanation required that agent A was in a certain mental state m or that percipient B was in state m'. If we had grounds for thinking that either A or B was not in the appropriate state, we would tend to favor a rival explanation more compatible with what we know (or believe we know) about the persons involved. Now in reiterative cases, the plausibility of telepathic explanations would hinge on the plausibility of attributing certain intentions or interests to a remote agent or group of agents. A prototypical reiterative case is one in which a succession of people – often independently of each other – report seeing a certain apparition at a given location over a period of time. But if the percipients have the apparitional experience as the result of telepathic interaction with some agent or agents, then presumably there is some reason why the culprit(s) should repeatedly produce the effects. A plausible telepathic explanation, then, would have to provide a reasonable conjecture as to whose interests are served by this state of affairs. One major problem, however, is that the interests in question – even if they are plausible or well-documented – may be more short-lived than the period during which the apparitions are experienced. That is, even if it is reasonable to attribute certain interests to agent A, in virtue of which A would find it beneficial to produce apparitional experiences telepathically in a sequence of percipients, it may be unreasonable to suppose that those interests are sufficiently urgent for A during the entire time the apparitions are reported. It may be more reasonable to suppose that A causes a perturbation at the location during the period when those interests are genuinely pressing, and that the effects of that action linger for some time after A's original interests have shifted or lost some of their force.

Perhaps the following analogy will make the point clear. Suppose Jones is feeling bitter over his bank's refusal to grant him a loan to buy a house he coveted. Suppose, further, that Jones is puerile enough to want to make the house unattractive to other prospective buyers. Accordingly, he concludes that his vindictive purposes would be served if he could make it appear that the house is haunted. Jones realizes, then, that he has a choice of two basic strategies. On the one hand, he could monitor the real estate agent's activities to discover when the house is to be shown to an interested party, and then arrive at the house to try to frighten the customers away. On the other hand, he could plant, say, a tape recording in the house, to be triggered into playing whenever someone opened the front door.

Now since we have been assuming that telepathy may have no inherent restrictions as to the scope or refinement of its interactions, let us suppose that Jones has plenty of free time to monitor the real estate agent's activities and lurk about the premises of the house. Even so, it is reasonable to suppose that Jones's anger may dissipate after a while, or at least that other interests (e.g., a love affair, a family tragedy) may assume an overriding importance in his life. He may thus lose the desire – either temporarily or permanently – to frighten away each prospective buyer of the house. His planted tape recording, however, could continue to work despite any such change in Jones's interests.

Unfortunately, the psychodynamics of apparitional cases are rarely, if ever, this clear cut. In fact, in reiterative cases we may not even have a good idea who the agent is, much less what underlying interests would be served by producing apparitions at the location in question. Still, the above analogy illustrates how one might choose between telepathic and objectivist explanations of a case of reiterative apparitions, even if all psi phenomena are unlimited in scope and refinement.

Reciprocal cases, too, can be explained fairly neatly by positing the existence of an entity capable of occupying positions different from that of the percipient(s). Whatever exactly that entity might be, and whatever exactly its connection might be with the subject whose physical body is at another location (e.g., whether it is a secondary or astral body, or a psychokinetic creation of the subject), it must at least be the sort of thing capable of experiencing or conveying information *as if* from a point of view.

The telepathic theory, by contrast, must explain how such location-specific information is acquired about a place where nobody or nothing sentient is. Proponents of that approach would presumably argue, as Gurney did, that this information may be *constructed* from memories and knowledge about the room and its occupants. Thus, even if agent A had never before visited the location where he seems to himself to be, and where his apparition is ostensibly seen, B *is* at that location, and is able to convey enough information – both from present perceptions and from knowledge and memories of the location from other points of view – for A to synthesize and construct for himself the appropriate location-specific apparent perception. Adherents to the telepathic theory might also claim that the agent's location-specific knowledge is easily within the scope of clairvoyance, and that when the agent produces an apparition in B he simultaneously acquires needed information about B's general location. Traditionally, however, proponents of telepathic theories have been loathe to grant ESP that degree of refinement or success, usually on the weak grounds that one never sees such high-quality ESP in formal experiments. (Of course, this is precisely the parochial attitude I have been arguing against.)

It would appear, then, that if both PK and ESP are potentially

211

unlimited in scope, neither of the two major analyses of reciprocal apparitions enjoys a clear advantage over the other. On the telepathic theory we need only posit first-rate ESP, and on the objectivist theory we need only posit first-rate PK (or the existence of a secondary or astral body).

This is perhaps the appropriate time to pause and consider briefly the concept of an astral body, since some have found it especially useful in connection with the evidence for apparitions and 'travelling' clairvoyance. Broad summarized the concept quite nicely:

> One's ordinary physical body, in its outward form and its inward constitution, is hardly at all affected, except cumulatively and very slowly, by one's habitual thoughts, emotions, and desires. Their only direct and immediate visible effects on it are variations of facial and other kinds of bodily expression, e.g., smiling, frowning, weeping, etc. One cannot, by taking thought, 'add a cubit to one's stature'; still less can one directly create or alter the clothing and material appurtenances of the physical body. But a person's secondary body (which, according to [this variant of the objectivist] theory, is what those concerned . . . are all perceiving in some non-sensory way) is very much more plastic and immediately responsive to his habitual thoughts, emotions, and desires. Its whole outward and visible form is moulded and clothed by, and in accordance with, his habitual mental picture of his physical body and its usual clothing and appurtenances. The secondary body as a whole, and its clothing, etc., automatically express that habitual mental picture of oneself, in somewhat the way in which a certain set cast of the countenance of the physical body may automatically express years of ill temper or of bodily pain. And the whole outward form and clothing and accoutrements of one's secondary body might vary with temporary variations of one's mental picture of oneself, in somewhat the way the face of one's physical body might pass from smiles to frown or to tears with changes in one's emotional mood. (Broad, 1962a, p. 237)

I am inclined to agree with Broad that the concept of an astral body, as described above, is at least intelligible. But I am not convinced that it is plausible to maintain that apparitions are astral bodies. As Gauld (1982, p. 228) observes, even if one accepts Broad's description of how astral bodies acquire (or perhaps more accurately, *create*) clothing, it is far from clear that a similar maneuver will explain why apparitional figures are often observed along with surrounding apparitional objects, such as fences, carriages, or automobiles.

In fact, supporters of the astral body hypothesis face an interesting dilemma. If they concede that the surrounding objects are temporary externalized entities created by an agent, they would seem to be endorsing the view that at least some apparitional figures are produced psychokinetically. And in that case one might just as well regard both the clothed human figure and the surrounding apparitional objects as materializations. The astral body hypothesis would be superfluous and unparsimonious. So perhaps it would be more advantageous for proponents of the astral body hypothesis to argue that parts of the apparitional experience may simply be telepathically induced. But in that case, the standard problems plaguing telepathic explanations of collective apparitions reappear. It is not clear why the various percipients' hallucinations of apparitional surroundings would be similar or simultaneous. It seems, therefore, that an appeal to PK more neatly explains collective apparitions of surrounding apparitional objects. But that option, we saw, renders the astral body hypothesis superfluous.

In any case, I shall not attempt to examine the astral body hypothesis further. Apart from the difficulties just noted, it enjoys the same theoretical advantages over the telepathic theory as the super-PK interpretation of apparitions. Whether the astral body hypothesis is more or less plausible than the super-PK hypothesis may depend on how indispensible the concept of a secondary body is to the interpretation of the evidence for survival. Since I shall not consider that evidence here, I shall make no further attempt to assess the merits of these two versions of an objectivist theory – with one exception. Quite clearly there is very strong evidence for large-scale and refined PK, though perhaps no experimental or semi-experimental evidence for PK of the magnitude and subtlety required for certain apparitional cases. But since we have no grounds for supposing that PK can only be as refined as our best non-anecdotal evidence suggests, we have no reason to think that PK is unable to account for the bulk of collective, reiterative, and reciprocal cases. The astral body hypothesis, by contrast, has no such clear evidence in its favor. Apart from its possible utility in connection with the evidence for survival (though I must add that super-PK strikes me as every bit as useful in that domain also), its main virtue with regard to apparitions seems merely to be psychological. It is simply less intimidating to suppose that apparitions are astral bodies than to suppose they are products of first-rate PK. In fact, the astral body hypothesis is actually rather hopeful or encouraging, whereas the super-PK hypothesis is frightening. Super-PK raises the spectre of near-omnipotence and the efficacy of death wishes; the concept of an astral body, on the other hand, suggests the existence of an entity that may survive bodily death.

When we turn to run-of-the-mill collective cases, we again find certain features that appear to favor an objectivist explanation over a telepathic explanation. For instance, in some cases one finds reports of the reactions of animals to the locations where the apparitions are ostensibly seen, and sometimes to locations where an apparently invisible presence is only felt or sensed. Regrettably, that phenomenon is not very well documented. But it is reported often enough to warrant consideration; and it does seem easier to explain by means of an objectivist theory. The reaction of animals to *locations* where apparitions are ostensibly seen or sensed suggests a genuine perturbation of a region of physical space, and not merely the existence of a telepathic stimulus to which both animals and humans may have been suscep-tible, and to which they would have had to respond in a similar fashion.

In fact, the difficulty posed for the telepathic theory by animal reactions may simply be a variant of one of the prominent difficulties with that theory generally – namely, its apparent inability to explain the uniformity of percipients' experiences. If the content of an hallucination results in part from the cognitive elaboration or distortion of the subject, and if telepathically-induced hallucinations may be subject to deferment, then it is unclear why a group of percipients should exhibit simultaneous or similar responses – in this case, responses to the same location.

Naturally, the objectivist theory handles the troublesome issues of simultaneity and similarity with no strain whatever. If the various percipients are responding, either by means of a familiar sense modality or by means of some hitherto unrecognized sensory modality, to an object located in the region of space apparently occupied by the apparition, then it is easy to understand why their experiences would occur at the same time and correspond in content. And if the objects are less like solid bodies and more like colored wisps of gas, rainbows, mirages, or electromagnetic fields, it is no mystery why only some of the potential percipients report experiencing the apparition. The major mystery, of course, would concern the precise nature of the apparitional objects and their means of production. But since PK is no better understood than telepathy, that nagging mystery poses no problem unique to the objectivist theory. Indeed, since we know equally little about telepathic states and their means of production, that puzzle has a clear counterpart in the case of the telepathic theory.

c. The 'Psychic Ether' theory

Before leaving the topic of apparitions, one last theory remains to be considered. Proposed in 1939 by H. H. Price, it is a kind of objectivist theory. But it differs considerably from the view that apparitions are materializations; and, oddly enough, it suffers from defects similar to those plaguing telepathic theories.

Price's theory deals with *mental images*, broadly conceived to include both visual and non-visual phenomena. He suggested that the main reason for calling mental images 'mental' is that 'they are not apprehended by means of the ordinary physical sense organs' (Price, 1939, p. 319). But to be mental in this minimal respect, mental images needn't have other properties traditionally ascribed to them. For example, they needn't be private, mind-dependent, or evanescent. Hence, mental images might be 'in' the mind, in the sense that we are directly aware of them non-sensorially; but in other respects they might exist 'out of' the mind.

Price suggested, in fact, that although every mental image is originated by a mental act, 'once it has come into being, the image has a tendency to *persist* in being; and . . . it is not dependent upon the mind for its continuance, as it was for its origination' (p. 319). He also proposed that a mental image is 'not necessarily *private* to the mind of its original author, but is capable of presenting itself in suitable circumstances to other minds as well' (p. 319). More specifically, he conjectured that an image might be endowed with causal properties, and in particular with a '*telepathic charge*, enabling it to modify or even perhaps to generate other mental contents, which need not be contents in the mind of its original author' (p. 320). These images, once originated, will exist in a kind of psychic ether of images. By appealing to this reservoir of images, Price hoped to explain collective and reiterative, and even reciprocal, apparitions.

The Psychic Ether theory is certainly novel and interesting; but it suffers from several outstanding flaws. One might wonder, first of all, to what extent it makes sense to talk of sensory qualities persisting independently of a mind, or of the person who experiences those qualities. For instance, are the acuteness of an itch, the timbre of a sound, the pungency of a smell, mere accidental properties of sensory experiences? Ordinarily, we suppose (say) that auditory waves have different timbral characteristics for different perceivers, and that the phenomenological properties of experiences produced by olfactory stimuli will depend on such things as whether one has a head cold. But in that case it would seem as if mental images (broadly speaking) are the kinds of things whose phenomenological characteristics generally are perceiver-dependent and perceiver-idiosyncratic. Would Price have wanted to maintain that a nearsighted person's visual mental image might have existed *out-of-focus* in the psychic ether? Secondly, is it plausible to claim that every mental image is brought into being by a mental act? Many result passively from external processes. And it is a *physical* deficiency that robs the blind and deaf of visual and auditory images.

Price admitted that his suggestions go against our ingrained linguistic habits; but he claimed this was to be expected, and that his theory would be antecedently more suspicious if it didn't give those habits a 'pretty violent tweak' (p. 323). Whether or not the oddness of Price's language is a virtue, as he suggests, let us in any case give him the benefit of the doubt, and assume that his conjectures about an ether of images are really defensible. Even so, serious problems remain.

And the problems look very much like those afflicting telepathic theories. Telepathic theories were unable to account satisfactorily for the similarity and simultaneity of percipients' experiences in collective and reiterative cases; they were unable to bridge the gap between telepathic interaction and the manifestation or experience of that interaction. Now in Price's theory, the persisting telepathically-charged image in the psychic ether plays the role of the telepathic stimulus. But even if we grant that those images are definite enough to produce uniform responses in the persons they affect – i.e., a dog image or the sound of a locomotive is likely to be recognized as such – certain other features of collective and reiterative cases remain mysterious.

Why, for example, should images in a non-physical psychic space direct the attention of several people (and even animals) to a specific region of *physical* space? Why should an image – say, of a person – be regularly or collectively projected onto the same region of physical space? Price claims merely that there is a sense in which psychic images can be physically 'localized' (329ff.). He suggests that just as one can, while in a mild altered state or during an hallucination, 'project' mental images onto a region of space, one might similarly project inhabitants of the psychic ether onto a room in a case of haunting. Price says, '. . . once an image has been projected into a certain region of space, it will remain there as long as it continues to exist' (p. 330). In that way, an image 'can come to be as it were "earth-bound" and tied to a particular place in the Physical World, by means of the mechanism of image-projection' (p. 330).

But Price's proposal seems to rest on a serious confusion. The projection of an image onto space is something that occurs only in the mind of the individual doing the projecting. Since *by hypothesis* items in the psychic ether are not in space, the projected image is not literally *at* that location. By hypothesis, it still resides in the psychic ether. Hence, the image cannot *remain* at that location; it was never there in the first place. Putting the point another way, *projection* is a three-term, and not merely a two-term, relation. We should not say simply that image *i* is projected onto space *s*; rather, we must say that *i* is projected onto *s* *in the mind of* person *p*. So it is of no help to Price to suggest that an image might unconsciously be projected onto *s* by its original author. It makes no sense to say that the image stays *there*, at *s*. By hypothesis, the image is *nowhere* in space, even when projected. The act of projection simply makes the image *appear* to be spatially localized, and then only for the individual doing the projecting. Hence, Price's suggestion does not explain why observers, either collectively or reiteratively, should project an image onto the same region of space.

The Psychic Ether theory also stumbles over telepathic deferment when applied to collective cases. Even if all the percipients are influenced by the same psychic image – and even if they all project it onto the same region of physical space – that would not explain why their experiences of it are simultaneous.

I suggest, then, that the Psychic Ether theory is not very promising. Not only does it require a highly questionable view of the autonomy of mental states, but it also has trouble explaining the reiterative cases for which it seems best designed. Moreover, it fares even worse for collective cases, and for the same reasons as the telepathic theories. Once again, a straightforward objectivist theory handles those cases with greater ease.

To sum up, then. Even if we needn't appeal to PK to explain all cases of apparitions, some seem plausibly explained in no other way. In collective and reiterative cases especially, telepathic theories face insuperable difficulties in accounting for the simultaneity and similarity of percipients' experiences. And in view of the wealth of decent evidence for PK – specifically, for materialization – we should take seriously the possibility that some apparitions are kin to the physical phenomena of the séance room.

4

TOWARD A THEORY OF PK

4.1 INTRODUCTION

In certain respects, the evidence for psychokinesis is similar to that in the case of an unsolved crime. We must determine whether it is reliable, and decide which clues are important and what they point to. This is no small task, however, considering the amount of material and the diversity of its sources and details. It is no wonder, then, that a central problem in assimilating the evidence is to determine what its underlying regularities are – i.e., to find theoretical frameworks that lend a high degree of systematicity to the data. After all, even the great physical mediums differed widely in their range and repertoire of phenomena, and in their modus operandi. And poltergeist cases differ from these in numerous and possibly relevant respects. Hence, one major job for the theoretician is to determine what such differences indicate about the nature of PK, and whether the differences are linked by deeper regularities.

But as crucial as this task may be, theoreticians must first grapple with some matters of considerable generality and abstractness. Behind every scientific theory is an implicit and complex network of philosophical assumptions about the structure of nature and its proper modes of investigation. The roots of every empirical scientific theory, then, are thoroughly non-empirical, and these rarely receive the attention they deserve. No matter how imposing the superstructure of a scientific theory may be, it can only be as strong as its foundations. I have lamented, on other occasions, how scientists tend either purposely to ignore the conceptual foundations of their theories, or else display no

219

awareness that they are implicitly philosophizing (sometimes quite badly) each time they theorize (see, e.g., Braude, 1979, 1982a, 1983). Likewise, parapsychologists have been either reluctant or ill-prepared to confront directly the deep philosophical issues underlying any theory of PK. Rather than belabor the point here, I will simply record my belief that this is one reason why PK theory is in such a sorry state, and why the current proliferation of theories is, at best, premature.

In this chapter, then, I want to discuss very general constraints on our theorizing about PK, and consider what form a PK theory should – or could – take. In fact, I want to address an issue which many parapsychologists assiduously avoid – namely, the extent to which a conventional scientific theory of PK is even *possible*. But before rushing headlong into the philosophical thicket, we must first examine some more thoroughly parapsychological issues, to which theoreticians likewise have given scant attention.

4.2 THE RANGE OF PK

A newcomer to parapsychology might reasonably expect theoreticians to have a more or less unified view of the proper scope of PK theory. But in fact, parapsychologists have displayed little agreement or clarity concerning the range of PK phenomena. Of course, one needn't know all the varieties of PK before developing a theory for the phenomena, any more than electromagnetic theory had to await an exhaustive inventory of electromagnetic phenomena. But in the case of PK, there remain serious doubts as to what *broad* ranges of phenomena PK theory must cover.

To begin with, it is far from clear how 'psychokinesis' should be defined, even provisionally (see Braude, 1979). But a reasonable beginning might be the following. Let us define 'PK' as 'the causal influence of an organism on a region r of the physical world, without any known sort of physical interaction between the organism's body and r'.

This definition obviously leaves certain questions open. For example, since it does not specify that region r is *extra-somatic*, it would seem to countenance the possibility that PK might operate on one's own body. Given our present state of ignorance, I consider this feature of the definition to be a virtue. Some have suggested that ordinary volition might be a case of PK, in which an intention directly produces a bodily change. Similarly, psychosomatic ailments and self-healing through hypnosis might be classed as types of PK. For now, I think it would be hasty to rule out these possibilities by definition.

Another open question is: How pervasive and extensive might PK effects be? Although many parapsychologists entertain the possibility of PK effects on ordinary visible objects (e.g., in poltergeist and mediumistic cases), they balk at the possibility of *significantly* larger effects, such as airplane crashes, weather changes, floods, earthquakes, and personal PK vendettas or death-at-a-distance (the 'evil eye'). But as I urged earlier, if we are willing to admit some PK into our universe, then at our present level of understanding we must be open to the possibility of PK on a grand scale. One reason is the abstract point made several times earlier (especially in Chapters 1.3 and 3.4), concerning the arbitrariness of deciding in advance what the limits of PK are. Another is that a serious case can be made for interpreting many instances of ostensible precognition as examples of PK on the part of the precognizer (see Braude, 1982b, and Eisenbud, 1982a; also Chapter 5), and for thinking that the advantages of this interpretation outweigh those of its rivals – particularly the retrocausal interpretation. But since precognitions often concern events on a very large scale, it again seems indefensible to rule out the possibility of PK operating on such a scale. One's intuitions concerning the limits of the empirically possible count for nothing here. Of course the *motivation* for denying the possibility may be powerful and very deep (see the penetrating discussions in Eisenbud, 1982a, 1984). But at best that would only explain the widespread resistance to PK on a grand scale; it does not excuse it.

Those who resist the possibiiity of PK on a grand scale sometimes protest that we never see any real evidence for it. But one must be circumspect in making that claim; it is only in the context of an overarching view of the place of psi in nature that one can have an idea of what evidence for super psi would even look like. Consider: if psi exists at all, then presumably its occurrence is not restricted to the artificial situations (lab experiments, séances, etc.) in which we *set out* to look for it. In fact, the reason people have set out to produce psi on demand is that it appears to have occurred in real life situations. But there is no reason to think that spontaneous psi must be restricted to the relatively infrequent occasions on which it hits one over the head with its conspicuousness. If psi-in-life may take dramatic and unusual forms, then it is reasonable to think that it might also assume more modest or less arresting forms as well. In that respect, psi would be continuous with other organic functions whose manifestations range from the dramatic and conspicuous to the mundane and inconspicuous. For example, we are all able to remember things; but some are able to perform prodigious feats of memory. Similarly, in our day-to-day activities we all display some degree of muscular coordination; but only a few of us make great athletes, jugglers, or tightrope walkers.

But once we entertain seriously the possibility that psi (like memory and muscular coordination) plays a role in everyday life, we can understand why evidence for psi on a grand scale might not be obvious in the way evidence for table levitations or small object movements is. For one thing, it is reasonable to suppose that everyday psi would result in ordinary sorts of events – not flagrant object levitations, materializations, or other events that automatically call attention to themselves. And clearly there needn't be any observable difference between (say) a normal heart attack or automobile accident and one produced by PK. The only relevant difference may be their distinct causal histories. Furthermore, conspicuous manifestations of everyday psi might be contrary to our psychological welfare or interests. In fact, the smooth integration of super-psi into day-to-day affairs might be *aided* by a lack of obviousness. For example, if my hostile thoughts cause someone to perish in a plane crash, then (in our culture at least) it is in my psychological interest for it to seem as if I had nothing to do with it. Similarly, it is easier for an apparently *unlucky* person to feel victimized by impersonal forces, or the universe at large, than to feel personally responsible for his accidents or disasters, or the victim of others' malevolent thoughts. Therefore, if super-PK occurs, and has a role in everyday life, one would expect evidence for it (in our culture at least)[1] to be anything but glaring. That is why studies of psi in the psychoanalytic setting are provocative and promising; they probe beneath its more overt manifestations in the surface dramas of life, and make an attempt to integrate psi with the deepest human needs and motives.

Toward a theory of PK

But even if we ignore the possibility that PK effects are virtually unlimited in magnitude, and restrict our attention just to the more widely recognized forms of PK, another nagging issue remains – namely, whether those forms of PK are nomologically continuous. Should we assume, for example, that PK influence on dice or RNGs results from processes fundamentally like those that produce object levitations, materializations, or D. D. Home accordion renditions? Should we, in other words, regard all these forms of PK as manifestations of a single, and as yet mysterious, process? Or, should we regard the superficial dissimilarities among the various PK phenomena as manifestations of deeper differences? Is it possible, in other words, that the classification of paranormal RNG or thermistor fluctuations with object levitations and materializations obscures deep differences in their underlying causal processes? Parapsychologists, no doubt, have hunches as to which of these two general pictures of PK is closest to the truth. But research in the field is nowhere near the point where we can confidently choose one over the other. One would think, then, that theorizing about PK would reflect or acknowledge our ignorance concerning the possible unity of PK phenomena.

But in fact, a great deal of recent PK research and theory seems oblivious to this issue. For example, some researchers study apparent PK effects on RNGs and develop elaborate theories to account for them, without considering whether the theories have anything at all to say about the most interesting phenomena reported in poltergeist and mediumistic cases. To be sure, some parapsychologists *do* attempt to extend their theories about laboratory PK to non-experimental phenomena. But with few exceptions, they feel the need to account only for small-scale and relatively non-dramatic effects, such as slight movements of small visible objects (e.g., compass needles or cigarettes). Certainly, none of the recent laboratory-based theories currently in vogue (most notably the various forms of the 'Observational Theory' – see the discussion in Braude, 1979) even pretends to explain, say, the materializations of Home and Palladino, or Home's accordion phenomena. As we will see below, there are good reasons for thinking that the theories are inappropriate to the phenomena from the start, and could not be used to explain them even if their proponents had tried. But their proponents have *not* tried, which is all the more striking when one considers that the theories are

223

allegedly theories of *PK*, and that we simply do not know whether the different forms of PK represent nomologically distinct classes of phenomena.

Under the circumstances, the rather widespread neglect of the most interesting physical phenomena strikes me as an inexcusable bit of scientific myopia. For all we know at this stage, the motley array of phenomena labeled 'PK' may be related in such a way that we cannot adequately understand one of them in isolation from the others. If so, PK phenomena would resemble, say, the various forms of humor or aggression. One cannot pretend to understand humor (much less propose a theory of humor) based on just one of its manifest forms – say, slapstick. Nor can one pretend to understand aggression (much less propose a theory of aggression) based on just one of its obvious forms – say, overt physical assaults. Similarly, it seems foolish and misguided to theorize about the nature and mechanics of PK while ignoring the achievements of Home and Palladino, or (on a grander scale), the potential relevance of people who claim to be able to change the weather, or those who are uncommonly lucky or unlucky.

Of course the neglect of large-scale physical phenomena is due in part to the misconceptions about the evidence that I addressed in the first part of this book. But to some extent it is aided by the currently fashionable professional jargon in parapsychology – in particular, the distinction between *micro-* and *macro*-PK. Parapsychologists often use these categories as if they marked a distinction between genuinely different and apparently independent kinds of phenomena. Perhaps the distinction was not originally intended to be used in this way. But it seems to me that by now it has succeeded primarily in codifying the unjustified neglect of the phenomena considered to be examples of macro-PK (especially the more dramatic sorts of phenomena covered in the first part of this book). Certainly it has offered nothing in the way of conceptual clarification. In fact, it seems to have produced considerable confusion. To see why, let us examine the distinction more closely.

Most parapsychologists these days would say that 'micro-PK' refers to PK phenomena whose existence can be demonstrated only by statistical tests. RNGs, if left to themselves, will inevitably produce apparently non-random sequences; and dice will land with a face up independently of any PK influence. What inclines us to regard certain such sequences or events as ostensible PK effects is their statistical improbability. But no quantitative analysis is needed to conclude that an apparent table levitation or materialization is an ostensibly paranormal phenomenon. The distinction between micro- and macro-PK, then, seems in practice to be no more than a distinction between two methods of determining ostensible paranormality. It would be more appropriate, I submit, to re-name it the distinction between quantitatively and qualitatively anomalous PK.

But there is more here than meets the eye. If the distinction is so straightforward, why use the terms 'micro' and 'macro'? Why, for example, should *dice* tests provide evidence of *micro*-PK? One can understand the use of 'micro' in connection with tests in which PK appears to affect radioactive decay or thermal noise. But dice are observable objects, and it seems odd to call PK influence on dice *micro*-PK simply because statistical tests are needed to determine whether a PK effect occurred. After all, if a die levitated, the phenomenon would *not* be considered an instance of micro-PK.

There may, however, be a reason for this peculiar terminology. I suggest that it is merely a holdover from the original use of the micro/macro distinction in PK research, one that reflects an underlying general view of how PK works. To the extent there is a received view in parapsychology on the nature of PK, it is that *every* observable PK effect is a causal consequence of *PK effects on systems too small to be observed by the naked eye.* And it seems that the original use of 'micro-PK' was to refer to this class of events, so that the class could be distinguished from PK effects on observable systems. But curiously, from that theoretical standpoint it would seem as if the term 'macro-PK' had no utility. One would think that if micro- and macro-PK were distinct types of phenomena, then macro-PK would be the direct PK influence on macroscopic systems, bypassing the sorts of microscopic causal interactions ordinarily thought to produce the macroscopic events in question. But PK on observable systems, unmediated by PK on the micro level, is precisely what the received view rejects.

It seems to me, then, that the present confused situation in PK theory has at least the following two outstanding features. First, parapsychologists tend to use the term 'micro-PK' in two distinct ways. According to one, it refers to

   (a) PK phenomena detectable only by means of statistical tests.

According to the other, it refers to

   (b) PK effects on systems too small to be observed by the naked eye.

Second, considering the prevailing view that primitive PK effects occur only on the micro level, sense (b) of 'micro-PK' has no corresponding contrast with 'macro-PK'. On the received view of PK, it would be a mistake to treat RNG deviations or thermistor fluctuations – but not table levitations, spoon bending, or material-izations – as evidence for micro-PK. According to the received view, *all* PK evidence is ultimately evidence for micro-PK. So when 'micro-PK' is used in sense (a), the micro/macro distinction has a limited taxonomic value, but no explanatory utility. And when it is used in sense (b), the distinction has at least possible explanatory value (since it entails that PK phenomena are nomo-logically continuous and all analyzable as due to direct small-scale PK), but no taxonomic utility.

   But in fact, the explanatory value of the second sense of 'micro-PK' is itself highly questionable. There are good reasons for doubting the prevailing view that all observable PK effects result from PK interactions on the level of the very small. But the weakness of the received view is not where some might have expected – namely, in the assumption that PK phenomena are nomologically continuous. Although that assumption may be false, it is at least intelligible. I see no serious confusion in the claim that there is no major theoretical difference between the processes responsible for PK effects on (say) thermal noise or radioactive decay and those responsible for PK effects on obser-vable systems. By contrast, it may well be a deep mistake to suppose that observable PK phenomena can be explained in terms of underlying processes or mechanisms. To see why, we must consider some additional general goals of and constraints on our theorizing about PK.

4.3 IS PK ANALYZABLE?

One elementary goal of a theory of PK is to explain certain causal connections between states of agents and resulting states of the physical world. But if the theory is to have any generality – i.e., if it hopes to make systematic sense of particular instances of PK, it must at least be able to state certain *regularities* or laws for PK. But what sort of regularity? The answer to this question is not as straightforward as it is with regard to the forms of ESP.

For example, a typical instance of telepathy is a case where there exists a certain non-fortuitous paranormal correlation or correspondence between the content of two mental states (e.g., both agent and percipient might think of Bugs Bunny). Similarly, in cases of clairvoyance there exists a correspondence between an agent's mental state and some state of the physical world (e.g., between the thought of a house on fire and a house's actually being on fire). If a conventional explanation of these cases is possible at all, it must make sense of the fact that it is non-fortuitous that the correlations obtain between mental states of the relevant *type*, or between a mental and physical state of the relevant *type*. For instance, it must explain how a telepathic agent's thought of *a* (or that *a* is *F*) can be a causal condition of the percipient's thought of *a* (or that *a* is *F*). Even more generally, a conventional theory of ESP must explain how *any* kind of telepathic or clairvoyant content-correspondence is possible. (See Braude, 1979, for a detailed discussion of telepathic content-correspondence.)

(I am supposing, at least for now, that we might actually be able to explain the forms of ESP in these conventional ways. Another possibility, defended in Braude, 1979, is that the regularities of ESP, like those of cognitive phenomena generally, have no analysis or explanation in terms of underlying processes or mechanisms. But whether or not ESP is primitive in this respect, it is nevertheless clear that the aforementioned sorts of regularities comprise the data to be identified and integrated systematically into the rest of our knowledge.)

When we turn to PK, however, it is somewhat more difficult to pinpoint the relevant causal regularities. For in these cases it is debatable, to say the least, whether we are dealing with similarities in the *content* of two different states. Even if we concede that

227

the cause of each PK event is an agent's *intention* (conscious or unconscious), we are by no means compelled to maintain that the agent brings about a state of the physical world similar to a state conceived or somehow envisioned (consciously or unconsciously) beforehand. /

Cognitivists in psychology and philosophy favor a view of action according to which results of action somehow represent the intended situation modeled beforehand in the agent's mind (or brain). But quite apart from philosophical objections to this approach to action theory, there are reasons for thinking that no such account of PK causal chains will apply generally to the evidence. For example, in some poltergeist cases it is plausible to treat the PK activity as analogous to brute flailings about, rather than cognitively elaborated plans (see Gauld and Cornell, 1979). Sometimes it seems as if poltergeist agents are simply releasing repressed feelings or pent-up hostilities when the phenomena occur. In these cases it may be reasonable to compare the agent's actions to those of an enraged, frightened, or otherwise over-stimulated infant, adult, or animal who instinctively strikes out or behaves wildly and erratically. Object shatterings or sudden object movements may thus be nothing more than a paranormal analogue to uncontrolled behavior of other sorts. Furthermore, in many cases of mediumship, one may plausibly argue that the medium had no idea (conscious or unconscious) of what phenomena were to occur. In many séances it appears as if a wait-and-see attitude prevailed instead. Here, of course, one may always maintain that the medium's modeling activity or preconceived plan was simply unconscious. But that interpretation will be particularly compelling only to those already committed to the cognitivist approach.

Nevertheless, in some cases of mediumship (and in experimental cases of apparitions) the ostensible agent seemed either to know which phenomena were to occur, or at least consciously *intended* certain phenomena to occur. Even those unsympathetic to cognitive science might wonder whether these cases are indeed ones in which the agent's mental state – i.e., the conception of the intended or apparently forseen state of affairs – causes a similar state of the physical world. So let us suppose, to see where it leads, that the causal connections to be explained in cases of PK *are* analogous to those in cases of ESP, and hence that we must somehow account for non-fortuitous similarities between a

PK effect and the mental state that causes it. If that approach helps us to get a grip on cases appearing to fit the cognitivist model, then perhaps it will help us with the other cases as well.

So let us consider what we may dub the *copy theory* of PK. According to this view, the cause of a PK event is a state S of the agent – a mental state or brain state, depending on one's degree of commitment to physicalism. State S is (or is a constituent of) a desire or intention to produce a certain similar state S' of the physical world; and the similarity between the two states will be explained with reference to their similar underlying structures. Just as a table levitation and the bending of a spoon are distinct sorts of events, *intentions* or *desires* to produce those states will likewise differ. The copy theory of PK maintains that the underlying differences between the intention to levitate a table and the intention to bend a spoon are analogous to the underlying differences between the two kinds of corresponding physical states of affairs. Agent's state S, then, will be *structurally isomorphic* to resulting state S', and one of the causal conditions of S' is that S has the structure it does. In other words, S' is the kind of event it is, because S is the (analogous) kind of event it is.

The reader may recognize that this theory of PK resembles what (in Braude, 1979) I called the *energy-transfer* (or *brain radio*) theory of telepathy.[2] Both assert the existence of, and attempt to analyze, *regularities* in the content or structure of two classes of states. In the case of telepathy, the regularities obtain between the mental states of agent and percipient. And according to the copy theory of PK they obtain between the agent's causally efficacious state S – let us call it an S'-*intention* for short – and the resulting state S' of the physical world. But the energy-transfer theory of telepathy, I argued, was deeply defective – in fact, fundamentally unintelligible. The same, it seems to me, must be true of the copy theory of PK. Both theories are vulnerable to crippling objections – in particular, (a) that similarity is not a static or inherent relation between things – hence, that it cannot be analyzed in structural or topological terms, and (b) that the function of a (mental or brain) state is not determined by its structure.

Actually, the scope of these objections extends well beyond the copy theory of PK. In fact, they are corollaries of another objection, which (if correct) explains why no theory – parapsychological or otherwise – can hope to *analyze* regularities involving mental states. So let us examine in detail the defects of the copy theory. The points we consider will help us to determine the extent to which conventional theories of PK are possible at all.

The copy theory posits a causal regularity between a *kind* of intention S in the agent and a corresponding kind of event S' in the physical world. But clearly, in order to analyze the causal relevance of S to S', as well as the similarity or correspondence between them, proponents of the copy theory must first be able to specify conditions for being an instance of the appropriate kind. As far as S'-intentions are concerned, identity theorists and epiphenomenalists would presumably appeal to the structures of associated brain-state kinds, while dualists might be more content to list phenomenological features of the appropriate mental-state kinds. Hence, if the copy theory cannot specify conditions for being an intention of kind S (say, the S'-intention to levitate a table), it cannot analyze in structural terms the causal regularities between kinds S and S', or the respect in which S' copies its corresponding S'-intention. Therefore, if S'-intentions, or mental states generally, happen to be the sorts of things for which – as a matter of principle – no necessary and sufficient conditions are specifiable, then the copy theory is stymied from the very beginning. For example, if in principle one cannot lay down necessary and sufficient conditions (physical or mental) for intending to levitate a table, then in principle one cannot analyze how mental states of that type are causally relevant or similar to some other type of state. In that case, obviously, the theory simply would not be viable.

Therefore, the copy theory presupposes that it is possible, at least in principle, to specify necessary and sufficient conditions for being S'-intentions. But this is virtually the same embarrassingly unscientific presupposition that sabotaged the energy-transfer theory of telepathy. Both theories are committed to a blatant form of Platonism with regard to the nature of mental states. Both require that thought or mental-state kinds have an essence, some property or set of properties without which a particular state would not be of that kind, and in virtue of which it is of that kind (rather than some other). Two distinct thought-tokens, then, will be of the same kind when they share the relevant property or set of properties. That is why it is imperative for the copy theory to be able to specify an essence for S'-intentions. If it cannot lay down conditions for being, say, an S'-intention to levitate a table, it cannot analyze relations between intentions *of that kind* and corresponding kinds of effects. And notice, if the copy theory could specify nothing more than necessary conditions for a certain kind of S'-intention, then it would not be able to explain why a state was that kind of S'-intention rather than some other sort of state (intention or otherwise). And if it could specify nothing more than sufficient conditions, then it might only be able to explain why certain states (but not others) were S'-intentions of that kind.

Let us consider, then, whether intention kinds or mental-state kinds generally have an essence, some property or set of properties both necessary and sufficient for being of that kind, something (say, in the case of old-fashioned physicalistic theories) with which to correlate a certain specifiable set of physical or physiological properties. And for simplicity, let us overlook the fact that a person may properly be described as being in mental state S in virtue of unconscious processes, or non-occurrent dispositional states, or solely in virtue of things the person is *doing* (rather than experiencing). Let us focus just on *conscious inner episodes*, and consider whether conscious inner-episode kinds have an essence. After all, one would think that if a certain kind of mental state S has an essence, then we should (in principle, at least) be able to provide criteria for being a *conscious inner episode* of that kind. Even if we succeeded, of course, our account would not qualify as an account of the mental state S; we would only have characterized one of its subsets. Still, we would at least have cause for optimism if we could carry out the more modest task of stating conditions necessary and sufficient for being an inner episode of the kind S.

But what if it turns out that virtually *any* inner episode may be of the kind S – i.e., if inner episodes of that kind need have nothing relevant in common except that when they occur they are taken or count as instances of that kind? In that case, I submit, we must grant that kind S has no essence. If in the appropriate circumstances any inner episode may be of kind S, then we cannot state general conditions in virtue of which some inner episodes (but not others) are of that kind, or in virtue of which an inner episode is of that kind (rather than another). For in that case, an inner episode will not be of the kind *S* in virtue of static conditions intrinsic to it, or in virtue of some antecedently specifiable property or set of properties it must have to be of kind *S*. Instead, membership in that kind will depend on loose and context-idiosyncratic relationships between the inner episode and the ongoing flow of events.

An example should help make this clear. In a moment I shall consider intentional states of the sort the copy theory takes to be the cause of PK effects. For now, however, let us suppose that I am thinking about Baltimore – i.e., that my mental state may be correctly described as being of the kind *thoughts about Baltimore*. Now it should be obvious that a person may properly be described as thinking about Baltimore *no matter what* his inner episodes happen to be. Even if we consider nothing but *images* in the person's mind, there is no reason to think that there is any limit at all as to what they may be. When thinking about Baltimore, I could have an image of a particular person (or any number of persons), a particular location, or (if I tend toward synesthesia) even of a sound, or smell. I could have an image of a scene recalled from personal experiences, or recalled from photographs or movies, or a scene constructed from descriptions I had read in Mencken or Poe, or perhaps just the image of those words on the printed page, or as sung by the Baltimore Orioles, and so on. And clearly, these subsets of images may likewise assume virtually any form. The varieties of feelings, smells, sounds, events, or persons I associate with Baltimore (either habitually or in the context of a discussion or some other particular situation) can no more be specified in advance than can the details of my life. And when we recall that *anyone* can think about Baltimore, and do so in ways totally idiosyncratic to the person's life and personality, the belief that one could lay down necessary and sufficient conditions merely for having mental images of Baltimore seems quite preposterous.

But if any mental image may be of or about Baltimore, given the appropriate surrounding history, then clearly the image has that function in virtue of the way it is integrated into a bit of life. Its function is not, so to speak, built-in. I might properly be described as thinking about Baltimore when I have a mental image of a certain politician. But if I were to have that image in a different setting or context, or if someone else were to have that image, it might be correct to describe it as being of something else – e.g., dishonest men, ugly men, dynamic men, men who have gone to prison, short men, men in 3-piece suits, men with blue eyes, pug noses, or just men in general. And of course the range of thoughts properly associated with my image may be quite arcane, depending on how it is embedded within a surrounding context. With that image before my mind, I might properly be described as thinking about, say, people who should never try to play a Schubert sonata, people incapable of savoring the subtleties of Strindberg, people I would like to see dropped into a tub of jello, people unlikely to win at Bowling for Dollars, people suited to host TV talk shows, objects softer than plywood but firmer than cotton, things that even a mother couldn't love, and so on. The image, then, is inherently *functionally ambiguous*, and the varieties of functions it may have is as limitless as the range of contexts into which it may fit, or into which a person may enter.

The same points apply, *mutatis mutandis*, to physicalistic theories that correlate brain-state kinds with mental-state kinds. The brain states that are allegedly either identical with or causally responsible for thoughts about Baltimore are states which we could say *represent* Baltimore. And clearly, what those states represent is no more intrinsic to them than it is to the mental states (e.g., images) with which they are correlated. In neither case can one tell, from the state alone, what it represents or what it is of or about. If an image may represent virtually anything, given its surrounding history, so may the brain state either identical with or causally responsible for it. (I develop these points in greater detail in Braude, 1979, where I also discuss, on pp. 177ff., why *anomalous monism* offers no solution). Moreover, as I argue below, similar observations count against so-called 'functionalist' theories, which attempt to take surrounding context into account.

Here we arrive at a fundamental point concerning the nature of *representation* or *meaning*. Whenever a thing represents (or means something), it does so solely in virtue of the way in which it is integrated into a slice of life. Representation (or meaning) is never a static relation between objects or events; nor is it an inherent property of a thing's internal *structure*. That is why *anything can represent (or mean) anything*, given the appropriate surrounding history. For example, a field commander may place a sugar cube on a map and say to his junior officers, 'Let this be the enemy'. A frustrated tennis player may reprimand himself by looking directly at his racquet and scolding it. An irate teacher may illustrate how he dealt with a student he despises by dramatically trampling a piece of chalk. A teenage girl may cradle a pillow lovingly in her arms, pretending it is the rock star she idolizes. To a fantasy-prone young boy, however, the pillow might represent a deadly virus he vanquishes while in the miniaturized form of 'Interferon Man'.

Naturally, contexts in which a sugar cube represents an enemy army, or in which a piece of chalk represents a despised student, are atypical in certain respects. But they are unusual only with regard to *what* the objects represent, not with regard to *how* representation comes about. Certain representational situations are so familiar that it is easy to overlook the fact that the acquisition of representational properties in those cases is every bit as context-dependent as it is in the more offbeat cases. That oversight, in turn, fosters the mistaken impression that representation in the more ordinary cases is built-in, and is merely *overridden* in less familiar contexts.

Moreover, it is important to remember that sugar cubes and tennis racquets acquire representational properties in the same way as more familiar bearers of representational properties, such as words or images. Given the appropriate surrounding history, a word can mean or an image can represent anything. And again, we should not be seduced by the familiarity of certain contexts into thinking that certain representations are inherent in the objects, or more fundamental to the objects than others. The familiarity of the contexts reveals more about us, about our patterns of life, than about the objects themselves.

Now it is easy to see how the foregoing observations undermine the copy theory of PK. For one thing, since an S'-intention can assume virtually any form, we cannot hope to specify conditions for being a state of that kind. For another, since there is no property or set of properties in virtue of which a state is an S'-intention, there will be no way to specify generally how a PK effect S' *copies* its corresponding S'-intention.

Consider, for example, the intention to levitate a table. Just as particular thoughts about Baltimore needed nothing in common with each other except that when they occurred they functioned

234

as thoughts about Baltimore, the same holds for intentions to levitate a table. First of all, intentions of that kind may, but needn't, involve mental imagery. The agent might merely feel a resolve to levitate a table. But even if we consider just the range of images an agent might employ, it is clear that they might be as diverse and idiosyncratic as thoughts about Baltimore. For instance, the agent might employ guided imagery when trying to levitate a table, and the images may be drawn from an idiosyncratic repertoire of symbols and associations, as well as from context-specific associations. To levitate a table, one agent might simply picture a table rising from the ground. Others, however, might picture tiny strongmen pushing up the table's legs from beneath, or a magnet pulling the table, or a spirit form pulling by means of ectoplasmic threads. Furthermore, the images selected by the agent needn't involve tables at all. Some might imagine, e.g., a crane pulling up on an unseen object below, or a rocket blasting off. Others might simply picture the *words* 'table up', or the heavenly choirs singing 'table up'.

And here, too, the relationship between the picture (or some associated structure such as a brain state) and the kinds of things it can represent or resemble, is never one-one. Although a certain object or state (mental or physical) functions in context c as an intention to levitate a table, in another context c' its function might be entirely different. And of course there is no reason to assume that the internal properties of the object or state must change from c to c'. Analogously, the same pillow can represent a rock star on one occasion and a virus on another without undergoing a structural transformation. Likewise, a photograph of a dog can represent the class of poodles on one occasion, the class of dogs on another, and the class of animals on another, again without changing its underlying structure. Hence, no matter what properties the copy theory proposes as criteria for being an S'-intention, a particular S'-intention needn't have those properties, and things that have those properties needn't be S'-intentions.

Moreover, just as *representation* cannot be explained in terms of properties inherent in the representing object and the thing represented, the same will be true of the related concepts, *similarity* or *resemblance*. Two things are never similar solely in virtue of static relations between the two objects, or in virtue of properties inherent in them. They must *count* or *be taken as* similar relative to some context of inquiry and criteria of relevance. For example, the movements of an elephant are not inherently similar or dissimilar to those of a flea. They might count as similar in a situation where the size of the organism is not relevant, but dissimilar in a context where size is a major concern. An isosceles triangle may be considered similar to a scalene triangle when the size of the interior angles is not relevant, but dissimilar in other contexts. In still other situations (say, when a child is asked to distinguish geometrical figures generally from pictures of fruit), a triangle may count as similar to a circle or square (see Braude, 1979, 1983, for a more detailed discussion of similarity).

The application of this point to theories of PK should be clear. No PK effect will be inherently similar to the mental or physical state (or some component thereof) we take to be its cause. What makes a mental image of a rocket blasting off similar to a table levitation is the fact that the image is used to help an agent levitate a table. But when used in a different context – say, where the PK agent slides a toy rocket across the floor – the image might be regarded as similar to something *other* than a rising table. Moreover, it is only in virtue of surrounding events, interests, etc., that we determine which features of the two similar things are relevant. In the case of the image of the rocket, for example, we focus on certain of its features and ignore others; and our choice always depends on the way we integrate the image into its surrounding history. In the context of an object levitation, the upward movement of the rocket might be relevant; but it might be irrelevant when the agent uses guided imagery to sabotage a stationary vehicle at Cape Canaveral. So once again, a PK theory will be unable to specify properties in virtue of which a PK effect S' will be similar to its corresponding S'-intention. No matter what properties the theory proposes, a given cause and effect may be regarded as similar without them, and even things that have all those properties needn't be taken as similar.

We see, then, that a theory of PK (or action theory of any kind) cannot simply correlate effects (actions) with *states of a person* (mental or physical). And it does not matter what the relevant 'hardware' of the agent is taken to be – for example, whether the states are sets of phenomenological, biochemical, or neurological properties. All such states, as we've seen, are functionally ambiguous; their functions can be disambiguated only relative to their position in a bit of life. Now I have been assuming that the copy theory would want to treat S'-intentions in this way – i.e., either as mental states (described phenomenologically) or as physiological correlates of those states. And in so doing I have merely been acknowledging what is still the dominant approach among scientists theorizing about action (paranormal as well as normal). In philosophy, however, old-fashioned dualist, identity, and epiphenomenalist theories have fallen out of favor; so-called 'functionalist' theories are now in vogue. Hence, some might suggest that since a mental image (or brain state) represents (or means) what it does in virtue of its position in a surrounding bit of history, what is needed is an analysis of that larger functional context, or perhaps an analysis of the causal history common to all instances of the appropriate kind of S'-intention (or mental-state kind generally). But it turns out that functionalist theories do not avoid the difficulties that sabotaged earlier mechanistic theories. Those problems are simply pushed back a stage. Indeed, anyone who thinks that functionalism is a promising theoretical alternative seems merely to have missed the point.

We have noted two important related features of mental states. First, an inner episode (mental or physical) is – or is correlated with – a certain kind of mental state, not in virtue of its topological features (or any inherent features), but in virtue of the way it is integrated into a surrounding history. Second, we cannot specify a set of necessary and sufficient conditions for a state of a person to be a certain kind of mental (or associated brain) state, since given the appropriate surrounding history, virtually any state of a person can be of that kind. Hence, no matter what properties we specify for being a mental state of a certain kind, a particular token of that kind needn't have those properties, and states that have those properties needn't be of that kind.

But analogous objections apply to the functionalist identification of mental- or brain-state kinds relative to a context. Suppose we attempt to specify some set F of functional or causal criteria for being a token of a certain mental-state kind M. The first point to observe is that, no matter how exhaustive or general we try to make set F, there is no end to the situations in which a person's mental state can properly be said to be of the kind M. The observations made earlier concerning thoughts about Baltimore still apply. Virtually anyone can think about Baltimore, and

237

in ways idiosyncratic to the person's history. Hence, the range of possible exemplifications of the kind *thoughts about Baltimore* is as open-ended and antecedently unspecifiable as the details of a person's history, or more generally, of human history itself. It is absurd, then, to think that there must be some antecedently specifiable set of functional properties for the kind *thoughts about Baltimore*, or for any mental-state kind. Moreover, no matter what set F of functional properties we specify, some episode meeting those criteria may fail to be of the appropriate kind. Relative to some wider context (e.g., a set of countervailing circumstances) or a different perspective (e.g., a set of needs, interests, or purposes), we might classify the episode as a different kind of state. Once again, therefore, no matter what functional properties we specify for being a mental state of a certain kind, a particular token of that kind needn't have those properties, and tokens that have the properties needn't be of that kind.

Approaching the matter from a somewhat different angle, we can see that the outer (extrinsic) states to which the functionalist appeals are every bit as functionally ambiguous as the inner episodes they are supposed to disambiguate. For example, a bit of behavior, considered solely with respect to its structure, can function in an endless number of ways. In itself, the structure is nothing; it counts as something only relative to a wider surrounding context and to a perspective or a positioning of the behavior within the context. There is no point at which we can specify some set of extrinsic properties or states that is inherently functionally unambiguous – i.e., that is of a certain kind solely in virtue of properties intrinsic to it. A bit of behavior is of a certain kind only relative to a wider context (say, further behavior) and a perspective from which they are integrated. And the wider behavior is of a certain kind only relative to a still wider context and a more global perspective. We usually don't need to think about the more global contextual features in everyday classifications of behavior, since we take a great deal for granted in those activities. But it is nevertheless true that a small bit of behavior is of a certain kind only relative to much wider contexts and ways of looking at things – indeed, to an entire perspective on life. The functionalist's problem, then, is not simply that no realistically feasible theory can specify a set of functional properties broad enough to disambiguate a certain inner episode (mental or physical). More seriously, no set of properties, however grand, could possibly do the job. No matter how the functionalist tries to disambiguate the extrinsic states to which he appeals (say, with reference to a wider context, or by linking the outer states to the inner states that produce them), he falls victim to a vicious regress of disambiguation. At no point can he stop the regress by specifying a set of conditions (inner, outer, or some combination) whose function is rigidly determined by its inherent properties or *structure*. No structure of any kind determines its function. Nothing can function in one and only one way (see Braude, 1979, pp. 168ff., for a more extended treatment of this point).

The prospects are bleak, then, for any theory attempting to analyze the causal connections between (on the one hand) kinds of PK effects and (on the other) intentions, desires, etc. to produce those kinds of effects. In fact, it appears that an entire theoretical tradition in parapsychology is deeply misguided. As a rule, parapsychologists have tended to analyze psi phenomena along lines familiar to the physical and biological sciences. They assume that observable psi phenomena have unobservable underlying structures, and that the former are thoroughly analyzable in terms of the latter. Just as we analyze heat (for example) as molecular motion or explain the heritability of physiological features in terms of genetic processes, parapsychologists have tried to analyze ESP and PK in terms of lower-level sorts of phenomena.

Perhaps the main reason for this widespread procedure is that parapsychologists have simply adopted the confused principle that vitiates a great deal of research in the behavioral sciences – namely, that organic phenomena generally (including cognitive and intentional phenomena) are analyzable in ways appropriate to (most) purely impersonal, mechanical, or non-organic phenomena. But behind this methodological assumption – or at least connected with it – is a deeper assumption about the nature of explanation and analysis that I believe to be false, and which certainly deserves to be brought clearly into the open.

4.4 THE SMALL-IS-BEAUTIFUL ASSUMPTION

Most scientists assume (either tacitly or explicitly) that there are no unanalyzable facts or phenomena (e.g., lawlike regularities) on the observable or macroscopic level. They embrace the broad mechanistic assumption that observable phenomena generally have underlying structures, and that it is possible (at least in principle) to analyze every such phenomenon in terms of its subsidiary processes or mechanisms. Scientists concede, of course, that *some* facts or phenomena are 'basic' or unanalyzable. They admit, in other words, that explanations in terms of lower-level processes cannot continue indefinitely, and that at the point where vertical explanation (explanation by analysis) stops, we will have reached phenomena neither identical with nor causally explicable in terms of still lower-level processes. At this point we arrive at scientific ground level, where the phenomena are *ultimate* or *primitive* in the sense that we can no longer profitably ask of them *how* they occur. The universe simply works in those ways, and no constitutive processes explain why. So far, this is all quite reasonable. But scientists tend to assume, further, that wherever explanation by analysis finally stops, wherever these fundamental phenomena occur, it will always be on the level of the very small – for example, at the neurological, biochemical, atomic, or subatomic level, and never closer to the surface, at the observable level. For convenience, let us call this the *small-is-beautiful assumption*. But although it is *only* an assumption, and although anti-mechanists have marshalled powerful arguments against it, scientists often treat it as if it were an empirically established fact.

One way to expose the defects of the small-is-beautiful assumption is to see how it fails for particular sorts of phenomena – for example, cognitive or intentional phenomena, including instances of personal behavior and large-scale social or behavioral regularities (such as the laws of economics). One could argue (as I did above, and as many others have done) that attempts to analyze such phenomena in terms of lower-level constitutive processes or mechanisms presuppose one or more deeply unacceptable theses – e.g., the Platonic or essentialist view that mental or psychological kinds can be specified by some set of necessary and sufficient conditions, the view that a brain state (or some other kind of state) can be functionally unambiguous, or else the view that a brain state (or some other kind of state) can be intrinsically isomorphic to the state of affairs it represents or produces (see e.g., Braude, 1979; Bursen, 1978; Goldberg, 1982; Heil, 1978, 1979, 1981, 1983; and Malcolm, 1977, 1980).

In addition, however, one could draw attention to some further and less heralded aspects and peculiarities of the small-is-beautiful assumption. The points I shall now make are not fatal to the assumption, as are the more specific anti-mechanistic arguments. The latter actually furnish counter-examples, while the considerations below are intended merely to illustrate more clearly just what sort of assumption we are dealing with, and in the process help rob it of its surface plausibility.[3]

To begin with, we must observe that the small-is-beautiful assumption is one form of the view that nature has a preferred (or inherently fundamental) level of description, a level at which we can identify absolutely primitive phenomena and their basic properties. And of course that assumption likewise may take different forms. Some (probably the majority of its supporters) hold that the preferred level is the province of physics, either in its present or in some perfected future form. But no matter what, precisely, the fundamental level of description is taken to be, the small-is-beautiful assumption is at least committed to the view that statements true of observable phenomena are inherently superficial, and that only statements true of the microcosm can be statements about primitive phenomena. Hence, partisans of the small-is-beautiful assumption are committed to the view that nature has some preferred or final inventory of objects, events, qualities, and relations. We may not at present know what that inventory is; but (they would say) we nevertheless know certain general things about it. We know that the primitive items on the list will inhabit the microcosm, and that the properties and relations will be of the sort exemplified by those kinds of things.

But this position strikes me as bizarre. It seems clearly false to say that there is a context-independent preferred descriptive scheme or way of talking about nature, an inherently or absolutely preferred (or final) inventory of events, objects, qualities, or relations. For one thing, nature may be given any number of different parsings, spanning a continuum running from the fine-grained to the coarse-grained. It may be characterized on different levels of description, each of which countenances certain things –

241

but not others – as objects, and certain descriptive categories (predicate and relational expressions) – but not others – as appropriate to those objects. More importantly, however, no one of these parsings or sets of categories is inherently more fundamental than any other. Some may be more appropriate or useful relative to a guiding set of interests or purposes. But none is justifiable – much less correct – *apart* from any contextual guidelines.

To see what is wrong with the idea that nature has a context-independent preferred parsing, consider the question: How many things are in this room? The important fact to observe here is that the question has no single correct answer. Before we can answer it, we need some idea of what is to count as a *thing*. In different contexts, different sorts of objects or entities may legitimately count as things. Independently of a set of interests or needs in which certain descriptions of the room (but not others) count as appropriate, the question simply has no answer. To a group of atomic physicists, it might be appropriate to consider atoms or their contituents to be things, in which case the number of things in the room would be enormous. But to interior decorators, household movers, or insurance agents, it might be more appropriate to parse the room into observable objects, in which case there would be far fewer things in the room.

Furthermore, by parsing nature a certain way into things or objects, we limit the range of predicate and relational expressions at our disposal. Household movers might use such terms as 'bulky', 'fragile', and 'hard to carry downstairs'; and interior decorators might use the terms, 'rustic,' 'garish,' 'casual', and 'matches the color of your eyes'. But these terms do not apply to atoms or their constituents. And just as the question 'How many things are in this room?' had no single correct answer, the same will be true of 'What properties and relations are exemplified in this room?' Since a set of descriptive categories applies only to an appropriate range of objects, we cannot say what the properties are without at least tacitly accepting a certain parsing of the room into things. But (as we've seen) a division of nature into units or objects is never intrinsically correct, or applicable independently of a set of interests and purposes relative to which certain parsings (but not others) count as appropriate. Apparently, then, our inventories of objects, properties, and relations are all perspective-relative and interdependent. Hence, neither properties nor their objects are items in a perspective-free warehouse of onto-logical furniture.

The same points apply to *states of affairs* or *events*, rather than objects. Bits of history may be parsed – legitimately – in an endless number of ways. And it does not matter whether we are concerned with so-called *objective* events or states of affairs, or a person's subjective states or inner episodes. For example, we might ask: How many events composed World War II (or Jones's memory of his first date)? Obviously, there is no single or preferred answer to the question. Either event, World War II or Jones's memory, may be subjected to numerous different sorts of fine-grained or coarse-grained parsings. In fact, the decision to treat World War II (say) as an event capable of further division already represents a decision to parse human history in one way rather than many others.

Furthermore, how we parse World War II into smaller event-units determines the range of descriptive categories applicable to those units. (Alternately, one could say that our choice of categories presupposes a range of parsings to which the categories apply.) If we divide World War II into battles or campaigns, we can apply such terms as 'decisive', 'cunning', 'victorious', and 'tragic'. However, if we are dealing instead with events on the scale of small muscle movements of individual soldiers, or events no longer than a few microseconds, we will have to employ different sets of descriptive categories.

It may be helpful to think of levels of description as *conceptual grids*[4] that we impose on reality. Different grids will parse reality differently and thereby permit us to map different sorts of connec-tions or regularities. Some grids, to be sure, may exhibit lawlike relations to others. For example, a grid through which we identify audible sounds will be nomologically related to one that parses reality into waveforms, sound-pressure levels, and attack and decay (envelope) characteristics. But some grids countenance or reveal objects, properties, and relations that have few (if any) connections to alternative grids. This kind of incommensurability obtains, I believe, between the diagnostic grids used in traditional Chinese medicine and that used by Western physicians (see e.g., Connelly, 1977, and Klate, 1980).

We must grant, then, that objects and phenomena are identified only with respect to a descriptive scheme or level of description, a set of categories that parses reality in a certain way and thereby takes certain relations (but not others) to exist in the universe – namely, the sort that can obtain between those elements. But then it would be surprising indeed if descriptive categories dealing with the microcosm were the only ones incapable of further analysis. In fact, we would *expect* a plurality of levels of description to countenance phenomena or regularities unique to those levels – i.e., not reducible to, derivable from, or capable of being mapped without residue onto, another level of description. For example, it would not be surprising if on the level(s) at which we identify psychological states, there are regularities or phenomena not analyzable at a lower level. (Of course, to judge by the arguments raised above in connection with the copy theory, this seems demonstrably to be the case.) In any event, apart from all the specific arguments designed to demonstrate the irreducibility of the mental to the physical, one cannot simply *assume* that psychological descriptions must be further analyzable (e.g., in biochemical or neurological terms, or in the language or physics). It would be more plausible to assume, right from the start, that there exists a plurality of irreducible descriptive schemes, each appropriate to a different domain of discourse or range of phenomena. But then we must concede that causal regularities among observable phenomena may not, after all, be further describable or analyzable on a level of description dealing with smaller-scale phenomena. (I remind the reader of the additional relevant points raised in Chapter 1.3, concerning the nature of abstraction and the corresponding limitations of the physical sciences. It should be clear that the foregoing comments simply approach the same topic from a different direction.)

Moreover, since our choice of descriptive schemes can be justified only with respect to a guiding set of interests or purposes, the view that nature has a preferred level of description presupposes that some such set of interests or purposes – some *perspective*, in other words – is inherently more fundamental, or more concerned with basic questions, than the rest. But that claim is simply incredible. For example, although the shifting perspectives of a theoretical physicist and an interior decorator might overlap or be related to one another in various ways, they might also be irrelevant to or nomologically independent of one another. To be sure, when an interior decorator explains the resilience of certain materials or colors in terms of manufacturing techniques, that explanation will be true *in virtue of* underlying truths about the chemical and atomic properties of matter. In that case, therefore, the perspective of the physicist might properly be said to undergird that of the interior decorator. But in other cases, one would look in vain for any heirarchical relationship between the perspectives of the physicist and interior decorator. No deeper physical explanation will explain why a pattern is *busy* or *garish*, or a decor *elegant*, *casual*, *contemporary*, *cold*, *daring*, or *unimaginative*. In some contexts, then, the physicist and interior decorator are interested in distinct and nomologically independent aspects of the world, each appropriate to a certain range of goals and interests. But then neither group has a monopoly on the basic questions. To suppose that the physicist's questions are inherently deeper or more fundamental is simply to be taken in by a kind of professional chauvinism. *Qua* physicist, we, focus on a certain range of objects and questions; *qua* interior decorator, our needs and interests change, and different and possibly independent entities, questions, and regularities command our attention. Similarly, and perhaps more pertinently, there is no reason to assume that the concerns, goals, and interests of the physicist must be either similar or related to, or deeper than, those of the behavioral scientist, or of people caught up in everyday matters of psychological survival.

In any case, since one can marshall strong arguments in support of the view that intentional or cognitive phenomena are not analyzable in terms of subsidiary processes or mechanisms, and since PK certainly seems to be such a phenomenon, let us consider how we might deal theoretically with PK, if we assume it to be non-analyzable as well.

4.5 TAKING PK AS PRIMITIVE

Let us assume, then – if only to see where it leads – that PK is not analyzable in terms of subsidiary processes or mechanisms. Far from obliterating all prospects of a PK theory, it seems to me that the assumption opens two main theoretical avenues.

(1) On the one hand, we might hold that while acts of PK are *mediated* by subsidiary processes or mechanisms, nevertheless

they do not *reduce* to some set of underlying phenomena. That is, we might claim that lower-level processes contribute causally to the occurrence of an observable PK event P, but that no set of such processes is either identical with P, or causally necessary and sufficient for its occurrence. We could put this briefly by saying that the production of P is *non-mechanistic*. From this point of view, we would expect certain small-scale physical or physiological conditions to be PK-conducive or even necessary for the exercise of PK, without there being a set of physical or physiological conditions necessary and sufficient for the production of a given kind of observable PK effect. Analogously, I might need a functioning brain in order to think about my brother (contrary to what spiritualists and Cartesian dualists maintain), even if no set of brain processes is identical with or necessary and sufficient for thinking about my brother.

As the foregoing discussion of the copy theory made clear, this is the respect in which I consider cognitive or intentional phenomena generally to be unanalyzable. Of course, that discussion focused on the presumed causes of PK effects – i.e., the agent's intention, desire, etc. But mental states are not the only kinds of events that resist mechanistic analysis; certain PK *effects* – i.e., physical states – appear to do so as well. That fact may easily be overlooked by those who dismiss the more interesting poltergeist and mediumistic phenomena. But consider the *gracefulness* of a D. D. Home accordion rendition, the *affection* in the touch of a materialized hand, or the *playfulness* or *hostility* of some poltergeist antics. These characteristics of the phenomena cannot be analyzed solely in terms of some antecedently specifiable set of properties inherent in all their instances. In part, at least, they can be understood only with respect to the way the phenomena are integrated into local as well as global (e.g., societal and cultural) contexts. For example, certain properties of a handshake may be affectionate in one setting but hostile or menacing in another. (Similarly, a father's loving kiss may be topologically indistinguishable from a syndicate hit-man's kiss of death.) Furthermore, there are no properties common to all affectionate handshakes, or affectionate acts generally. Even a punch in the mouth, or knocking someone unconscious, can be affectionate in some situations. (Recall the old movie lines: 'I had to do it; it was for your own good', 'I can't let you go up in a rig like that', or 'Thanks, I needed that'.)

Even table levitations may display context-sensitive characteristics. Richet, a seasoned and keen observer of the phenomena, once remarked,

> the table answers as if it was alive; the emotions of the
> subconscious are faithfully translated by the kind of
> movements made by the inert object. This lifeless table seems
> to have a mind; it hesitates, it shows irritation; it affirms
> energetically; or it sways solemnly. No one who has witnessed
> such séances can imagine how well diverse sentiments can be
> expressed by the frequency or the forcefulness, the slow,
> hesitating, vigorous, or gentle movements. It is an actual
> language and always interesting. . . . (Richet, 1923/1975,
> pp. 401–2)[5]

In any case, if PK phenomena are fundamental and unanalyzable in the sense outlined above, then scientists will be able to analyze only those aspects of the PK process that *can* be described mechanistically. This may not take us very far, just as an analysis of the processes underlying the production of vocal sounds or hand movements in writing ultimately tells us very little about communication (see the remarks on telepathy in Braude, 1979). But at least there would be processes to study.

(2) But observable PK may be unanalyzable in a more interesting and radical way. There might be no *process* to PK, at least in a familiar sense of 'process'. That is, there might be no set of lower-level events intervening between the PK effect and the state of mind causing it, almost as if a phenomenon could be produced instantaneously by waving a magic wand. One reason for taking this suggestion seriously has to do with some abstract issues concerning the nature of causal connections; and I will address these shortly. Another is that certain mediumistic and poltergeist phenomena – some of those conspicuously ignored by PK-theoreticians – render the option more plausible than it would seem had our attention been limited to laboratory experiments (e.g., RNG tests). The currently fashionable (and in many ways justifiable – see Braude, 1979) practice of generating PK targets by means of radioactive decay or electronic noise makes it seem (and *only* seem) as if PK is forced to work initially on the micro level,

and that macroscopic effects are outcomes of a resulting 'chain reaction'. But a somewhat different picture emerges from non-experimental cases – e.g., apports and some cases of ostensible materializations, in which complex and well-formed objects appear (and sometimes disappear and reappear) apparently instantly.

If this more radical approach to PK has any merit, it could turn a great deal of current theorizing on its head. We might then want seriously to consider the possibility that phenomena classified as examples of micro-PK (in sense (b) above) are really instances of direct, unmediated interactions between organisms and observable objects of states of affairs. For example, we would be more open to the suggestion that spoon bending (say) is a phenomenon whereby macroscopic deformation of the spoon produces a corresponding microstructural change, rather than a process in which a change in the spoon's microstructure produces a corresponding macroscopic change. By the same token, we would be prepared to consider the possibility that changes on the quantum level are by-products of PK effects on the observable level, rather than the reverse. Or, more modestly, we might simply say that a macro-PK effect *is* (the same as) a corresponding micro-PK effect, identified relative to a different level of description. But whichever option we choose, the point to remember is that we are not forced to treat macroscopic changes as causal outcomes of earlier micro-PK effects.

Quite understandably, few will yield very easily to this suggestion. And the source of their discomfort is not difficult to fathom. They would protest that all PK phenomena seem to involve a mysterious connection between a mental state and a resulting physical state. Even die-hard physicalists would concede that they all involve a mysterious physical $\rightarrow$ physical connection over an apparent spatial gap. So in one form or another, a certain question seems to cry out for an answer – roughly, 'How do we bridge the gap between the intention and the effect?'

But is it clear that this question *must* have an answer? Apparently, the question presupposes that cause and effect must be spatiotemporally contiguous – i.e., that all causal connections are explicable (at least ultimately) according to something like a billiard-ball model of causality. But that position is contentious, to say the least. For example, some have argued that the phenomena of memory demonstrate that cause and effect are frequently non-contiguous, and that the positing of memory traces (in order to close the gap) simply promulgates various incoherent or otherwise indefensible philosophical positions (see Braude, 1979; Bursen, 1978; Heil, 1978; and Malcolm, 1977). Others have simply observed that there is not just one correct account or acceptable or fundamental concept of causality, and that causal explanations may properly assume different forms in different contexts (see, e.g., Collingwood, 1948/1966, and Scriven, 1975).

Recently, physicists have been fond of making a similar observation. They note that quantum physics has had to replace old-fashioned mechanical billiard-ball causality with statistical or probabilistic causal laws. The majority of PK-theoreticians, in fact, are either physicists or people deeply influenced by recent developments in physics. And they embrace quite happily the possibility of at least a spatial gap between a PK effect and the mental state causing it. Curiously, however, they find the gap acceptable only so long as the PK effects are quantum-level phenomena. The fundamental sort of PK effect, they argue, is that of a mental state collapsing the state vector (see, e.g., Mattuck, 1982; Mattuck and Walker, 1979; Schmidt, 1984; and Walker, 1975, 1984). On their view, PK interactions between an organism's state of mind and observable states of affairs cannot be primitive occurrences – i.e., connections unmediated by lower-level processes. They apparently feel that we can take some of the mystery out of PK by analyzing observable PK phenomena in terms of fundamental PK events at the quantum level.

But this strikes me as a clear example of blind adherence to the small-is-beautiful assumption. For one thing, insofar as both sorts of interaction posit a causal link running from the mental to the physical, neither is less mysterious than the other. In fact, partisans of this approach seem to be impaled on the horns of a dilemma (see Beloff, 1980, and Thakur, 1979). Either they must reduce states of consciousness to physical states and then construe the causal efficacy of mental states as merely a form of purely physical causation, or they must admit that collapse of the state vector by consciousness is a form of mental $\rightarrow$ physical causation. The first horn of the dilemma, outright reduction of the mental to the physical, is implausible for a number of reasons, including those outlined earlier in this chapter. Beside, Mattuck and Walker make a point of rejecting the reductionist platform, and claim explicitly that consciousness is non-physical. This leaves the second horn of the dilemma. But that option retains the principal mystery which the retreat to quantum physics was intended to avoid. The causal link between the mental and the physical remains, and presumably the physicist must concede that this particular mental → physical link is one that resists further analysis. *How* it is that consciousness directly brings about collapse of the state vector is a question without an answer. It is simply the way the universe works. But that form of mental → physical causation is every bit as mysterious as any other direct link from a mental state to a physical state of affairs.

So the popular quantum physical approach offers no further insight into the causal link between consciousness and the physical world. It merely restricts attention to one of the mind's possible stages of operation, the quantum level. But once we allow a mental → physical gap to be primitive *at all*, it needn't be on any one level exclusively. In other words, once we grant (i) that it is possible for primitive or unanalyzable facts about organisms to be facts about observable phenomena, and (ii) that there may be unanalyzable causal interactions between states of mind and the physical world, we are simply no longer constrained to locate those fundamental interactions on the quantum level.

Nevertheless, some parapsychologists have a certain intuition about the difference between the micro- and macro-level, which disposes them to look to the former – and not the latter – for fundamental PK interactions. They think that because of quantum-level indeterminacy, there is 'room' on the micro-level for an otherwise mysterious mental → physical 'push'. The macro-world, however, they take to be a deterministic function of those indeterministic micro-phenomena; hence it has no room in it for mental → physical pushing.

But not only is this intuition highly controversial, it also fails to support the alleged primacy of the micro-level. For one thing, many physicists maintain that neither the macro- nor the micro-world is fully deterministic. They argue that quantum physics shows that nature generally follows only probabilistic laws. Heisenberg's uncertainty relations, they would say, still apply to the macro-world, although the measurement problem does not arise there in an acute form. Hence, if fundamental PK interactions occur only in an indeterministic domain, then from this respectable alternative point of view, they can occur on the macro-level.

Furthermore, let us suppose (reasonably) that macroscopic PK is a genuine phenomenon. If so, then either it requires 'room' somewhere for a mental → physical push, or it doesn't. If it requires room for a mental → physical push, then either it is there already in the macro-world, or else it is in the micro-world (by reference to whose underlying phenomena we analyze or explain the macro phenomena). But observable PK, as we have seen, is not susceptible to explanation or analysis in terms of underlying processes or mechanisms. Hence, either macro-PK requires room in the macro-world for a mental → physical push and it is there already, or else it requires no such room. And in neither case is there a compelling reason to locate fundamental PK interactions exclusively on the quantum level.

Finally, we have no reason to assume that PK phenomena must respect our distinction between observable and unobservable. After all, the distinctions between macroscopic and microscopic, and observable and unobservable, are not sharp; they are merely matters of degree. In fact, they do little more than allow us to systematize phenomena in terms of the limitations of our sense organs. But, to put it somewhat colloquially, these limitations are something *we* are stuck with. Nature could care less about them. It is completely implausible to suppose that nature's laws must make a sharp distinction where mere humans are forced to make an unsharp distinction – that is, that nature inherently divides into ontologically distinct or nomologically independent domains of phenomena corresponding to the domains marked off by our perceptual limitations. So perhaps fundamental PK interactions can occur *anywhere* on the observable/unobservable continuum; perhaps PK is a phenomenon that involves primitive interactions between organisms and physical systems generally, whether observable *or* unobservable.

4.6 CONCLUSION

I suggest, then, that the quest for a unified analysis of PK phenomena is misguided. It is misguided in the same way as attempts to frame mechanistic theories for more ordinary sorts of intentional phenomena (e.g., aggression, compassion, or communication). They all presuppose a deeply mistaken view of the nature of intentional states, or mental states generally. No matter how scientific they might appear when dressed up in some appropriately imposing technical vocabulary, underneath they remain only bad philosophy.

I reassert, however, that the futility of these projects should not prevent scientists from studying whatever processes mediate *certain forms* of the phenomena. But the study of PK, like the study of most interesting human capacities or regularities, belongs primarily to the realm of the behavioral-science analogue of the biological naturalist (Eisenbud is probably the only theoretician today who comes close). There is plenty of room in parapsychology for someone to classify phenomena and map regularities – i.e., to offer modes of description that systematize the domain in question. But there is no need, and apparently no possibility, of explaining the phenomena or regularities by means of underlying processes or mechanisms. For that reason, no science modeled after physics or chemistry can offer much of interest to parapsychology.

To some, these remarks will undoubtedly seem like an admission of failure, an assertion that there can be no scientific study of PK – hence, a plea to abandon the quest for understanding the phenomenon. But that would be a serious misconstrual of my position. And it would probably rest on an indefensibly limited conception of what a science is, and what *understanding* and *explanation* are. For one thing, stopping the search for vertical explanation at the level of behavior (or observable phenomena) is no more unscientific (or prescientific), nor more of a failure in understanding, than taking phenomena at the quantum level to be primitive and unanalyzable. In fact, it would be a *victory* of understanding to figure out where analysis ends in a given domain. That is why sensible folk do not try to further analyze the laws of economics (say) in terms of the laws of physics (see also J. Fodor, 1975, pp. 2–26, and 1981). Besides, we needn't abandon all hope of explanation once we identify ground-level phenomena; only vertical explanation (explanation by analysis) will grind to a halt. But that still leaves forms of horizontal explanation (e.g., explanation by analogy) and covering-law explanation, as options.

Hence, other forms of explanation should remain viable and may still prove profitable.

Moreover, parapsychological theoreticians should resist the tendency, manifested by thinkers in all disciplines, to begin theorizing with what appear to be the 'simple' cases, to treat these as closest to a theoretical ideal, and then to regard the more complex cases as their degenerate forms. While there is good reason to adopt this method in certain sciences, it is as inappropriate to the behavioral sciences as the easy reliance on mechanistic explanation, and for similar reasons.

The procedure to which I refer should be familiar to most readers. In the philosophy of language, for example, one can see it in attempts to treat simple sentences like 'the cat is on the mat' as paradigmatic, and then with the aid of models developed from these initial cases, to analyze sentences that seem less clear-cut on the surface (for a more enlightened approach, see Goldberg, 1982). In parapsychology, it appears in attempts to base theories of psi on results of lab tests (e.g., card-guessing, thermistor or RNG fluctuations). But these theoretical programs strike me as almost completely wrongheaded. The superficially simple laboratory examples of ESP and PK may be far from basic or close to an ideal. Their apparent simplicity may reveal nothing more than that the essentials of the cases are thoroughly obscure. For example, the crucial relationships between psi-functioning and a person's needs and interests are never as clear in the lab as they can be in real life situations. Similarly, laboratory psi offers no indication of the richness, flexibility, or refinement of psi-functioning. I suggest we consider cases of laboratory psi to be degenerate instances of real-life psi, and that we take the latter to be theoretically paradigmatic. Laboratory psi draws on contrived and limited needs and interests of the agent, and forces psi to manifest itself in artificial and exceedingly restricted forms. These cases of straightjacketed psi-functioning are no more close to a theoretical ideal than laboratory examples of human behavior.

And quite apart from abstract arguments (of the sort given earlier) showing the futility of building behavioral or intentional theories from the bottom up, it seems as if the major attempts thus far have been conspicuous failures – enough so to suggest that history is offering a lesson to be learned. But relatively few seem to have noticed. The philosophical theories of language, perception, knowledge, and action that adopt the approach have been notoriously inadequate, as have been similarly structured scientific theories (e.g., memory-trace, learning, and generative linguistic theories, and cognitive or computational psychological theories generally). In fact, the latter are merely variants of the former, couched in a particular limited technical vocabulary. What history shows, I believe, is that in any discipline for which human beings and their activities provide the data, starting with 'simple' cases tends to lead to simplistic and procrustean theoretical constructs into which the more interesting and illuminating cases never fit.

If the study of PK is to make any progress, it must reflect the fact that there is more than one way of being scientific – i.e., of systematizing and generating predictions about a domain of phenomena. Regrettably, however, parapsychologists – like many scientists – display a slavish adherence to the methods and goals of physics and chemistry, as if those sciences achieved a preferred form of understanding, or offered a preferred form of explanation. Researchers remain blind to points made more than two thousand years ago by Aristotle: that there are different – and equally legitimate – forms of explanation and understanding, and that different domains require different methodologies. It is this blindness (among other things) that leads many to embrace the small-is-beautiful assumption.

I suggest, then, that the lack of progress in PK theory is an inevitable consequence of (a) the misguided application of the analytic and quantitative methods of physics and chemistry to a domain where those methods lose nearly all their utility, and (b) taking as paradigmatic the small-scale and thoroughly unintimidating (and relatively uninteresting) phenomena occurring in the lab. The major, currently fashionable theoretical approaches in parapsychology all suffer from at least one of these defects. The observational theories of Schmidt, Mattuck and Walker (and variants thereof) fail on both counts (see e.g., Schmidt, 1975, 1976, 1978, 1982, 1984; Houtkooper, *et al.*, 1980; Mattuck and Walker, 1979; Millar, 1978; Walker, 1975, 1984). So does the systems-theoretical approach of Kornwachs and von Lucadou (Kornwachs and von Lucadou, 1979; von Lucadou and Kornnwachs, 1980), although in a somewhat different way. And although Stanford's *Conformance Behavior* theory (Stanford, 1978) suffers primarily from the second defect, it is still seriously flawed in a way related to the first. Like behaviorist theories generally, it is couched in a pseudo-precise, and fatally narrow and coarse-grained terminology spawned in an attempt to emulate the 'tough-minded' theories of physics and chemistry. Hence, in addition to their fatal lack of scope, the leading theories all attempt to apply crisp theoretical constructs to a domain whose most interesting – and probably deepest – features are neither precisely nor quantitatively describable.

In my view, significant contributions to our understanding of PK will come only from those who have mastered more than the experimental data, and who can think in terms broad enough to systematize the totality of evidence for paranormal physical phenomena. Furthermore, they must be able to relate the phenomena to matters that no precise terminology or formal system can represent or capture – namely, the nuances and dynamics of organic behavior. In fact, the true trail-blazers of PK (or psi) theory will probably be masters, not just of the data, but also of human psychology and the subtleties of life. They will have to explain the role of psi *outside* the situations in which parapsychologists try to harness it for the purposes of investigation. Experiments are designed merely to elicit contrived and artificially conspicuous manifestations of capacities that undoubtedly continue to operate when the experimenters are no longer looking. Quite probably, then, experimental psi is no more than the tip of the iceberg. In fact, as I mentioned earlier, it might well be characteristic of psi to function in ways that do not command one's attention. The crucial issue about PK (or psi), therefore, is not *how* the phenomena occur; indeed, as we have seen, attempted lower-level explanations of that sort cannot possibly succeed. Rather, the central issue seems to be *why* the phenomena occur, both in general and in specific kinds of situations. We need, then, fewer technicians and more parapsychological naturalists, people with an eye for regularities and connections, and a gift for qualitative analysis, researchers whose keen perceptions and descriptive powers will help reveal illuminating patterns and relationships in the data. And once researchers realize how pointless it is to look for mechanisms underlying the observable regularities, the project will lose its apparent air of superficiality.

5

PRECOGNITION WITHOUT RETROCAUSATION

5.1 INTRODUCTION

When I originally examined the concept of precognition (in Braude, 1979), I had just begun to take seriously the evidence for large-scale PK. Although I acknowledged that the evidence for precognition could in principle be explained in terms of pervasive and refined PK on the most subtle and intimate matters of everyday existence, I considered that option a 'mere' logical possibility, one whose probability approached zero. But it should be clear by now that I am prepared (though not necessarily happy) to assign extensive and refined psi a much higher probability. As I have already insisted many times throughout this work, we are not currently entitled to suppose that psi (PK *and* ESP) has any limits at all; if mundane psi is possible, then for all we know super psi is possible as well. Moreover, what helps to lift this position out of the realm of mere abstract philosophizing is the evidence for PK surveyed in Chapter 2. Since we have outstanding evidence for a degree of PK far surpassing that apparently demonstrated in laboratory experiments, and since we still know very little about PK (or psi generally), it seems arbitrary to impose antecedent restrictions on the phenomenon's range or refinement. And in that case, we might well profit from an examination of evidence suggesting even greater PK refinement or control (for example, psychoanalytic case studies; see e.g., Eisenbud, 1970, 1982a, 1983).

But that task goes beyond the scope of this book. My present concern is to engage in some preliminary conceptual house-cleaning. Because I had underestimated the possibility of super psi in my earlier treatment of precognition, I perpetuated the view that the concept of precognition presupposed that of retrocausation. I thereby effectively dismissed what now seems to me to be an additional serious – and probably a more viable – approach to the analysis of that concept: the appeal to a combination of super ESP and super PK. Accordingly, I shall begin this chapter with a re-examination of the concept of precognition, in light of the possibility of super psi. Then I shall consider the extent to which the evidence for precognition may plausibly be interpreted as evidence for PK, or at least the extent to which it may be explained without an appeal to retrocausation.

5.2   THE ANALYSIS OF PRECOGNITION

As I now see it, precognition admits of three major types of analysis, each of which (no doubt) may assume various forms.

I. *Retrocausal*. This, of course, is the traditional view of precognition. In its most naive form, it takes the unfortunate term 'precognition' literally and considers the phenomenon to be non-inferential for*knowledge* of a future state of affairs. Some have even taken the cognitive model so far as to define 'precognition' as 'the *perception* of a future state of affairs'. But as most parapsychologists now recognize, the evidence for precognition lends little support to this approach (see Braude, 1979). To the extent that the evidence for precognition points at all to retrocausal ESP, it suggests what Broad (1962a) called telepathic or clairvoyant *interaction* rather than telepathic or clairvoyant *cognition*. A more enlightened retrocausalist, then, drops the requirement that precognition be a form of knowledge, and maintains simply that a precognitive experience E at time t is the effect of some event E' occurring at $t' > t$. For example, whether or not it counts as an instance of knowledge, my precognitive vision or dream of an airplane crash could be interpreted as the effect of a retrocausal process initiated by the subsequent crash. (After all, I might have no idea why I had the experience, or that it 'referred' to the future. I might mistakenly believe someone was playing real-time telepathic games with me.)

Of course the concept of retrocausation is highly controversial, and those who consider it indefensible will reject this approach from the start. That leaves them with two alternatives. On the one hand they can argue that the evidence for precognition is, therefore, evidence for no psi phenomenon at all – i.e., that it consists of a body of interesting coincidences, nothing more. Obviously, partisans of this approach would not be taking seriously the possibility of super psi, and hence the viability of a non-retrocausal psi analysis of precognition. Of course, for reasons mentioned frequently throughout this book, I consider the dismissal of super psi to be groundless. But quite apart from the issue of whether appeals to super psi are plausible, and also quite apart from the issue of whether appeals to retrocausation are defensible, this first alternative has little merit. It seems to me that there is simply no justification for dismissing the evidence for precognition – *whatever* its proper interpretation – as nothing more than a body of interesting coincidences. Moreover, it is highly implausible that some set of more or less familiar non-paranormal causal hypotheses can account for the totality of the evidence, experimental and anecdotal. (See, e.g., Broad, 1962a; Cox, 1951; Dunne, Jahn and Nelson, 1983; Eisenbud, 1982a; Krippner, *et al.*, 1971, 1972; Puthoff & Targ, 1979; Richet, 1923/1975; E. Sidgwick, 1888; and Tyrrell, 1938/1961.) In any case, those theoretically opposed to retrocausation have another option – namely, to explain precognition in terms of clockwise ESP and PK. Eisenbud (1982a) calls this option the 'active' analysis, as opposed to the 'passive' retrocausal approach. He chooses that terminology because the retrocausal approach explains precognition in terms of mere information reception, whereas the active analysis appeals to something the subject *does*.

The active analysis consists of two component analyses, which may be used together or separately, depending on the nature of the case to be explained.

II. *Psi-Mediated Inference*. The first regards precognition as formally analogous to a familiar kind of normal inference. Consider the case of an engineer who, after examining a building under construction, claims 'this building will collapse'. The first thing to observe is that the engineer's statement is a tacit *conditional* or hypothetical. He is not maintaining that the building will collapse *no matter what*. Rather, he is making a claim of the form, 'the building will collapse unless—'; and, in context, one usually knows which conditions are being taken for granted.

Presumably, the engineeer means that unless (say) the design is modified, or unless different materials are used, collapse is probable (if not inevitable). The next thing to observe is that the engineer bases his judgment on *contemporaneous* information. His conditional assertion, 'the building will collapse', is justified with respect to, or inductively inferred from, presently available information regarding the blueprints, the state of the building, or the materials being used to build it.

Now according to Analysis II, the situation is much the same when a person precognizes a plane crash. First, the precognizer's judgment that the plane will crash is a tacit conditional, 'the plane will crash unless—' (e.g., unless repairs are made, unless the plane takes a different flight path, or unless a different air traffic controller is on the job). Second, this judgment is based on contemporaneous information gained via real-time ESP of relevant states of affairs (e.g., the mental state of the pilot or air traffic controller, the projected flight path, or the condition of the plane's engines or electrical system). The principal difference (apart from the use of psi) between the precognitive case and that of the engineer is that in the former, neither the precognizer nor anyone else will (usually) know how to fill in the blank in the conditional 'event E will occur unless—'. Presumably this is because not even the precognizer need be consciously aware of the data on which his inference is based.

In fact, the inference itself needn't be conscious. It may occur unconsciously as part of the subject's ongoing need-determined psi-scanning, and simply lead to various kinds of overt manifestations. For example, the precognizer might cancel his reservation on a train that he unconsciously infers will crash (see Cox, 1951). Consciously, however, he needn't be aware of so much as a 'hunch' that the train will derail. It might be in his best interest psychologically to mask the source or nature of his information, in which case he might simply appear to lose his desire to make the trip. In other cases, the paranormally acquired information and unconscious inference might find their way into a dream, or even produce a somatic disorder. For example, rather than ride on the train he unconsciously fears will crash, the ticket holder might suddenly develop a disabling migraine headache.

III. *Psychokinesis*. Some opponents of the retrocausal approach may also find Analysis II unsatisfactory for some or all cases of precognition, at the very least those in which precognitive targets are selected after the precognition by random processes (whose outcomes, we may assume, are non-inferable in principle). They may prefer to suppose that the precognizer *brings about* the state of affairs precognized – e.g., that the precognizer of the plane crash actually disposes events in such a way that the crash occurs (or will occur unless appropriate countervailing measures are taken). Clearly, this view encourages us to take very seriously the deep psychodynamical factors that would explain why one or more ostensible precognizers might (probably unconsciously) want to bring about the (sometimes unfortunate if not tragic) events in question. It is no wonder, then, that the best case for the PK analysis has been made by a psychoanalyst, Eisenbud (see 1982a, 1984).

Eisenbud recognizes that one can never be certain about underlying motives, much less that one could ever know the full story – i.e., the complete array of relevant unconscious goings-on and under-the-surface interactions (normal and paranormal). At best, one can proceed as in other speculative areas of science, by generating hypotheses that tie together systematically as many loose ends as possible. Eisenbud also counters the predictable objection that people are unlikely to will or wish for – even unconsciously – the tragic large-scale disasters that from time to time are ostensibly precognized (e.g., the sinking of the Titanic, or the Aberfan mine disaster). According to some, even if people *were* able psychokinetically to bring about events of that magnitude, it is implausible to suppose that they would. Eisenbud's response, in addition to pointing out that psi-mediated inference is still an alternative to the retrocausal hypothesis, is simply to deny that humans are incapable of such a degree of malevolence.

There is no disaster, of whatever magnitude of degree or horror, that has ever been foreshadowed in dream, premonition, or Delphic utterance that cannot be matched in effect by one that has been brought about by some individual deliberately and with full awareness of the consequences. . . . The record on this score is so extensive and so clear – from fatal child abuse to Hiroshima, from capriciously started wars to shocking acts of political terrorism – that there can be no reasonable argument about human propensities in this domain.

The only question is whether there is a hidden part of the average well-acculturated human being, who cannot consciously imagine himself battering a child or bombing a school building, that is subject to the same impulses that actuate persons who are openly destructive. (Eisenbud, 1982, p. 175)

5.3 PROBLEMS WITH RETROCAUSATION

Twice before I addressed the topic of precognition (see Braude, 1979, 1982b), and on neither occasion did I see any serious problem with the concept of retrocausation. (In my later discussion, I considered a possible difficulty with the retrocausal analysis; but it did not have to do with the very positing of retrocausal connections.) That's not to say I felt at home with the idea of backwards causation; in fact, I found it puzzling and counter-intuitive. But it seemed to me (and still does) that the arguments leveled against its intelligibility were unconvincing (see, e.g., Brier, 1974 and Fitzgerald, 1974 for criticisms of the usual arguments). Hence, I attributed my lingering uneasiness to my own conceptual limitations.

Now, however, I believe I understand the basis for my uneasiness. I have come to suspect that the concept of retrocausation suffers from a deep and interesting defect. This shift in perspective was provoked by Eisenbud's all too brief criticism of the retrocausal account of precognition in 1982a, and by some interesting supplementary remarks he offered in correspondence.

But before discussing what seems to be the problem, I must first make some general observations about causation. In so doing, I am not attempting to sketch a theory of causation. I have no general theory to offer, and in fact I believe that the concept of causation cannot be fully analyzed, or captured in a general theory. To that extent, at least, I agree with Scriven (1975) that the concept of causation is largely pragmatic. But be that as it may, the claims I make below about causal relations and causal explanations should be compatible with a wide range of views about the nature of causality. Indeed, it is the relative independence of these claims from any particular theory of causation that gives my subsequent arguments against retrocausation much of their force.

The first point to notice, then, is that when we individuate events C and E, and relate the two causally, we are *not* identifying two discrete events or a single event, $C \to E$, that may be completely isolated from the surrounding mass of happening which we parse according to our needs and interests. Both C and E have their own individual causal histories running from earlier to later; each is the outcome of an enormous number of converging causal lines. Of course we never identify all those lines when considering what caused the event; we identify only those relevant to the context of inquiry.

Consider some examples. Suppose we want to know what caused my heartburn. That request may be *correctly* answered in a number of different ways, depending on such things as who is asking, and how much and what sort of knowledge of the situation is presupposed or even relevant to the request for an explanation (i.e., how much one *needs* to know). For example, if we simply want to isolate which of my activities that day was causally relevant to my heartburn, it might be enough to observe that I had eaten Mexican food for dinner. But in response to different requests for explanation or needs to understand, it might be more appropriate and illuminating to trace different causal lines. For example, we might prefer to connect my heartburn to the ingredients present in my dinner, the chemical structure of those ingredients, or the physiological disposition of my body (or of my stomach in particular). Or, it might be more appropriate to connect my heartburn to the psychological factors (say, my relationship with my parents) that contributed to my developing a nervous or weak stomach, or the way in which the chef's preoccupation with his divorce led to an excess of hot spices in my meal, or perhaps even the cultural tradition and geographical factors that culminated in a Mexican propensity for preparing 'picante' dishes, etc.

Or suppose we want to explain what caused the frequent 'drop-outs' of sound during playback of an audio cassette. Once again, different sorts of explanation will be appropriate to different needs to understand. For example, it might be enough to point out that the cables from the cassette player to the preamplifier were not fastened securely. But in some contexts we might need to present a more complex causal picture. It might be more appropriate and helpful to mention that the cassette player had recently been disconnected and reconnected somewhat hastily, or that a young child had been playing behind the audio hookups and might have inadvertently (or intentionally) loosened the connection. Or, we might need to mention the poor quality control of the cable manufacturer, which led to the construction of interconnects that fatigue easily or seldom fit securely, and which accordingly require the continued vigilance of the user.

But no matter which specific causal history suits our purposes, whenever we relate two events as cause and effect, we inevitably *presuppose* that there is a surrounding network of events leading to and away from them. Any causal connection we identify will always be part of a larger causal nexus spreading indefinitely into the past and future. The particular causal connections we find worthwhile to single out are individuated, on pragmatic grounds, out of an intrinsically seamless web of happening running from earlier to later and leading to and away from the events we relate causally. And from out of that web we can distinguish numerous different causal lines, some converging toward the individual events and others spreading out from them.

And as the two examples above help illustrate, when we identify a causal connection and presuppose its surrounding causal history, we needn't have in mind some specific additional story or set of stories to tell about the component events. Rather, we presuppose simply that there is more we *could* say if we had to. In fact, we face a situation analogous to that of persons who plot travel routes for the Automobile Association. When asked to trace a route from Cincinnati to Cleveland (for example), they know that both cities are points on a complex system of roads, and that there are different ways of getting from one city to the other. Then they select a path suiting the needs and interests of the traveller. For example, they might select a direct and quick route, rather than one more convoluted and (allegedly) more scenic. Similarly, when we identify events as cause and effect, we presuppose the *possibility* of tracing an indefinite number of different sets of connections leading to and away from them – different stories or causal maps, each appropriate to an associated range of interests and requests for explanation and understanding. That, I believe, is the respect in which an event may be a causal condition (or product) of an enormous number and variety of other events.

263

In fact, that events are embedded in this way into a surrounding nexus of related happenings seems to be a central presupposition, not just of the activity of giving causal explanations, but also of the ordinary concept of an *event*. Generally speaking, events are determinate slices of an intrinsically undifferentiated mass of happening running clockwise from earlier to later, a whole onto which we may trace different causal maps or grids, relevant to different associated needs and interests. That is why my heartburn may be explained relative to different causal histories – e.g., a socio-cultural explanation concerning the origin of the use of chili in Mexican cooking, a psychoanalytic explanation concerning the development of my nervous stomach, or simply an account of how my friends and I chose to eat at a Mexican restaurant. That is also why ordinary events may typically be embedded in a chain of transitive causal links. The loose audio connectors might be traced to my having hastily reconnected my audio components; and that event in turn might be traced to my having cleaned all my audio contacts, which in turn might be the outcome of my wanting to remedy an audible degredation in the sound of my system, and so on. And of course various sorts of causal histories and transitive causal chains lead away from the event explained as well. My heartburn may lead to a confrontation with the chef, and a curtailed evening with my friends, etc. And the drop-outs from my cassette player might lead me to believe that the problem is with my player, and that might result in my taking it to a repair shop for unnecessary service, etc.

Of course, thus far I have been concerned only with an event's temporally *conventional* causal history.[1] But we are now in a position to evaluate the view of the retrocausalist. As one might expect, retrocausalists tend to urge that retrocausal links are merely *mirror images* of temporally conventional causal links – i.e., that they are just like ordinary causal connections except for the temporal direction of the causal arrow. And that position is not idiosyncratic to those who worry about precognition; it is often embedded in general philosophical speculations about the nature of time and causality.[2] Some consider causes to be necessary conditions (at least in the circumstances) of their effects (e.g., Beloff, 1977a; Mackie, 1974, Chapter 7), or the member of a pair of events that explains the other (e.g., Newton-Smith, 1980, pp. 28ff.; Scriven, 1975), or the member of a pair of events the control of which can bring about or prevent the other (e.g., Brier, 1974; Dummett, 1954, 1964; possibly Scriven, 1975); and they argue that these construals of the notion of a cause are inherently atemporal. Others buttress their position with the observation that certain equations of physics require backwards causation, or at very least that they are time-reversal invariant or time-indifferent (e.g., Earman, 1974; Fitzgerald, 1974; Mehlberg, 1971, pp. 43–45; Sklar, 1977, pp. 375–78). Lucas even claims that 'date-indifference' is a 'precondition of our having any causal laws at all' (1973, p. 72). But whatever the justification of their position might be, retrocausalists nevertheless want to maintain that except for the causal arrow's temporal direction, retrocausal connections are quite orthodox.

But that seems to me to be false. Naturally, it is to the retrocausalists' advantage to propose a type of causal link differing from conventional causality only in temporal direction. If that proposal were defensible, it would boast a kind of disarming simplicity. But despite the assurances of retrocausalists, I suspect that retrocausal connections are not, after all, mirror images of conventional causal connections, and that the differences are both deep and fatal to the retrocausalist position. Indeed, I now believe that retrocausalists have not clearly grasped just what sort of view they are favoring.

In the case of a humdrum conventional (clockwise) causal connection $C \rightarrow E$, E may have any number of different sorts of causal consequences, spreading out in a variety of ways to events of all sorts; but the retrocausal link $E \leftarrow C'$ seems to be different. Retrocausalists treat $E \leftarrow C'$ as if it were an almost completely isolated connection – for example, as if the precognitive dream had no further retrocausal influence, or as if there was almost no *possibility* of tracing further retrocausal consequences from the dream. I say 'almost' here because I suspect that retrocausalists might claim that any event (precognitive experiences included) may be precognized, or that retrocausal links might be parts of surrounding small-scale local retrocausal perturbations (although we are never told what they are). But when one looks at the proposed examples of retrocausation, the retrocausalist view seems to be that – apart from these possible exceptions – retrocausal connections are isolated causal links. They do not spread extensively back into the future and out into the past as conventional causal links spread extensively back into the past and out into the future. That is why retrocausal effects (say, precognitive dreams) seem to have no further retrocausal repercussions, although they have plenty of conventional causal consequences. A precognitive dream may cause the dreamer to be upset, or to enter the experience into a diary, and so on. But I know of no account, either of precognition or of retrocausation generally, according to which the effect of a later cause has additional – much less extensive – retrocausal consequences. Rather than being conveniently individuated from a mass of happening running counterclockwise from later to earlier, retrocausal connections seem to stand out like a sore thumb on any causal map.

For example, the cases drawn from physics (e.g., involving advanced potentials and tachyon interactions) invariably concern isolated retrocausal connections. And the stories concerning human agency are likewise abruptly truncated, including those that do not involve precognition. Dummett (1964) imagines a case where an Indian chief's dancing *after* his warriors have been hunting causes them to have acted bravely on the hunt. And in an earlier paper (1954), he imagines a case in which every time a man says 'Click!' before opening an envelope received in the mail, he finds it does not contain a bill. But in neither case does he suggest how the proposed cause and its earlier effect might fit into an overall retrocausal history leading counterclockwise both to and away from the events in question. Indeed, he treats the events retrocausally related as parts of an ongoing mass of *clockwise* happening.

In the latter case, for example, one would expect an account of the events that contributed retrocausally to the saying of 'Click!' – in fact, to the *repeated* saying of 'Click!' over a period of months (Dummett's explanation of the motivation for continuing the experiment is given in clockwise causal terms). Similarly, one would expect a retrocausal account of how the saying of 'Click!' or the absence of a bill in envelopes (even from creditors?) is retrocausally connected to the earlier events that ordinarily would have caused bills to be received in the mail. If this story is to have any real explanatory force, it must say something about the relationship between the utterance of 'Click!' and the inexorable processes by which people are billed for their purchases. The process of billing has a complex conventional causal structure, involving the selection of items to be purchased, the act of charging one's purchases, the computation of interest, the initial sending of bills in the mail, the subsequent warnings for unpaid bills, and eventually the instigation of legal action for non-payment. Hence, one must say a great deal more than that the word 'Click!' 'prevents anyone from sending me a bill the previous day' (1954, p. 44). Dummett's example, then, seems to be a poor excuse for a causal story of any sort; we have no idea at all how the alleged cause and effect fit into a surrounding bit of history running in the same temporal direction. But we always have some idea how to fill in a surrounding history for clockwise regularities that we take to be causal, even when (as in Dummett's case) we don't understand the nature of the connection.

Consider the following imaginary case. Suppose that every time I said 'Click!' my next door neighbor would fall asleep (if awake) or awaken (if asleep). Even if we are mystified about the nature of the causal connection, we at least know how to trace conventional causal histories to and away from the events related. For example, we can trace various causal lines leading to my neighbor's falling asleep over his dish of spaghetti. He was born to Italian parents, developed a love of Italian cuisine, was divorced and consequently concerned about his diminished financial resources, was neither adept in the kitchen nor willing to go out for dinner, and so was preparing an easy and inexpensive Italian dish for himself. And from his falling asleep suddenly we might trace his face plunging into the spaghetti, breaking his nose, soiling his clothing, and all these events setting the stage for an embarrassing interview later at the hospital.

It almost seems as if retrocausalists are dimly aware (or afraid) that making retrocausal connections mirror images of conventional causal connections would have undesireable consequences. To put it metaphorically, perhaps their intuition is that a retro-causal history would interfere with, swallow up, or cancel out the conventional causal history which it interpenetrates. But whatever their reason might be for treating precognitive connections as virtually isolated retrocausal links, retrocausalists must at very least defend the view of causality they seem tacitly to endorse. They must explain why an isolated link deserves to be considered a causal link of *any* sort, never mind its temporal direction. No other sort of putative causal connection lacks an extensive surrounding causal history running temporally in the same direction.

Retrocausalists might reply that in talking about retrocausal connections, they are introducing a new sense of 'cause', appropriate to the unique way in which later events can be causal conditions of earlier events. Or, they might argue that the conventional concept of causality is simply defective, and that it needs to be replaced by one that allows cause and effect to have no surrounding causal history running in the same temporal direction. But the retrocausalist position cannot be salvaged by means of a superficial terminological fiat, or by the straightforward replacement of one concept by a new improved version.

First of all, no *data* require positing retrocausation. Outside of the parapsychological cases, the proposed examples are all highly contrived thought experiments or controversial suggestions concerning the interpretation of physical equations. And the parapsychological cases can all be accomodated by means of the active analysis, which appeals only to large-scale extensions of phenomena for which we already have evidence. Second, the concept of causation, we must recall, is intimately linked to many others in a larger network of concepts; concepts are no more isolated individuals than are events or causal links. That is why retrocausalists cannot be content with mere terminological or conceptual patchwork. In order to revise or supplement the concept of causation, they would have to refashion a larger cluster of related concepts, all of them central to our conceptual framework (e.g., explanation, understanding, event, decision, action, intention). They would no longer be endorsing the apparently simple view that the retrocausal arrow is just like the regular causal arrow except for its temporal direction. They would have to defend a sweeping and fundamental revision of our conceptual framework, one that is neither required by the data nor more parsimonious than its alternatives.

Perhaps it is in the retrocausalists' interest to appeal to a 'block universe' cosmology, according to which the history of the universe is already laid out atemporally in its entirety. From this point of view, temporal direction, temporal becoming, and causal maps are at best pragmatically justifiable fictions – i.e., ways of imposing order on the universe as a whole. Hence, it would appear that no feature of the universe inherently forbids the telling of retrocausal stories. But it seems to me that a block universe cosmology does not help the retrocausalist. At best it will provide a controversial and shaky foundation, and at worst it is of no more help to retrocausalists than to their opponents.

To begin with, the conception of a block universe faces some well-known and serious problems – most notably the need to make sense of consciousness and the awareness of temporal passage, and perhaps also the need to deflect the insistence of some physicists on the fundamentality of indeterminacy. More importantly, however, the block universe seems indifferent to the debate between retrocausalists and non-retrocausalists. If causal talk and the ordinary individuation of events are merely ways of ordering and systematizing an atemporal spacetime, it nevertheless remains true that causal connections and events have the features discussed above – i.e., that ordinary events (the kind involved in ostensible precognitive connections) have numerous different causal antecedents and repercussions, and that causal links are therefore not isolated connections. Retrocausalists, then, must still justify a massive revision of a pragmatically highly-justified conceptual framework. The active interpretations of precognition would still seem to fit more easily and parsimoniously into our world view. Naturally, they would make a significant *difference* to the prevailing scientific world view, and they might force some hefty revisions of certain scientific theories. But we would not have to scuttle or overhaul the central concepts of event and causation, as well as revise the cluster of concepts with which they are intimately connected. (I remind the reader that we need not suppose, even ordinarily, that cause and effect must be spatio-temporally contiguous. See my remarks in Chapter 4.5, and in Braude, 1979, pp. 184–210.)[3]

At this point some might wonder whether I have been stacking the deck against the retrocausalist. After all, why give up the mirror image view so easily? Granted, the literature makes it look as if retrocausal connections are isolated links between events; but retrocausalists might be able to explain that away. They could insist that retrocausal links are, indeed, parts of larger retrocausal stories, but that due to our conceptual bias in favor of conventional causality, we have simply failed to think in retrocausal terms, or develop a repertoire of retrocausal concepts. And that is why (they might say) we have difficulty filling out the retrocausal histories of which precognitions and other putative retrocausal connections are a part. I suspect that this response would appeal most strongly to those who initially defended retrocausation on the grounds that the equations of physics are time-reversible or time-indifferent, or who argued for 'the irrelevance of temporal sequencing to the essential nature of the cause-effect relationship' (Scriven, 1975, p. 5).

But just as before it was the retrocausalists' responsibility to show why an isolated link deserved to be considered a causal link, or why we should accept a major revision of our entire conceptual framework, once again the burden of proof belongs to the retrocausalist. If retrocausal connections are not isolated, and if (like conventional causal connections) they may be parsed out of a web of happening running in the same temporal direction, one would think that retrocausalists could at least make some reasonable proposals about what a surrounding retrocausal history might look like. They wouldn't need to know precisely what it would be for any given case, any more than we must know precisely the conventional causal history surrounding conventional causal links between ordinary events. But just as we could tell different conventional causal stories (as I did above) for ordinary events, one would expect the retrocausalist to be able to suggest a variety of retro-histories in which the events involved in precognitions play a part. But it seems to me that we have no idea at all how to do this, and that a retrocausalist making the above argument is offering a worthless promissory note.

I propose, then, that we consider an example of precognition, in order to make this discussion less relentlessly abstract, and to see more clearly how formidable are the problems facing the retrocausalist.

5.4   AN EXAMPLE

Suppose that I visit my neighborhood psychic, Jones, whom I ask to 'see' into the future of my friend Smith (whom Jones doesn't know). We may suppose that I'm worried about Smith because he has been depressed for quite a while, although I feel reasonably certain (based on my familiarity with Smith's history) that my friend would never exhibit suicidal behavior. But suppose that

Jones tells me that Smith will try to take his life, and that Jones then has a mental image of a man lying near a bottle of pills. Knowing Smith as I do, I'm naturally skeptical about the accuracy of Jones's forecast. But suppose that the next day I'm startled to learn that Smith has just unsuccessfully attempted to do away with himself by taking an overdose of barbiturates.

The first thing to observe about this story is that conventional causality is presupposed by our very description of the case and the individuation of its constituent events. Every suicide attempt, for example, has a temporal direction running from earlier to later. In Smith's case it might involve, say, a sequence including his deciding to do away with himself, determining how to go about it, writing a note, taking the pills, etc. Moreover, like its constituent events, the suicide attempt as a whole has various conventional causal antecedents and consequences. Let us suppose that it was the outcome of Smith's continuing failures in love and business, combined with a depressive personality initially developed during his childhood. And let us suppose that it was the cause of (among other things) the suffering and concern of Smith's family and friends, of Smith's later seeking psychiatric counseling, collecting disability compensation, and so on.

Furthermore, the experience had by the psychic, Jones, is likewise part of a larger network of happening running from earlier to later. It was caused in part by my request for information about Smith, and more remotely (let us suppose) by Jones having won my confidence with the accuracy of his psychic readings over the years, and more remotely still by Jones's psychic experiences leading him to become a professional psychic. And it is easy to imagine various conventional causal consequences of Jones's mental image of a man lying near a bottle of pills, such as the heightened concern I felt for Smith's welfare, Jones's wondering whether his experience was veridical, and (more remotely) Jones's finding employment as a clairvoyant with the police, and later becoming a national celebrity.

In fact, what makes Jones's mental image *about* Smith and his attempted suicide, rather than someone else, or someone merely sleeping after taking medicine for an infection, is the sequence of events *preceding* it. The very intelligibility of the precognitive vision, its representing what it does rather than something else, is partly a function of the events causally leading up to it. That

271

the experience corresponds to Smith's subsequent suicide attempt is not what makes the experience *about* (or 'refer' to) Smith. That is merely what makes it veridical; the experience would still have been about Smith even if he had not attempted to kill himself.

Now it seems to me that anyone who attempts to explain Jones's precognition in retrocausal terms is impaled on the horns of a dilemma. The proposed retrocausal link leading from Smith's attempted suicide to Jones's precognitive experience will either be – or not be – a mirror image of a conventional causal link – i.e., part of a surrounding causal history having the same temporal direction. And it seems that neither option admits of a reasonable justification.

Suppose, to begin with, that the retrocausalist maintains that the link from the later to the earlier event is a mirror image of a conventional causal connection. In that case, he must show two related things: (a) that just as events individuated in the incident play a part in an indefinite number of conventional causal stories and have a variety of conventional causal antecedents and consequences, the events retrocausally connected have an analogous set of diverse retrocausal antecedents and consequences in a surrounding nexus of happening running counterclockwise from later to earlier; (b) that the events playing a part in these retrocausal stories (including, presumably, Smith's suicide attempt, the event precognized) can be *individuated* in such a way that their descriptions presuppose analogously extensive and variegated retrocausal histories – i.e., that they can be parsed out of a surrounding mass of counterclockwise happening.

For example, Smith's suicide attempt is a pivotal occurrence on either the conventional or the retrocausal account. Partisans of the active and retrocausal interpretations all would agree that it is the event ostensibly precognized. Of course, in describing it as a suicide attempt, we presuppose that the event has a conventional causal history. Indeed, one would think that retrocausalists would consider that description inherently misleading, if not downright question-begging. Hence, one would reasonably expect the retrocausalist to be able to individuate – in retrocausal terms – Smith's attempted suicide, or at least some bit of retro-happening roughly coterminous with it. In order for the retrocausalist proposal to seem like anything more than wishful thinking or empty speculation, proponents must identify the event precognized in such a way that one could trace a set of retrocausal stories which lead counterclockwise to and away from it. It may also be fair to demand retrocausal analogues to familiar *kinds* of conventional causal situations, such as causal pre-emption and overdetermination.

Moreover, a great deal of conceptual stage-setting would be required in order to construct even a half-baked retrocausal story. For example, when we describe the event precognized as a suicide attempt, we are not simply slicing the pie of clockwise happening into spatiotemporal parts. We are identifying one of those parts in such a way that we can see how it might fit or does fit into a larger story or set of stories. Describing it as a suicide attempt presupposes various concepts which already have considerable conceptual and explanatory utility. The very concept of a suicide is but a small part in a large network of psychological or intentional ascriptions with which we are able to discriminate illuminating patterns, regularities, and connections within the mass of clockwise happening. Therefore, the retrocausalists' job will be to provide an analogous set of retrocausal concepts and explanatory tools, and then to individuate the event precognized in a way that gives it a place within that system of descriptions or retroconceptual framework. In other words, the job is not to show how a *suicide* attempt fits into different retrocausal stories; suicides do not occur counterclockwise. It is to redescribe or reindividuate the event conventionally described as a suicide attempt – or at least some bit of retro-happening roughly coterminous with it – and show how we can fit that bit of happening, *described in that way*, into a set of retrocausal stories.[4]

I don't know how to demonstrate that this cannot be done (although the argument in the next section may be one way). But the retrocausalist must give some reason for thinking that it can. If the best the retrocausalist can do is proffer assurances that one could develop appropriate analogous retrocausal explanatory grids given suitable conceptual evolution, then those assurances, I suggest, count for very little. In fact, considering that no one has ever sketched out even a partial retrocausal analogue to a set of ordinary causal concepts, one can only wonder why retrocausalists should have any confidence at all that the task can be pulled off. If we are to take seriously the suggestion that we have stunted our conceptual growth by clinging obdurately to a conventional causal framework, retrocausalists must support the claim that the limitation has been with us, and not in the nature of their proposal.

The second horn of the retrocausalist dilemma would be to defend the view that retrocausal links are not mirror images of conventional causal chains – in particular, that they can be isolated from the surrounding mass of happening, and that they are not necessarily parts of larger retrocausal stories. But as I mentioned earlier, the concept of causality cannot be amended or abandoned in that way without forcing deep revisions elsewhere in an extensive network of related concepts. Hence, proponents of a retrocausal interpretation of precognition must justify the need for a large-scale conceptual revision, when the data can be explained without it, and when the alternative active analysis requires much less sweeping changes to our world view (although the changes are still highly significant). Hence, retrocausalists must defend what at best seems to be an unnecessary and extremely unparsimonious position.

5.5   A FURTHER PROBLEM FOR THE MIRROR IMAGE VIEW

The foregoing considerations suggest that the retrocausal interpretation of precognition is highly implausible at best, and demonstrate that it has never been developed in the kind of detail necessary to give it even a fighting start. Still, we might wonder whether the concept of retrocausation suffers from even more pernicious defects. We might wonder, in fact, whether there is something to the intuition that retrocausal connections would potentially swallow up or cancel out the conventional causal history it allegedly interpenetrates. How might we unpack these metaphors? I would like now to offer an argument which seems to me to be sound, and which may help to do just that. Even more important, however, it shows why retrocausation cannot be a mirror image of conventional causation – hence, why the most popular and allegedly most plausible concept of retrocausation is untenable.

Consider first a perfectly familiar feature of conventional causality. When we identify an event C as the cause of E, we seldom, if ever, regard C as sufficient for E. Usually, we suppose that C

274

is one of many conditions which are jointly sufficient for E. These additional causal conditions are sometimes irrelevant to our requests for causal explanations. But often they are simply too mundane to mention or consider in any real-life context of inquiry. For example, as Hausman (1984) correctly observes, we usually take for granted the *persisting of properties* of matter throughout causal episodes involving physical objects. When we want to explain what caused my heartburn, or the drop-outs in the play-back of my cassette, we usually don't need to consider that I needed to be alive throughout the causal episode leading to the heartburn, or that the atomic structure of my audio components remained stable. Rarely, then, do we ever identify *total* causes.

But once we grant that causes are seldom (if ever) sufficient for their effects, we can understand why for any ordinary causal connection $C \rightarrow E$, it is usually the case that some other event C' can prevent the occurrence of E. Moreover, an intervening causal process can typically prevent E even after C has already occurred. For example, my heartburn would not have resulted from the chef's excess of chili if an event in the restaurant made me lose my appetite before I began to eat, or if I died of a heart attack before the spices had begun to work their magic in my tummy. The loose audio connectors would not have led to the drop-outs if I had discovered and tightened them before playing the tape, or if an irate neighbor destroyed my audio system before I could play the tape.

Now if retrocausation is a mirror image of conventional causation – i.e., if retrocausal connections belong to a web of retro-happening running counterclockwise (even if we are impotent to describe it), then the following problem emerges. Presumably, retrocauses are no more total causes than are the events we conventionally identify as causes; like ordinary causes, they are not sufficient for the occurrence of their effects. Hence, one would think that intervening retrocausal chains could retro-prevent any given effect from occurring. The retrocausal mirror image of the familiar situation just considered is this. Suppose C occurs at t_3 and its earlier effect E occurs at t_1. Then at some intermediate time t_2 it is possible that another event C' intervenes and retro-prevents the occurrence of E. But presumably that is *not* possible at any time later than t_1, since *ex hypothesi*, E has already occurred.[5] Apparently, then, retrocausation cannot be – at least in this respect – a mirror image of conventional causation. To suppose otherwise leads to the intolerable conclusion that future events could *change* – not merely *affect* – the past (see Dummett, 1964).

Diehards might urge that retrocausation simply fails to mirror the aforementioned kind of conventional causal intervention, but that otherwise the two forms of causation are analogous. But to concede that retrocausation does not mirror this feature of ordinary causation is to admit defeat. It is to abandon the view that the former is analogous in *any* deep and interesting way to the latter. The possibility of the sort of causal intervention we've just considered is entailed by the deeper truth about causality noted above – namely, that ordinary causes are not sufficient for their effects. And the insufficiency of causes can be explained by reference to our earlier observation that causal connections are individuated out of an intrinsically seamless web of happening running in the same temporal direction, and that the component events have an indefinite number of causal lines leading to and away from them. That is why events typically can figure in various and sundry different causal stories.[6] Apparently, then, if the retrocausalist relinquishes the possibility of retrocausal intervention, he's committed to abandoning the view that retrocausation does not mirror these deep and pervasive features of conventional causation.

We may conclude, therefore, that retrocausation is not analogous to conventional causation. Hence, retrocausalists seem forced to revert to the unpromising second option considered earlier. They must claim either that we need a second concept of causation to capture the peculiar features of retrocausal connections, or that we must overhaul the old one substantially. But as we saw earlier, that option requires a sweeping and deep revision of our conceptual framework, one that is neither required by the cases allegedly explained by retrocausation, nor more parsimonious than its alternatives.

5.6   CONCLUSION

I have argued that the concept of retrocausation is more problematical than its proponents have realized. To begin with, alleged retrocausal explanations seem not to be *genuine* explanations. One reason conventional causal accounts explain at all is that particular causal links may be embedded within a surrounding matrix of connections; any particular causal connection is always part of a larger set of stories we could tell if we needed to. And I suggest that a putative causal explanation is genuinely explanatory only when it satisfies this condition. But as we have seen, the striking defect of retrocausal connections is that they appear to play a part in no larger retrocausal story at all, much less a set of stories.

The reason for this, I have argued, is that retrocausation cannot be a mirror image of conventional causation, contrary to what most retrocausalists like to believe. The mirror image view of retrocausation seems to entail that future events can change the past. The remaining option, however, is to embrace a view according to which retrocausal links are isolated connections; but that would force retrocausalists to carry out and defend a major facelift on our conceptual framework as a whole. And that job, as we have seen, is neither demanded by the evidence nor more parsimonious than its alternatives.

It appears, then, that there are strong reasons for rejecting the retrocausal account of precognition. But since the data seem to require a paranormal explanation, we have no choice but to seriously consider the active analysis. Now as I have argued, nothing at present justifies placing limits on the range or efficacy of psi. Furthermore, the evidence surveyed in this book suggests strongly that PK can be considerably more refined and extensive than most of us have wanted to believe, and that the overt manifestations of PK may only be the tip of the iceberg. It would seem, therefore, that the active analysis is a promising approach to explaining precognition, however unpalatable the spectre of super ESP and PK might be.

6

CONCLUSION

I have been arguing that we should accept as genuine some apparently very peculiar phenomena, and that we should accordingly expand our conception of the range and variety of human capacities. Furthermore, I have urged that we accept – if only provisionally – the hypothesis that psi phenomena are unlimited in magnitude and refinement. But it would be irresponsible, I feel, to leave matters there, and say nothing about the world view to which I believe this all leads. Regrettably, I have not developed anything like a robust conception of the role of psi in nature. But I am able to sketch some very general positions which I think we should seriously entertain.

As I argued in Chapters 1 and 4, psi functioning is probably not the sort of thing that occurs only in conspicuous ways. Generally speaking, human faculties or capacities occur in degrees; and their manifestations run the gamut from the mundane to the arcane, and the inconspicuous to the conspicuous. It would be unprecedented, then, if psi did not likewise manifest itself along similar continua. Quite probably, if psi occurs at all, we notice only its more striking occurrences. For example, instances of telepathy are likely to be noticed only between persons who know and communicate with one another. And cases of apparent precognition or real-time clairvoyance are likely to command our attention only when they concern events that are arresting for some reason (usually because they are crises or other sorts of unexpected or unpleasant occurrences). But we might be interacting all the time with the minds of strangers, and acquiring information by ESP of events to which we give little or no conscious attention.

Similarly, one would not expect typical PK effects to be

flagrantly obvious. But once we entertain the possibility that small- or large-scale PK might insinuate itself into everyday affairs, we can see how an appeal to PK might explain phenomena or regularities that would otherwise be considered mysterious or fortuitous. Pervasive and refined PK (and ESP) could explain why some people are healthier than others, or remarkably luckier or unluckier than others. For example, it could explain why some soldiers escape serious injury, despite taking repeated heroic risks on the battlefield. It might explain why incompetent or reckless drivers continue to avoid the automotive catastrophes that befall others, and emerge unscathed from those which they initiate. It might even explain why some always seem to find parking spaces. And however distasteful the thought might be, consistent bad luck or misfortune could be an external PK analogue to psychosomatic illness. We should perhaps explore the relationship between a person's misfortune and his self-image (e.g., his degree of self-hatred), and be prepared to see him as disposing events to reinforce his image as a victimized, cursed, or unworthy individual. Of course, an even more sinister possibility is that others are the cause of the misfortune. We should perhaps investigate the deep relationships between unlucky persons and their acquaintances and relatives – possibly even connections with strangers whose interests conflict with theirs. But on the brighter side, again, refined unconscious psi might undergird the careers of those who are successful in business and finance, and who seem to have a knack for speculation. It might even play a role in athletics (see Murphy and White, 1978).

I must emphasize that in making these suggestions, I do not wish to license the cavalier use of psi hypotheses to explain everyday events. Indeed, if psi really is operative under the surface, its role is probably anything but straightforward. That is why psi is probably *not* responsible for *every* bit of luck or misfortune. That is why it might not be the reason we find a lost article of jewelry, or happen to meet 'by chance' someone we needed to see.

Consider, for example, the role of the 'evil eye' in everyday affairs, and let us suppose (for reasons mentioned earlier) that thoughts can kill. Now, to claim that thoughts *can* have that kind of causal efficacy is not to claim that they always will. Once we grant that psi might work under the surface, there is no reason to suppose it must all be malicious, or that all psi effects are directed toward the same (or compatible) goals. Presumably, paranormal hostilities would be only part of a wider nexus of covert psi interactions, subject (like other types of influence) to various countervailing forces. In fact, it would be reasonable to expect hostile psi to parallel normal forms of hostility. For example, not every insult or attempt at ridicule hurts its intended victim. Ordinarily, people have ways of deflecting the malevolence; some are insensitive, inattentive, or simply able to brush it aside. Similarly, not every attempted physical assault produces its intended result. Many people are able to defend themselves, and sometimes others intervene and restrain the attacker. Analogously, one would think that people may likewise draw on a reservoir of defenses against covert hostile psi. In general, our hostile actions (whether verbal or physical) can hurt; but they often don't, even when the aggressor is formidable. Analogously, even if thoughts can kill, they often won't, no matter how prodigiously psychic the assailant happens to be. A hostile word, blow, or thought will be effective only if other conditions permit. Indeed, hardly a person would now be alive (or intact) if every hostile thought were to reach fruition. Hence, even if psi is theoretically unlimited in scope, power, or refinement, there is reason to think it might be severely limited in practice.

Another disturbing aspect of acknowledging the possibility of even modest psi in life is that it might constantly be contaminating otherwise clean experiments in science. Why suppose that PK on machines or quantum processes is confined only to parapsychology experiments? Orthodox scientists are at least as motivated as parapsychologists to get their desired results. And since they are not engaged in parapsychological experimentation, they probably do not suffer from the aroused and inhibiting fear of psi that might keep lab results in parapsychology at marginally significant and non-threatening levels. But then what is to prevent covert psi interference or influence in orthodox laboratory experiments, especially when *many* scientists are hoping for a certain result? It would not be surprising if the resistance of some scientists to parapsychology is partly related to the unacknowledged fear of this possibility.

But let us not focus (again) only on the bleak side of psi. If psi can do harm or mischief, it presumably can also do good. Whether or not conscious control of psi is attainable, we might nevertheless be able to improve or maintain our health and fortune by cultivating the appropriate goals, attitudes, and feelings. Perhaps we cannot be the ultimate masters of our destiny, and perhaps we are as incompetent in or resistant to using psi for our benefit as we are in the case of our other capacities (see Chapter 2.1). Nevertheless, we might be far from impotent, much less pawns or helpless victims of larger 'karmic' or impersonal forces whose inexorable tendencies and direction we are powerless to divert. Although psi might not make us gods, we might be more powerful than we realize.

But with that power, of course, comes responsibility for the things it can achieve. And responsibility for our actions is something few care to assume, and many others fear. Accordingly, one would think that the greater the power of psi, the greater the potential responsibility for our use of it – hence, the greater the fear or degree of resistance, either to using it or simply to acknowledging its existence. Indeed, the fear of assuming responsibility for large-scale (or any) psi might be one major reason why its manifestations are rarely conspicuous. Covert psi would perpetuate the useful illusion that we are merely spectators rather than agents. Moreover, the fear of responsibility might also be a serious constraint on the very use of psi, even under the surface; it might be one of the countervailing circumstances I mentioned earlier. We often curb our normal aggressive tendencies in order to avoid responsibility for the actions they would produce. Similarly, not only might we be inhibited from using psi conspicuously; the burden of responsibility might be great enough to prevent us from using it at all. (For interesting comments on the fear of psi, see Eisenbud, 1982a, 1983; and Tart, 1982, 1984.) Perhaps (as I suggested in Chapter 2.1) it contributed to the reduction in quantity and quality of PK phenomena with the demise of the spiritualist movement; and today the fear might express itself in the chance or small-scale effects obtained in parapsychology experiments. In fact, since parapsychologists are as likely as others to suffer the fear of psi, one would expect progress in parapsychology to be made by those who possess, not just the requisite amount of intelligence and perceptivity, but also a hefty and profound dose of moral courage.

NOTES

Chapter 1 THE IMPORTANCE OF NON-EXPERIMENTAL EVIDENCE

1 See Gauld and Cornell, 1979 for a good discussion of these features of poltergeist and haunting phenomena.

2 To contest this point now would make no difference with regard to the more important underlying issue I want to address in this chapter. The distinction between experimental and semi-experimental evidence is, to a great extent, *normative*. The latter class of evidence is typically held to be inferior to the former precisely because the procedures considered appropriate for conducting experiments are thought to yield a more reliable body of data than the apparently looser procedures tolerated in séances, poltergeist investigations, etc. (This is one of the prejudices I examine in this chapter.) And clearly, we don't undercut this point of view by calling the best studies of mediums (say) experiments. The normative distinction would simply have to be expressed another way in that case – for example, by claiming that there are different *classes* of experiments, some better than others. One purpose of this chapter is to evaluate the claim that the semi-experimental material is evidentially inferior to the experimental material. Therefore, I prefer not to indulge in question-begging reclassification, and shall attack directly the normative wedge driven between the semi-experimental and experimental evidence.

3 Nicol (1972) makes an interesting case for concluding that the S.P.R. has traditionally displayed a bias against evidence about or provided by those he calls 'the Peasants'. He argues, however, that the Society's double standard turned out to be a piece of good fortune, since some excellent cases were scrutinized much more thoroughly than they would have been had the psychics been from a higher class. But despite those benefits, other good cases may have been passed by, such as that of Jack Webber (see Edwards, 1962). In fact, the Society's bias against physical phenomena and the work of outsiders has resulted in several lost opportunities to examine apparently

outstanding phenomena, such as those investigated by Crawford, (1918, 1919, 1921), and those reported to have occurred in the presence of Carlos Mirabelli (see, e.g., Dingwall, 1930). (See also Chapter 2.4) For an overview of the S.P.R.'s handling of evidence for physical phenomena, see Inglis, 1977, and especially 1984.

4 Dobbs makes several good observations on this point. The most important is that the only way to tell whether telepathy (say) obeys the inverse square law would be to determine the precise amplitude and exact departure and arrival times of the telepathic signal. But we have no idea at all when or at what level of intensity the presumed signal departs or arrives, much less some device – a telepathy meter – for measuring those parameters. The evidence for telepathy consists only of subjects' verbal reports or other physiological responses (e.g., blood volume changes and EEG readings). And of course we have no idea when a signal would be transmitted following an experience or response of the 'sender', or how long it takes a 'receiver' to respond to the signal's arrival. Moreover, since a response to a telepathic signal may be partly a function of its *relevance* or *importance* to the receiver, there may be no correlation between intensity of signal and intensity of response. For example, a weak signal (at the threshold of detectability) could provoke an intense response, and a strong signal could provoke a weak response.

5 In many cases there was no body of literature, and certainly no widely-distributed body of literature, to be familiar with. Only in recent years, in fact, has there been any substantial body of technical, and even popular, literature on poltergeists; and the most detailed and accurate examples of these are known primarily to parapsychologists. Much of the better evidence for poltergeists antedates these works.

6 Also interesting is Randi's failure to keep a promise to pay '$1,000 to any named charity should Targ and/or Puthoff be able to substantiate any of the 24 "facts" they alleged concerning statements I made about their Geller research fiasco in my book *The Magic of Uri Geller*'. For more details, see Fuller, 1979. More recently, and more significantly, the credibility of the allegedly impartial Committee for Scientific Investigation of Claims of the Paranormal has apparently been destroyed by its own Watergate-type scandal. See Rawlins, 1981, Curry, 1982, and Kammann, 1982.

   For additional details about the dishonorable behavior of prominent nineteenth-century skeptics, see Podmore, 1902/1963, vol. 2, pp. 145ff.

7 See Hastings and Krippner, 1961 for an account of the role of expectancy in poltergeist cases. But it should be noted that the case described in this article is not strongly evidential, and was not taken to be such by seasoned and wary psychical researchers.

8 I grant that it is difficult to establish conclusively that what improves is the witnesses' observational, rather than literary, skills. Here, as in all written testimony, there is no substitute for reading the documents

and attempting, with as much impartiality as one can muster, to get a 'feel' for them.

9 See Richet, 1888, 1889 for reports of his work on hypnosis and ESP.

10 In the parapsychological literature the experiences of apparitions (whether individual or collective) are often called *hallucinations*. In fact, Broad (1962a) follows this convention, which I find somewhat surprising. The problem with the term 'hallucination' in these contexts is that the experiences in question sometimes prove to be veridical. But many would take hallucinations to be non-veridical *by definition*. See Chapter 3 for a discussion of this terminology.

11 I discuss the slippery meaning of 'paranormal' in Braude, 1979.

Chapter 2   PHYSICAL MEDIUMSHIP

1 I submit, in fact, that this is why James Randi has never made good on his much-touted acceptance of Eisenbud's challenge to reproduce the Serios phenomena. Neither Randi nor anyone else can fraudulently duplicate the Serios results on Polaroid film under the most stringent of the conditions in which Serios succeeded. See Eisenbud, 1967, 1977; and Fuller, 1974.

2 The reader will recall that I argued in the last chapter that conditions were *not* especially loose. But whether or not the prevailing opinion was correct, it *was* the prevailing opinion.

3 The reader should keep in mind, when reading accounts of phenomena that might initially seem to be caused by the medium exerting an undetected effort of his own, that at no time in his life was Home a strong person. He was always frail, and often sick (usually suffering from consumption).

4 Crookes was fortunate to have this handy means of setting his researches before the public. Alfred Russel Wallace, another prominent scientific investigator of physical phenomena, and sitter at some of Crookes's séances with Home, had been unable to persuade scientific journals to publish reports of his own studies.

5 Crookes and Wallace, by the way, were not the only major scientists to have gone on record about Home's phenomena, and accordion phenomena in particular. Francis Galton apparently attended several séances supervised by Crookes. In a letter to Charles Darwin dated April 19, 1872, he wrote,

> I have had only one seance since I wrote, but that was with Home in full gas-light. The playing of the accordion, held by *its base* by one hand under the table and again, away from the table and behind the chair was extraordinary. The playing was remarkably good and sweet. It played in Serjeant Cox's hands, but not in mine, although it shoved itself, or was shoved under the table, into them. There were other things nearly as extraordinary. What

surprises me, is the perfect apparent openness of Miss F. [Kate Fox] and Home. They let you do whatever you like, within certain reasonable limits, their limits not interfering with adequate investigation. I really believe the truth of what they allege, that people who come as men of science are usually so disagreeable, opinionated and obstructive and have so little patience, that the seances rarely succeed with them. . . . Crookes, I am sure, so far as it is just for me to give an opinion, is thoroughly scientific in his procedure. I am convinced the affair is no matter of vulgar legerdermain and believe it well worth going into, on the understanding that a *first rate medium* (and I hear there are only 3 such) puts himself at your disposal.

. . . Home *encourages* going under the table and peering everywhere (I did so and held his feet while the table moved). . . . (quoted in Medhurst and Goldney, 1964, p. 42)

6 The occurrence of musical phenomena during Home's séances is an important and potentially revealing feature of his mediumship. Although it is not clear how musically talented Home was, he nevertheless played the piano reasonably well. Hence, one might wonder what that indicates about the origin of the phenomena. My understanding of the evidence for mediumship generally is that other famous mediums both lacked musical abilities and did not manifest musical phenomena (at least in the form of impressive *performances* of pieces). Of course, hard-line spiritualists might contend that musical phenomena are most easily produced *through* a medium who possesses the requisite musical abilities. But I suspect that most would interpret the facts differently, and consider Home's PK phenomena to be an extension of and continuous in form and style with his normal abilities.

Regrettably, the evidence from cases of mental mediumship only makes it more difficult to interpret the facts. In many of those cases, mediums behave in ways that appear to transcend their normal physical and cognitive capacities. Female mediums sometimes speak in distinctly male voices, exhibiting timbral characteristics that are perhaps not producible normally through their vocal organs. Moreover, mediums often exhibit personality traits (e.g., degrees or qualities of humor or discernment) quite unlike those they normally display, and arguably well beyond or discontinuous with their normal abilities or character.

7 Mere verbal assurances to the contrary from a magician are not enough. Let the magician do the trick, under conditions similar to those in which Home's phenomena occurred. Until then, the magician's pronouncements – no matter how confident their tone – are worthless. Confidence is easier to fake than a Home table levitation. And this caveat against the judgment of magicians applies with equal force today. In my view, laymen, scientists, and even parapsychologists, settle too easily for the opinions of magicians (e.g., James Randi has not felt constrained to prove his claim that he could

duplicate the Serios phenomena under Serios' test conditions; see Fuller, 1974). Often – and certainly in the case of Randi (currently the most outspoken of the lot) – the opinions are incompetent, ill-informed, and sometimes dishonest, betraying more about the magician's professional or philosophical fears than about his expertise.

8 I shall, below, discuss the grounds for Feilding's confidence in the genuineness of the phenomena connected with the 'cabinet'. But I should mention, here, that many of Eusapia's phenomena (e.g., table levitations and some object movements) seem to be independent of her relationship with the 'force' inside. If these phenomena must be treated as genuine, as the best evidence compels us to believe, it is simply unnecessary to suppose that the cabinet is merely a prop for Eusapia's bag of tricks, or that it casts doubt on her phenomena generally.

9 For example, it may be, as many mediums have claimed, that light interferes with the force producing the phenomena. On the other hand, since Eusapia and others have in fact produced phenomena in bright light, and since Home often made objects move and instruments play above or away from the table, the occasional utility of darkness, reduced illumination, or the protection of a table may not point to generalizable features of a PK force or process. It may instead reveal more about the psychological atmosphere of the séance in question, or perhaps about the belief system of the medium.

10 Although Crawford found similar weight increases and decreases with another medium, he did not obtain the same correspondences with decreases and increases of weight in the table. Crawford suggested that another sitter may have had some mediumistic influence; and, in fact, certain figures suggest that the combined weight loss of the two people was approximately equal to the weight gain of the table (Crawford, 1919, pp. 170ff).

Chapter 3   APPARITIONS

1 Sidgwick (1889c, p. 9) also claims that 'apparition' may appropriately be applied only to visible phenomena. Whether or not his feel for the proper use of the term was correct – and I question whether it was – I think it is fair to say that nowadays both common usage and theoretical expediency justify a broader application of the term.

2 Quite possibly, Broad's definition was influenced by that of Sidgwick (1889c, p. 9), who defined 'hallucination of the senses' as 'a sensory effect which we cannot attribute to any external physical cause of the kind that would ordinarily produce this effect.' But Sidgwick – at least on this occasion – was concerned only with waking experiences; hence he was not countenancing dreams as hallucinations. On this issue, then, he parts company with Broad and with his colleagues (including his wife) who compiled the case material.

Gurney (1885) adopted a similar position. He defined 'sensory hallucination' as 'a percept which lacks but which can only by distinct reflection be recognized as lacking, the objective basis which it suggests . . .' (p. 154). And, he says, 'objective basis' is 'a short way of naming the possibility of being shared by all persons with normal senses' (p. 154). Gurney also realizes that his definition seemed inadequate to deal with collective cases; but he made no attempt to revise or replace it.

3 Interestingly, although the pioneers of the S.P.R. established a tradition of allowing hallucinations to be veridical, they disagreed over whether hallucinations must be erroneously believed to be normal perceptions. Gurney, for example, argued that

> . . . belief in their reality, though a frequent, is by no means an essential feature; a *tendency* to deceive is all that we can safely predicate of them. (Gurney, 1885, p. 152)

Henry Sidgwick, on the other hand, claimed that,

> . . . in every experience that we call a Hallucination there is an element of erroneous belief, though it may be only momentary, and though it may be the means of communicating a truth that could not otherwise have been known. If I seem to see the form of a friend pass through my room, I must have momentarily the false belief that his physical organism is occupying a portion of the space of my room, though a moment's reflection may convince me that this is not so, and though I may immediately draw the inference that he is passing through a crisis of life some miles off, and this inference may turn out to be true. In the case of a recurrent Hallucination known to be such, we cannot say that the false belief ever completely dominates the percipient's mind; but still, I conceive, it is partially there; here is an appearance that has to be resisted by memory and judgment.
>
> It is, then, this element of error – perhaps only momentary and partial – which is implied in our term 'Hallucination'. . . . (H. Sidgwick, 1889c, p. 8)

I suspect that veterans of drug-induced hallucinations (among others) would be quick to challenge Sidgwick. Many of those who use hallucinogens regularly or recreationally know, during the entire time the hallucinations are occurring, that the experiences are non-veridical. In fact, many take the drugs precisely because they want to have non-veridical experiences.

4 Gurney (1885) recognized that his definition also applied to some illusions. His response was to claim (unconvincingly, in my opinion) that 'illusions are merely the sprinkling of fragments of genuine hallucination on a background of true perception' (p. 154).

Chapter 4   TOWARD A THEORY OF PK

1 In cultures (e.g., so-called 'primitive' societies) where psi or super-natural phenomena are widely considered available for everyday uses (e.g., hexing an enemy, helping one's crop or love life), people will naturally be more on the lookout for the intrusion of psi into day-to-day affairs. They might also be better able to cope with the implications of the pervasive role of human agency (their own and that of others) in those affairs.

2 The copy theory is also strongly reminiscent of trace theories of memory, according to which different things in the world (the events or objects remembered) leave corresponding traces (representational states) in the agent. The major difference between the two theories, in fact, seems to be the location of mental states on the causal arrow. Memory theories posit causal connections *resulting* in mental states, whereas the copy theory posits connections *beginning* with mental states. For a discussion of the deep errors underlying trace theories, see Braude, 1979; Bursen, 1978; Heil, 1978; and Malcolm, 1977;

3 For additional sorts of comments along these lines, see J. Fodor, 1975, pp. 9–26, and 1981. Interestingly, however, Fodor doesn't see that his own cognitive science program commits many of the standard mechanist errors.

4 I owe this useful image to Bruce Goldberg.

5 Similar observations were made in connection with the 'Philip' experiments. See Owen, 1975; Owen and Sparrow, 1974, 1977.

Chapter 5   PRECOGNITION WITHOUT RETROCAUSATION

1 As far as I can see, these points also apply to alleged cases of *simultaneous* causation. Some philosophers wonder whether those cases are merely improperly described instances of ordinary forward causation (see, e.g., Beauchamp & Rosenberg, 1981, pp. 237ff). But we needn't worry about that issue here. What matters for our purposes is that cases of ordinary forward and putatively simultaneous causation are such that the component events figure in a surrounding set of stories running from earlier to later. If analogous counterclockwise stories can be told at all – and I argue that they cannot – then we could happily admit the possibility of individuating cases of simultaneous causation from a surrounding mass of counterclockwise happening.

2 For example, Fitzgerald (1974, p. 513) writes, 'The interesting question is whether we could conceive of something very closely analogous to the usual kind of (temporally prior) cause except that it was later than its effect.'

3 For additional difficulties in explaining precognition in the block universe, see Werth, 1978.

4 Since writing this, I have discovered that a related point has been made by Waterlow (1974). Unfortunately, her overall discussion turns on the needlessly obscure (in her hands, at least) notion of *temporal continuing*, and is further seriously marred by reliance on the unclear and probably indefensible concept of a *whole* event. On the other hand, she seems to be one of the few to appreciate that discussions and examples of retrocausation are always couched in terms that presuppose conventional clockwise causality.

5 We may, I think, fearlessly endorse the principle that once event E has occurred, it is impossible that a later event cause E not to have occurred. Similarly, we may embrace the tense-logical principle 'CpGPp' (if p, then it will always have been that p).

6 Ehring (1982) and Hausman (1984) have drawn attention to a related feature of conventional causality in their recent and interesting accounts of causal priority. A similar point may also undergird Lewis's recent discussion (1979). As Ehring puts it, 'a cause is a member of a set of events that possess, within that set, a certain causal independence, whereas the effect event is not causally independent of any of these events' (1982, p. 770). As Hausman puts it, 'everything causally connected to the particular cause is causally connected to the effect, but there is something causally connected to the effect, but not to the cause' (1984, p. 265). For example, my heartburn was caused by eating Mexican food, and is connected causally to events connected causally to my eating Mexican food, such as my hunger and desire for it. But other events causally connected to my heartburn, such as the chef's extremely liberal use of chili, are causally independent of these other causes.

Interestingly, Ehring thinks his account can tolerate retrocausation. For the reasons given above, I believe he is mistaken. Hausman is not quite sure, apparently, what to say on the subject.

BIBLIOGRAPHY

Alvarado, C. S. (1980). 'On the "Transference" of Psychic Abilities: A Historical Note'. *European Journal of Parapsychology* 3: 209–11.

Alvarado, C. S. (1982). 'Notes on Seances with Eusapia Palladino after 1910'. *Journal of the Society for Psychical Research* 51: 308–9.

Alvarado, C. S. (1983). 'Historical Notes on a Seance with Eusapia Palladino in 1912'. *Zetetic Scholar* No. 12.

Alvarado, C. S. (1984). 'Palladino or Paladino?: On the Spelling of Eusapia's Surname'. *Journal of the Society for Psychical Research* 52: 315–16.

Baggally, W. W. (1910). 'Discussion of the Naples Report on Eusapia Palladino'. *Journal of the Society for Psychical Research* 14: 213–28.

Barrett, W. F. (1886). 'On Some Physical Phenomena, Commonly Called Spiritualistic, Witnessed by the Author'. *Proceedings of the Society for Psychical Research* 4: 25–42.

Barrett, W. F. (1919). 'Report of Physical Phenomena Taking Place at Belfast with Dr. Crawford's Medium'. *Proceedings of the Society for Psychical Research* 30: 334–7.

Barrett, W. F. and Myers, F. W. H. (1889). Review of *D. D. Home, His Life and Mission*. *Journal of the Society for Psychical Research* 4: 101–36.

Batcheldor, K. J. (1966). 'Report on a Case of Table Levitation and Associated Phenomena'. *Journal of the Society for Psychical Research* 43: 339–56.

Batcheldor, K. J. (1984). 'Contributions to the Theory of PK Induction from Sitter-Group Work'. *Journal of the American Society for Psychical Research* 78: 105–22.

Beauchamp, T. L. and Rosenberg, A. (1981). *Hume and the Problem of Causation*. New York, Oxford: Oxford University Press.

Beloff, J. (1977a). 'Backward Causation'. In Shapin and Coly (eds) *The Philosophy of Parapsychology*. New York: Parapsychology Foundation.

Beloff, J. (1977b). 'Historical Overview'. In B. B. Wolman (ed.) *Handbook of Parapsychology*. New York: Van Nostrand Reinhold.

Bibliography

Beloff, J. (1980). 'Could There Be a Physical Explanation for Psi?'. *Journal of the Society for Psychical Research* 50: 263–72.

Bender, H. (1975). 'Modern Poltergeist Research'. In J. Beloff (ed.) *New Directions in Parapsychology*. Metuchen, N. J.: Scarecrow Press.

Bergson, H. (1915). Presidential Address to the S.P.R. *Proceedings of the Society for Psychical Research* 27: 157–75.

Berry, T. E. (1984/1985). 'Séances for the Tsar: Spiritualism in Tsarist Society and Literature, Part IV'. *Journal of Religion and Psychical Research* 7: 218–30, 8: 52–65.

Besterman, T. (1930). Review of *Mensagens do Além obtidas e controladas pela Academia de Estudios Psychicos "Cesar Lombroso" atravez do celebre Medium Mirabelli*. *Journal of the Society for Psychical Research* 26: 142–4.

Besterman, T. (1932a). 'The Psychology of Testimony in Relation to Paraphysical Phenomena: Report of an Experiment'. *Proceedings of the Society for Psychical Research* 40: 363–87.

Besterman, T. (1932b). 'The Mediumship of Rudi Schneider'. *Proceedings of the Society for Psychical Research* 40: 428–36.

Besterman, T. (1935). 'The Mediumship of Carlos Mirabelli'. *Journal of the Society for Psychical Research* 29: 141–53.

Besterman, T. (1936). Letter to the *Journal*. *Journal of the Society for Psychical Research* 29: 235–6.

Besterman, T. and Gatty, O. (1934). 'Report of an Investigation into the Mediumship of Rudi Schneider'. *Proceedings of the Society for Psychical Research* 42: 251–85.

Brandon, R. (1983). *The Spiritualists*. New York: Alfred A. Knopf.

Braude, S. E. (1979). *ESP and Psychokinesis: A Philosophical Examination*. Philadelphia: Temple University Press.

Braude, S. E. (1980). Reply to Ray Hyman. *Zetetic Scholar* No. 6: 42–3.

Braude, S. E. (1981). 'The Holographic Analysis of Near-Death Experiences: The Perpetuation of Some Deep Mistakes'. *Essence* 5: 53–63.

Braude, S. E. (1982a). Review of D. Bohm, *Wholeness and the Implicate Order*. *Journal of the American Society for Psychical Research* 76: 67–75.

Braude, S. E. (1982b). 'Precognitive Attrition and Theoretical Parsimony'. *Journal of the American Society for Psychical Research* 76: 143–55.

Braude, S. E. (1983). 'Radical Provincialism in the Life Sciences: A Review of Rupert Sheldrake's *A New Science of Life*'. *Journal of the American Society for Psychical Research* 77: 63–78.

Braude, S. E. (1985). Review of T. Hall, *The Enigma of Daniel Home*. *Journal of the Society for Psychical Research* 53: 40–6.

Brier, B. (1974). *Precognition and the Philosophy of Science*. New York: Humanities Press.

Broad, C. D. (1962a). *Lectures on Psychical Research*. London: Routledge & Kegan Paul.

Broad, C. D. (1962b). 'Some Notes on Mr Roll's "The Problem of

Precognition," and on the Comments Evoked By It'. *Journal of the Society for Psychical Research* 41: 225–34.

Broad, C. D. (1964). 'Cromwell Varley's Electrical Tests with Florence Cook'. *Proceedings of the Society for Psychical Research* 54: 158–72.

Brookes-Smith, C. (1973). 'Data-Tape Recorded Experimental PK Phenomena'. *Journal of the Society for Psychical Research* 47: 69–89.

Brookes-Smith, C., and Hunt, D. W. (1970). 'Some Experiments in Psychokinesis'. *Journal of the Society for Psychical Research* 45: 265–81.

Bruck, C. (1936). Letter to the *Journal*. *Journal of the Society for Psychical Research* 29: 202–3.

Bursen, H. A. (1978). *Dismantling the Memory Machine*. Dordrecht, Boston, London: D. Reidel.

Carington, W. (1934). 'The Quantitative Study of Trance Personalities, Part I'. *Proceedings of the Society for Psychical Research* 42: 173–240.

Carrington, H. (1907). *The Physical Phenomena of Spiritualism*. Boston: H. B. Turner & Co.

Cartwright, N. (1980a). 'The Truth Doesn't Explain Much'. *American Philosophical Quarterly* 17: 159–63. Revised for Cartwright (1983).

Cartwright, N. (1980b). 'Do the Laws of Physics State the Facts?'. *Pacific Philosophical Quarterly* 61: 75–83. Revised for Cartwright (1983).

Cartwright, N. (1983). *How the Laws of Physics Lie*. Oxford, New York: Oxford University Press.

Collingwood, R. G. (1948/1966). *An Essay on Metaphysics*. Oxford University Press.

Collins, H. M. (1981). 'Science and the Spoon Benders'. Lecture delivered to the S.P.R., London, Feb. 10, 1981.

Connelly, D. M. (1977). *Traditional Acupuncture: The Law of the Five Elements*. Columbia, Md.: Centre for Traditional Acupuncture.

Courtier, M. (1908). 'Rapport sur les séances d'Eusapia Palladino à l'Institut Général Psychologique en 1905, 1906, 1907, 1908'. *Bulletin de l'Institut Général Psychologique* 8: 415–546.

Cox, W. E. (1951). 'Precognition: An Analysis, II'. *Journal of the American Society for Psychical Research* 50: 99–109.

Crandon, M. (1928). Statement to the S.P.R. *Proceedings of the Society for Psychical Research* 36: 515–16.

Crawford, W. J. (1918). *The Reality of Psychic Phenomena*. New York: E. P. Dutton & Co.; reprinted, Mokelumne Hill, Calif.: Health Research, 1970.

Crawford, W. J. (1919). *Experiments in Psychical Science*. London: Watkins.

Crawford, W. J. (1921). *The Psychic Structures at the Goligher Circle*. New York: E. P. Dutton & Co.

Crookes, W. (1870). 'Spiritualism Viewed by the Light of Modern Science'. *Quarterly Journal of Science* 7 (July). Reprinted in Medhurst *et al.* (1972).

Crookes, W. (1871a). 'Experimental Investigation of a New Force'. *Quar-*

terly Journal of Science 8 (July): 339–49. Reprinted in Medhurst *et al.* (1972).

Crookes, W. (1871b). 'Some Further Experiments on Psychic Force'. *Quarterly Journal of Science* 8 (Oct.): 484–92. Reprinted in Medhurst *et al.* (1972).

Crookes, W. (1874). 'Notes on an Enquiry into the Phenomena called Spiritual During the Years 1870–1873'. *Quarterly Journal of Science* 11 (Jan.): 77–97. Reprinted in Medhurst *et al.* (1972).

Crookes, W. (1889). 'Notes of Séances with D. D. Home'. *Proceedings of the Society for Psychical Research* 6: 98–127. Reprinted in Medhurst *et al.* (1972).

Crookes, W. (1897). Presidential Address to the S.P.R. *Proceedings of the Society for Psychical Research* 12: 338–55.

Curry, P. (1982). 'Research on the Mars Effect'. *Zetetic Scholar* 9: 34–53.

Dingwall, E. (1921). 'Dr. W. J. Crawford's "The Psychic Structures at the Goligher Circle" '. *Proceedings of the Society for Psychical Research* 32: 147–50.

Dingwall, E. J. (1922). 'Physical Phenomena Recently Observed with the Medium Willy Schneider at Munich'. *Journal of the American Society for Psychical Research* 16: 687–98.

Dingwall, E. J. (1926a). 'A Report on a Series of Sittings with the Medium Willy Schneider'. *Proceedings of the Society for Psychical Research* 36: 1–33.

Dingwall, E. J. (1926b). 'A Report on a Series of Sittings with the Medium Margery'. *Proceedings of the Society for Psychical Research* 36: 79–158.

Dingwall, E. J. (1930). 'An Amazing Case: The Mediumship of Carlos Mirabelli'. *Psychic Research* 34: 296–306.

Dingwall, E. J. (1936). Letter to the *Journal. Journal of the Society for Psychical Research* 29: 169–70.

Dingwall, E. J. (1953). 'Psychological Problems Arising from a Report of Telekinesis'. *British Journal of Psychology* 44: 61–6.

Dingwall, E. J. (1961). Review of *Das Medium Carlos Mirabelli: Eine Kritische Untersuchung. Journal of the Society for Psychical Research* 41: 80–2.

Dingwall, E. J. (1962a). *Some Human Oddities*. New Hyde Park, N.Y.: University Books.

Dingwall, E. J. (1962b). *Very Peculiar People*. New Hyde Park, N.Y.: University Books.

Dingwall, E. J. (1967). (ed.) *Abnormal Hypnotic Phenomena: A Survey of Nineteenth-Century Cases*, 4 vols. New York: Barnes & Noble.

Dingwall, E. J. (1974). 'The End of a Legend'. *Parapsychology Review* 5.

Dingwall, E. J., Goldney, K. M., and Hall, T. H. (1956). *The Haunting of Borley Rectory*. London: Duckworth. Also in *Proceedings of the Society for Psychical Research* 51 (1956).

Dobbs, A. (1967). 'The Feasibility of a Physical Theory of ESP'. In J. R. Smythies (ed.) *Science and ESP*. London: Routledge & Kegan Paul.

Bibliography

Driesch, H. (1930). 'The Mediumship of Mirabelli'. *Journal of the American Society for Psychical Research* 24: 486–7.

Ducasse, C. J. (1951). 'Paranormal Phenomena, Nature, and Man'. *Journal of the American Society for Psychical Research* 45: 129–48.

Ducasse, C. J. (1954a). 'Some Questions Concerning Psychical Phenomena'. *Journal of the American Society for Psychical Research* 48: 3–20.

Ducasse, C. J. (1954b). 'The Philosophical Importance of "Psychic Phenomena" '. *Journal of Philosophy* 51: 810–23.

Ducasse, C. J. (1956). 'Science, Scientists, and Psychical Research'. *Journal of the American Society for Psychical Research* 50: 142–7.

Ducasse, C. J. (1958). 'Physical Phenomena in Psychical Research'. *Journal of the American Society for Psychical Research* 52: 3–23.

Dummett, M. A. E. (1954). 'Can an Effect Precede its Cause?'. *Proceedings of the Aristotelian Society* supp. vol. 28: 27–44.

Dummett, M. A. E. (1964). 'Bringing About the Past'. *Philosophical Review* 73: 338–59.

Dunne, B. J., Jahn, R. G., and Nelson, R. D. (1983). *Precognitive Remote Perception*. Princeton: Princeton University School of Engineering/Applied Science.

Dunraven, Earl of (1925). 'Experiences in Spiritualism with D. D. Home'. *Proceedings of the Society for Psychical Research* 35: 1–285.

Earman, J. (1974). 'An Attempt to Add a Little Direction to "the Problem of the Direction of Time" '. *Philosophy of Science* 41: 15–47.

Edwards, H. (1962). *The Mediumship of Jack Webber*. Guildford, Surrey: The Healer Publishing Co., Ltd.

Ehring, D. (1982). 'Causal Asymmetry'. *Journal of Philosophy* 79: 761–4.

Eisenbud, J. (1956). 'Psi and the Problem of the Disconnections in Science'. *Journal of the American Society for Psychical Research* 50: 3–26. Reprinted in Eisenbud (1983).

Eisenbud, J. (1963a). 'Psi and the Nature of Things'. *International Journal of Parapsychology* 5: 245–69. Reprinted in Eisenbud (1983).

Eisenbud, J. (1963b). 'Two Approaches to Spontaneous Case Material'. *Journal of the American Society for Psychical Research* 57: 118–35. Revised for Eisenbud (1983).

Eisenbud, J. (1966a). 'The Problem of Resistance to Psi'. *Proceedings of the Parapsychological Association* 3: 63–79. Reprinted in Eisenbud (1983).

Eisenbud, J. (1966b). 'Why Psi?'. *The Psychoanalytic Review* 53 (4): 647–53. Reprinted in Eisenbud (1983).

Eisenbud, J. (1967). *The World of Ted Serios*. New York: Morrow.

Eisenbud, J. (1970). *Psi and Psychoanalysis*. New York & London: Grune & Stratton.

Eisenbud, J. (1972). 'Some Notes on the Psychology of the Paranormal'. *Journal of the American Society for Psychical Research* 66: 27–41. Reprinted in Eisenbud (1983).

Eisenbud, J. (1977). 'Paranormal Photography'. In B. B. Wolman (ed.) *Handbook of Parapsychology*. New York: Van Nostrand Reinhold.

Eisenbud, J. (1979). 'How to Make Things Null and Void'. *Journal of Parapsychology* 43: 140–52.

Eisenbud, J. (1982a). *Paranormal Foreknowledge: Problems and Perplexities*. New York: Human Sciences Press.

Eisenbud, J. (1982b). 'The Flight That Failed'. *The Christian Parapsychologist* 4: 211–17.

Eisenbud, J. (1983). *Parapsychology and the Unconscious*. Berkeley: North Atlantic Books.

Estabrooks, G. H. (1957). *Hypnotism*. New York: Dutton.

Feilding E. (1926). 'Review of Mr Hudson Hoagland's "Report on Sittings with Margery" '. *Proceedings of the Society for Psychical Research* 36: 159–70.

Feilding, E. (1963). *Sittings with Eusapia Palladino and Other Studies*. New Hyde Park, N.Y.: University Books.

Feilding, E., Baggally, W. W., and Carrington, H. (1909). 'Report on a Series of Sittings with Eusapia Palladino'. *Proceedings of the Society for Psychical Research* 23: 309–569. Reprinted in Feilding (1963).

Feilding, E. and Marriott, W. (1911). 'Report on a Further Series of Sittings with Eusapia Palladino at Naples'. *Proceedings of the Society for Psychical Research* 25: 57–69.

Fitzgerald, P. (1974). 'On Retrocausality'. *Philosophia* 4: 513–51.

Fodor, J. A. (1975). *The Language of Thought*. Cambridge, Mass.: Harvard University Press.

Fodor, J. A. (1981). 'Special Sciences', in *Representations: Philosophical Essays on the Foundations of Cognitive Science*. Cambridge, Mass.: The MIT Press.

Fodor, N. (1966). *Encyclopaedia of Psychic Science*. New Hyde Park, N.Y.: University Books.

Fournier d'Albe, E. E. (1922). *The Goligher Circle*. London: Watkins.

Franklin, R. L. (1980). 'On Taking New Beliefs Seriously: A Case Study'. *Theoria to Theory* 14: 43–64.

Fukurai, T. (1931/1975). *Clairvoyance and Thoughtography*. New York: Arno Press.

Fuller, C. (1974). 'Dr Jule Eisenbud *vs* the Amazing Randi'. *Fate* (Aug.): 65–74.

Fuller, C. (1979). 'Randi Rides Again'. *Fate* (July): 37–44.

Gauld, A. (1968). *The Founders of Psychical Research*. London: Routledge & Kegan Paul.

Gauld, A. (1978). Review of A. Gregory's 'Anatomy of a Fraud' [Gregory (1977)]. *Journal of the Society for Psychical Research* 49: 828–35.

Gauld, A. (1979). Letter to the *Journal*. *Journal of the Society for Psychical Research* 50: 46–7.

Gauld, A. (1982). *Mediumship and Survival: A Century of Investigation*. London: Heinemann.

Gauld, A. and Cornell, A. D. (1979). *Poltergeists*. London and Boston: Routledge & Kegan Paul.

Geley, G. (1922). 'Les expériences d'ectoplasmie de la "Society for

Psychical Research" de Londres avec Mlle Eva C.'. *Revue Métapsychique*, No. 2: 103–31.

Geley, G. (1927/1975). *Clairvoyance and Materialisation*. London: T. Fisher Unwin; reprinted, New York: Arno Press.

Goldberg, B. (1982). 'Mechanism and Meaning'. In Ginet and Shoemaker (eds) *Knowledge and Mind*. Oxford and New York: Oxford University Press.

Gordon, M. (1869). *The Home Life of Sir David Brewster*. Edinburgh: Edmonston & Douglas.

Gregory, A. (1977). 'Anatomy of a Fraud'. *Annals of Science* 34: 449–549.

Gregory, A. (1979). Letter to the *Journal*. *Journal of the Society for Psychical Research* 50: 40–2. Comment on Gauld (1978).

Gregory, A. (1982). 'Investigating Macro-Physical Phenomena'. *Parapsychology Review* (Sept.–Oct.): 13–18.

Gregory, A. (1985). *The Strange Case of Rudi Schneider*. Metuchen, N.J.: Scarecrow Press.

Gurney, E. (1885). 'Hallucinations'. *Proceedings of the Society for Psychical Research* 3: 151–89.

Gurney, E. (1889a). 'Recent Experiments in Hypnotism'. *Proceedings of the Society for Psychical Research* 5: 3–17.

Gurney, E. (1889b). 'Hypnotism and Telepathy'. *Proceedings of the Society for Psychical Research* 5: 216–59.

Gurney, E. (1889c), completed by F. W. H. Myers. 'On Apparitions Occurring Soon after Death'. *Proceedings of the Society for Psychical Research* 5: 403–85.

Gurney, E., Myers, F. W. H., and Podmore, F. (1886). *Phantasms of the Living*. London: Society for Psychical Research.

Haight, D. F. (1984). '1884 Revisited: Levitation and the Fourth Dimension – Notes from the Overground'. *Journal of Religion and Psychical Research*, 7: 242–50.

Hall, T. H. (1962). *The Spiritualists*. London: Duckworth & Co. Ltd.

Hall, T. H. (1984). *The Enigma of Daniel Home*. Buffalo: Prometheus.

Hambourger, R. (1980). 'Belief in Miracles and Hume's Essay'. *Noûs* 14: 587–604.

Hart, H., *et al.* (1956). 'Six Theories About Apparitions'. *Proceedings of the Society for Psychical Research* 50: 153–239.

Hart, H. and Hart, E. B. (1933). 'Visions and Apparitions Collectively and Reciprocally Perceived'. *Proceedings of the Society for Psychical Research* 41: 205–49.

Hastings, A. and Krippner, S. (1961). 'Expectancy Set and "Poltergeist" Phenomena'. *ETC: A Review of General Semantics* 18: 349–60.

Hausman, D. (1984). 'Causal Priority'. *Noûs* 18: 261–79.

Heil, J. (1978). 'Traces of Things Past'. *Philosophy of Science* 45: 60–7.

Heil, J. (1979). 'Making Things Simple'. *Critica* 11: 3–33.

Heil, J. (1981). 'Does Cognitive Psychology Rest on a Mistake?'. *Mind* 90: 321–42.

Bibliography

Heil, J. (1983). *Perception and Cognition*. Berkeley & Los Angeles: University of California Press.

Hodgson, R. (1892). 'Mr Davey's Imitation by Conjuring of Phenomena Sometimes Attributed to Spirit Agency'. *Proceedings of the Society for Psychical Research* 8: 253–310.

Hodgson, R. (1895). 'The Value of Evidence for Supernormal Phenomena in the Case of Eusapia Paladino', with replies by Myers, Lodge, Richet, and Ochorowicz. *Journal of the Society for Psychical Research* 7: 36–79.

Hodgson, R. and Davey, S. J. (1887). 'The Possibilities of Mal-Observation and Lapse of Memory from a Practical Point of View'. *Proceedings of the Society for Psychical Research* 4: 381–495.

Home, D. D. (1863/1972). *Incidents in My Life*. Secaucus, N. J.: University Books.

Home, Mme. D. D. (1888/1976). *D. D. Home, His Life and Mission*. London: Trübner & Co.; reprinted, New York: Arno Press.

Honeyman, J. (1904). 'On Certain Unusual Psychological Phenomena'. *Proceedings of the Society for Psychical Research* 18: 308–22.

Hope, Lord C., *et al* (1933). 'Report on a Series of Sittings with Rudi Schneider'. *Proceedings of the Society for Psychical Research* 41: 255–330.

Hope, Lord C. (1934). 'A Note on the Recent Experiments with Rudi Schneider'. *Proceedings of the Society for Psychical Research* 42: 310–15.

Hope, Lord C. (1936). Letter to the *Journal*. *Journal of the Society for Psychical Research* 29: 183.

Houtkooper, J. M., Andrews, R., Ganzevles, P. C. J., and van der Sijde, P. C. (1980). 'A Hierarchical Model for the Observational Theories: A Study of Subject Identity and Feedback in Repeated Retroactive Psychokinesis'. *European Journal of Parapsychology* 3: 221–46.

Hyman, R. (1980). 'Pathological Science: Towards a Proper Diagnosis and Remedy'. *Zetetic Scholar* No. 6: 31–9.

Inglis, B. (1977). *Natural and Supernatural*. London: Hodder & Stoughton.

Inglis, B. (1983). Review of R. Brandon, *The Spiritualists*. *Journal of the Society for Psychical Research* 52: 209–12. Review of Brandon (1983).

Inglis, B. (1984). *Science and Parascience: A History of the Paranormal 1914–1939*. London: Hodder & Stoughton.

Isaacs, J. (1984). 'The Batcheldor Approach: Some Strengths and Weaknesses'. *Journal of the American Society for Psychical Research* 78: 123–32.

Jenkins, E. (1982). *The Shadow and the Light: A Defence of Daniel Dunglas Home the Medium*. London: Hamish Hamilton.

Johnson, A. (1909). 'The Education of the Sitter'. *Proceedings of the Society for Psychical Research* 21: 483–511.

Kammann, R. (1982). 'The True Disbelievers: Mars Effect Drives Skeptics to Irrationality'. *Zetetic Scholar* No. 10: 50–65.

Keil, H. H. J., Herbert, B., Ullman, M., and Pratt, J. G. (1976). 'Directly

Observable Voluntary PK Effects'. *Proceedings of the Society for Psychical Research* 56: 197–235.

Klate, J. (1980). *The Tao of Acupuncture*. Amherst, Mass.: Pioneer Valley Center for the Healing Arts.

Kornwachs, K. and von Lucadou, W. (1979). 'Psychokinesis and the Concept of Complexity'. *Psychoenergetic Systems* 3: 327–42.

Krippner, S., Honorton, C., and Ullman, M. (1972). 'A Second Precognitive Dream Study with Malcolm Bessent'. *Journal of the American Society for Psychical Research* 66: 269–79.

Krippner, S., Ullman, M., and Honorton, C. (1971). 'A Precognitive Dream Study with a Single Subject'. *Journal of the American Society for Psychical Research* 65: 192–203.

Lambert, G. W. (1956). 'The Use of Evidence in Psychical Research'. *Proceedings of the Society for Psychical Research* 50: 275–93.

Lambert, G. W. (1976). 'D. D. Home and the Physical World'. *Journal of the Society for Psychical Research* 48: 298–314.

Lang, A. (1900). 'The Fire Walk'. *Proceedings of the Society for Psychical Research* 15: 2–15.

Leroy, O. (1928). *Levitation: an Examination of the Evidence and Explanations*. London: Burns Oates & Washbourne, Ltd.

Lewis, D. (1979). 'Counterfactual Dependence and Time's Arrow'. *Noûs* 13: 455–76.

Lin Shuhuang, *et al.* (1981). 'Some Experiments on the Transfer of Objects Performed by Unusual Abilities of the Human Body'. Abridged version published in *Psi Research* 2 (1981): 4–24. *Nature Journal* (China) 4, no. 9.

Lodge, O. (1894). 'Experience of Unusual Physical Phenomena Occurring in the Presence of an Entranced Person (Eusapia Paladino)', with discussion'. *Journal of the Society for Psychical Research* 6: 306–60.

Lodge, O. (1911). 'On the *A Priori* Argument Against Physical Phenomena'. *Proceedings of the Society for Psychical Research* 25: 447–54.

Lodge, O. (1929). 'On the Asserted Difficulty of the Spiritualistic Hypothesis from a Scientific Point of View'. *Proceedings of the Society for Psychical Research* 38: 481–516.

Loftus, E. (1979). *Eyewitness Testimony*. Cambridge, Mass.: Harvard University Press.

Lombroso, C. (1908). 'Psychology and Spiritism'. *Annals of Psychical Science* 7: 376–80.

London Dialectical Society (1871/1976). *Report on Spiritualism*. London: Longmans, Green, Reader and Dyer; reprinted, New York: Arno Press.

Lucas, J. R. (1973). *A Treatise on Time and Space*. London: Methuen.

Luria, A. R. (1975). *The Mind of a Mnemonist*. Harmondsworth, Middlesex: Penguin.

Mackie, J. (1974). *The Cement of the Universe*. Oxford University Press.

Malcolm, N. (1977). *Memory and Mind*. Ithaca: Cornell University Press.

Bibliography

Malcolm, N. (1980). ' "Functionalism" in the Philosophy of Psychology'. *Proceedings of the Aristotelian Society* 80: 211–29.

Mattuck, R. (1982). 'A Crude Model of the Mind-Matter Interaction Using Bohm-Bub Hidden Variables'. *Journal of the Society for Psychical Research* 51: 238–45.

Mattuck, R. D. and Walker, E. H. (1979). 'The Action of Consciousness on Matter: A Quantum Mechanical Theory of Psychokinesis'. In A. Puharich (ed.) *The Iceland Papers*. Amherts, Wisc.: Essentia Research.

Mauskopf, S. H. and McVaugh, M. R. (1980). *The Elusive Science*. Baltimore & London: The Johns Hopkins University Press.

Maxwell, J. (1906). 'Concerning the Criticisms on Professor Richet's Algerian Experiences'. *Annals of Psychical Science* 3: 283–335.

Medeiros, T. de A. (1935). 'The Mediumship of Carlos Mirabelli'. *Journal of the American Society for Psychical Research* 29: 15–18.

Medhurst, R. G., *et al.* (1972). *Crookes and the Spirit World*. New York: Taplinger.

Medhurst, R. G. and Goldney, K. M. (1964). 'William Crookes and the Physical Phenomena of Mediumship'. *Proceedings of the Society for Psychical Research* 54: 25–157.

Mehlberg, H. (1971). 'Philosophical Aspects of Physical Time'. In Freeman and Sellars (eds) *Basic Issues in the Philosophy of Time*. LaSalle, Ill.: Open Court.

Millar, B. (1978). 'The Observational Theories: A Primer'. *European Journal of Parapsychology* 2: 304–32.

Murphy, G. and Ballou, R. O. (1960). *William James on Psychical Research*. New York: The Viking Press.

Murphy, M. and White, R. A. (1978). *The Psychic Side of Sports*. Reading, Mass.: Addison-Wesley.

Myers, F. W. H. (1890). Review of *The Gift of D. D. Home*. *Journal of the Society for Psychical Research* 4: 249–52.

Myers, F. W. H. (1894). 'The Character of D. D. Home'. *Journal of the Society for Psychical Research* 6: 176–9.

Myers, F. W. H. (1903). *Human Personality and its Survival of Bodily Death*. London: Longmans, Green, & Co.

Newton-Smith, W. H. (1980). *The Structure of Time*. London and Boston: Routledge & Kegan Paul.

Nicol, F. (1972). 'The Founders of the S.P.R.'. *Proceedings of the Society for Psychical Research* 55: 341–67.

Osis, K. and Haraldsson, E. (1976). 'OOBEs in Indian Swamis: Sathya Sai Baba and Dadaji'. In Morris, Roll, and Morris (eds) *Research in Parapsychology 1975*. Metuchen, N.J.: Scarecrow Press: 147–50.

Osty, E. (1933). *Supernormal Aspects of Energy and Matter*. London: Society for Psychical Research.

Osty, E. and Osty, M. (1931/1932). 'Les Pourvoirs Inconnus de L'Espirit sur la Matière'. *Revue Métapsychique* 11: 393–427; 12: 1–59, 81–122.

Owen, I. M. (1975). ' "Philip's" Story Continued'. *New Horizons* 2 (1): 14–20.

Owen, I. M. and Sparrow, M. H. (1974). 'Generation of Paranormal

Physical Phenomena in Connection with an Imaginary "Communicator" '. *New Horizons* 1 (3): 6–13.

Owen, I. M. and Sparrow, M. H. (1977). *Conjuring Up Philip*. New York: Harper & Row.

Perovsky-Petrovo-Solovovo, M. (1908). 'Review: Mr Hereward Carrington's "Physical Phenomena of Spiritualism" '. *Proceedings of the Society for Psychical Research* 21: 392–404.

Perovsky-Petrovo-Solovovo, M. (1909a). 'The Hallucination Theory as Applied to Certain Cases of Physical Phenomena'. *Proceedings of the Society for Psychical Research* 21: 436–82.

Perovsky-Petrovo-Solovovo, M. (1909b). 'Note on Miss Johnson's Paper'. *Proceedings of the Society for Psychical Research* 21: 512–15. Comment on Johnson (1909).

Perovsky-Petrovo-Solovovo, M. (1909c). 'M. Courtier's Report on the Experiments with Eusapia Palladino at the Paris "Institut Général Psychologique" and Some Comments Thereon'. *Proceedings of the Society for Psychical Research* 23: 570–89.

Perovsky-Petrovo-Solovovo, M. (1910). 'Discussion of the Naples Report on Eusapia Palladino'. *Journal of the Society for Psychical Research* 14: 228–31.

Perovsky-Petrovo-Solovovo, M. (1912). 'On the Alleged Exposure of D. D. Home in France'. *Journal of the Society for Psychical Research* 15: 274–88.

Perovsky-Petrovo-Solovovo, M. (1930). 'Some Thoughts on D. D. Home'. *Proceedings of the Society for Psychical Research* 39: 247–65.

Playfair, G. L. (1975). *The Flying Cow*. London: Souvenir Press.

Podmore, F. (1902/1963). *Mediums of the Nineteenth Century*, 2 vols. New Hyde Park, N.Y.: University Books. Reprint of *Modern Spiritualism*, 1902.

Podmore, F. (1910/1975). *The Newer Spiritualism*. London: T. Fisher Unwin; reprinted, New York: Arno Press.

Price, H. H. (1939). 'Haunting and the "Psychic Ether" Hypothesis. . .'. *Proceedings of the Society for Psychical Research* 45: 307–43.

Price, H. H. (1960). 'Apparitions: Two Theories'. *Journal of Parapsychology* 24: 110–28.

Puthoff, H. E. and Targ, R. (1979). 'A Perceptual Channel for Information Transfer over Kilometer Distances. . .'. In Tart, Puthoff, and Targ (eds) *Mind at Large*. New York: Praeger.

Randall, J. L. (1982). *Psychokinesis: A Study of Paranormal Forces Through the Ages*. London: Souvenir Press.

Rawlins, D. (1981). 'Starbaby'. *Fate* (Oct.): 2–32.

Rayleigh (père), Lord (1919). Presidential Address to the S.P.R. *Proceedings of the Society for Psychical Research* 30: 275–90.

Rayleigh (fils), Lord (1938). 'The Problem of Physical Phenomena in Connection with Psychical Research'. *Proceedings of the Society for Psychical Research* 45: 1–18.

Reichbart, R. (1977). 'Group Psi: Comments on the Recent Toronto

PK Experiment as Recounted in *Conjuring Up Philip*. *Journal of the American Society for Psychical Research* 71: 201–12.

Rhine, L. E. (1977). 'Research Methods with Spontaneous Cases'. In B. B. Wolman (ed.) *Handbook of Parapsychology*. New York: Van Nostrand Reinhold.

Rhine, L. E. (1981). *The Invisible Picture: A Study of Psychic Experiences*. Jefferson, N.J.: McFarland & Co., Inc.

Richet, C. (1888). 'Relation de Diverses Expériences sur la Transmission Mentale, la Lucidité, et Autres Phènoménes non Explicables par les Données Scientifiques Actuelles'. *Proceedings of the Society for Psychical Research* 5: 18–168.

Richet, C. (1889). 'Further Experiments in Hypnotic Lucidity or Clairvoyance'. *Proceedings of the Society for Psychical Research* 6: 66–83.

Richet, C. (1895). Letter to F. W. H. Myers concerning Eusapia Palladino. *Journal of the Society for Psychical Research* 7: 178–80.

Richet, C. (1899). 'On the Conditions of Certainty'. *Proceedings of the Society for Psychical Research* 14: 152–7.

Richet, C. (1905). 'Concerning the Phenomenon Called Materialization'. *Annals of Psychical Science* 1: 207–10, 269–89.

Richet, C. (1923/1975). *Thirty Years of Psychical Research*. New York: Macmillan; reprinted, New York: Arno Press.

Rogo, D. S. (1979). 'Reassessing the Poltergeist'. *Journal of Parapsychology* 43: 326–40.

Rogo, D. S. (1982). 'The Poltergeist and Family Dynamics: A Report on a Recent Investigation'. *Journal of the Society for Psychical Research* 51: 233–7.

Roll, W. G. (1972). *The Poltergeist*. New York: New American Library.

Salter, W. H. (1948). 'A Commentary on "The Investigation of Spontaneous Cases" '. *Proceedings of the Society for Psychical Research* 48: 301–5. Commentary on West (1948).

Schatzman, M. (1980). *The Story of Ruth*. New York: Kensington Publishing Co.

Schmidt, H. (1975). 'Toward a Mathematical Theory of Psi'. *Journal of the American Society for Psychical Research* 69: 301–19.

Schmidt, H. (1976). 'PK Effect on Pre-Recorded Targets'. *Journal of the American Society for Psychical Research* 70: 267–91.

Schmidt, H. (1978). 'Can an Effect Precede its Cause? A Model of a Noncausal World'. *Foundations of Physics* 8: 463–80.

Schmidt, H. (1982). 'Collapse of the State Vector and Psychokinetic Effect'. *Foundations of Physics* 12: 565–81.

Schmidt, H. (1984). 'Comparison of a Teleological Model with a Quantum Collapse Model of Psi'. *Journal of Parapsychology* 48: 261–76.

Schouten, S. A. (1979). 'Analysis of Spontaneous Cases as Reported in "Phantasms of the Living" '. *European Journal of Parapsychology* 2: 408–55.

Schrenck Notzing, Baron von (1923a). *Phenomena of Materialisation* (trans. E. E. Fournier d'Albe). New York: Dutton; reprinted, Mokelumne Hill, Calif.: Health Research, 1970, and New York: Arno Press, 1975.

Schrenck Notzing, Baron von (1923b). 'Concerning the Possibility of Deception in Sittings with Eva C.' *Proceedings of the Society for Psychical Research* 33: 665–72.

Scriven, M. (1975). 'Causation as Explanation'. *Noûs* 9: 3–16.

Sheldrake, R. (1981). *A New Science of Life: The Hypothesis of Formative Causation*. London: Blond & Briggs.

Sidgwick, E. M. (1886). 'Results of a Personal Investigation into the Physical Phenomena of Spiritualism'. *Proceedings of the Society for Psychical Research* 4: 45–74.

Sidgwick, E. M. (1888). 'On the Evidence for Premonitions'. *Proceedings of the Society for Psychical Research* 5: 288–354.

Sidgwick, E. M. (1891). 'On the Evidence for Clairvoyance'. *Proceedings of the Society for Psychical Research* 7: 30–99.

Sidgwick, E. M. (1917a). Review of W. J. Crawford's *The Reality of Psychic Phenomena*. *Journal of the Society of Psychical Research* 18: 29–31.

Sidgwick, E. M. (1917b). Reply to Correspondence [regarding Sidgwick, E. M., (1917a)]. *Journal of the Society for Psychical Research* 18: 65–7.

Sidgwick, E. M. (1922). 'Phantasms of the Living. An Examination and Analysis of Cases of Telepathy between Living Persons printed in the *Journal* of the Society since the Publication of the Book *Phantasms of the Living* by Gurney, Myers, and Podmore, in 1886'. *Proceedings of the Society for Psychical Research* 33: 23–429.

Sidgwick, H. (1889a). 'Opening Address at the Thirtieth General Meeting'. *Proceedings of the Society for Psychical Research* 5: 399–402.

Sidgwick, H. (1889b). 'The Canons of Evidence in Psychical Research'. *Proceedings of the Society for Psychical Research* 6: 1–6.

Sidgwick, H. (1889c). 'The Census of Hallucinations'. *Proceedings of the Society for Psychical Research* 6: 7–12.

Sidgwick, H. (1895). 'Eusapia Paladino'. *Journal of the Society for Psychical Research* 7: 148–59.

Sidgwick, H. (1896). Statement on Eusapia Palladino. *Journal of the Society for Psychical Research* 7: 230–1.

Sklar, L. (1977). *Space, Time, and Spacetime*. Berkeley, Los Angeles & London: University of California Press.

Smith, W. W. (1919). ' "The Reality of Psychic Phenomena" '. *Proceedings of the Society for Psychical Research* 30: 306–33.

Society for Psychical Research (1884). 'A Theory of Apparitions', Parts I & II. *Proceedings of the Society for Psychical Research* 2: 109–36, 157–86.

Society for Psychical Research (1894). 'Report on the Census of Hallucinations'. *Proceedings of the Society for Psychical Research* 10: 25–422.

Society for Psychical Research (1895). Notes of the 75th General Meeting. *Journal of the Society for Psychical Research* 7: 131–35.

Society for Psychical Research (1922). 'Report on a Series of Sittings with Eva C.' *Proceedings of the Society for Psychical Research* 32: 209–343.

Society for Psychical Research (1926). Correspondence Concerning H. Hoagland's 'Report on Sittings with Margery'. *Proceedings of the Society for Psychical Research* 36: 414–32.

Stanford, R. G. (1978). 'Toward Reinterpreting Psi Events'. *Journal of the American Society for Psychical Research* 72: 197–214.

Stephenson, C. J. (1966). 'Further Comments on Cromwell Varley's Electrical Test on Florence Cook'. *Proceedings of the Society for Psychical Research* 54: 363–417.

Stevenson, F. McC. (1920). 'An Account of a Test Séance with the Goligher Circle'. *Psychic Research Quarterly* 1: 113–17.

Stevenson, I. (1968). 'The Substantiality of Spontaneous Cases'. *Proceedings of the Parapsychological Association* 5: 91–128.

Stewart, B. (1886). Note on Barrett, 1886. *Proceedings of the Society for Psychical Research* 4: 42–4.

Swanson, J. W. (1967). 'Religious Discourse and Rational Preference Rankings'. *American Philosophical Quarterly* 4: 245–50.

Tart, C. T. (1982). 'The Controversy about Psi: Two Psychological Theories'. *Journal of Parapsychology* 46: 313–20.

Tart, C. T. (1984). 'Acknowledging and Dealing with the Fear of Psi'. *Journal of the American Society for Psychical Research* 78: 133–43.

Thakur, S. C. (1979). 'Hidden Variables, Bootstraps and Brahman'. *Journal of the Society for Psychical Research* 50: 135–48.

Thurston, H. (1920). 'The Conversion of Home the Medium'. *The Month* 135: 434–45.

Thurston, H. (1952). *The Physical Phenomena of Mysticism*. Chicago: Henry Regnery Co.

Tietze, T. R. (1973). *Margery*. New York: Harper & Row.

Turner, J. (1973). (ed.) *Stella C*. London: Souvenir Press.

Tyrrell, G. N. M. (1938/1961). *Science and Psychical Phenomena*. New Hyde Park, N.Y.: University Books. Published with Tyrrell (1942/1961).

Tyrrell, G. N. M. (1942/1961). *Apparitions*. New Hyde Park, N.Y.: University Books. Published with Tyrrell (1938/1961).

Verrall, H. (1914). 'The History of Marthe Béraud'. *Proceedings of the Society for Psychical Research* 27: 333–69.

von Lucadou, W. and Kornwachs, K. (1980). 'Development of the System Theoretic Approach to Psychokinesis'. *European Journal of Parapsychology* 3: 297–314.

Wagner, M. W. and Monnet, M. (1979). 'Attitude of College Professors Toward Extra-Sensory Perception'. *Zetetic Scholar* No. 5: 7–16.

Walker, E. H. (1975). 'Foundations of Paraphysical and Parapsychological Phenomena'. In L. Oteri (ed.) *Quantum Physics and Parapsychology*. New York: Parapsychology Foundation.

Walker, E. H. (1984). 'A Review of the Criticisms of the Quantum Mechanical Theory of Psi Phenomena'. *Journal of Parapsychology* 48: 277–332.

Walker, M. C. (1935). 'Psychic Research in Brazil'. *Journal of the American Society for Psychical Research* 28: 74–8.

Wallace, A. R. (1896/1975). *Miracles and Modern Spiritualism*. London: George Redway; reprinted, New York: Arno Press.

Wallace, A. R. (1905). *My Life: A Record of Events and Opinions*, 2 vols. London: Chapman & Hall.

Waterlow, S. (1974). 'Backwards Causation and Continuing'. *Mind* 83: 372–87.

Werth, L. F. (1978). 'Normalizing the Paranormal'. *American Philosophical Quarterly* 15: 47–56.

West, D. J. (1948). 'The Investigation of Spontaneous Cases'. *Proceedings of the Society for Psychical Research* 48: 264–300.

Wolman, B. B. (1977). (ed.) *Handbook of Parapsychology*. New York: Van Nostrand Reinhold.

Woolley, V. J. (1926). 'An Account of a Series of Sittings with Mr George Valiantine'. *Proceedings of the Society for Psychical Research* 36: 52–77.

Woolley, V. J. and Brackenbury, E. (1931). 'The Margery Mediumship, and the London Sittings of December 1929'. *Proceedings of the Society for Psychical Research* 39: 358–73.

Woolley, V. J. and Dingwall, E. J. (1926). 'Luminous and Other Phenomena Observed with the Medium Janusz Fronczek'. *Proceedings of the Society for Psychical Research* 36: 34–51.

Zöllner, J. C. F. (1888/1976). *Transcendental Physics*, trans., C. C. Massey. Boston: Colby & Rich; reprinted, New York: Arno Press.

Zorab, G. (1964). 'Foreign Comments on Florence Cook's Mediumship'. *Proceedings of the Society for Psychical Research* 54: 173–83.

Zorab, G. (1970). 'Test Sittings with D. D. Home at Amsterdam'. *Journal of Parapsychology* 34: 47–63.

Zorab, G. (1971). 'Were D. D. Home's "Spirit Hands" Ever Fraudulently Produced?' *Journal of the Society for Psychical Research* 46: 228–35.

Zorab, G. (1973). 'ESP Performance of D. D. Home'. In Roll, Morris, and Morris (eds) *Research in Parapsychology 1972*. Metuchen, N. J.: Scarecrow Press: 171–3.

Zorab, G. (1975). *D. D. Home the Medium: A Biography and a Vindication*. Unpublished in English; published in Italian as *D. D. Home, il Medium* (Milano: Armenia Editore, 1976); revised and published in Dutch as *D. D. Home, het krachtigste medium aller tijden . . .* (Den Haag: Uitgeverij Leopold, 1980).

Zorab, G. (1978). 'Have We Finally Solved the Enigma of D. D. Home's Descent?' *Journal of the Society for Psychical Research* 49: 844–7.

Zorab, G. (1980). *The Enigma of 'Katie King': Living Woman or Phantom?* Unpublished in English. Published in Italian as *Katie King Donna o Fantasma?* Milano: Armenia Editore.

Zorab, G. and Inglis, B. (unpublished). *D. D. Home the Medium*. New version of Zorab (1975).

INDEX

305

Index